THE BEAT OFFICER'S COMPANION

6th Edition

GW00708341

Gordon Wilson

BA (Law), MSc

By the same author
The Traffic Officer's Companion

1st edition 1983
2nd edition 1986
3rd edition 1988
4th edition 1992
5th edition 1994
reprinted 1996
reprinted 1997
6th edition 1998

ISBN 0 85164 0656 0

Police Review Publishing Co

Celcon House
289-293, High Holborn
London WC1V 7HZ

Illustrations by Rich King, Ashton Under Lyne
Typeset by Hairy Toffee Design, London
Printed and bound in Great Britain by
The Cromwell Press, Trowbridge, Wiltshire.

Contents

Contents

Contents

Contents

Contents

Contents

Preface

This book is presented in a manner similar to that adopted by 'The Traffic Officer's Companion'. The diagrammatic and pictorial format provides an easily read and understandable interpretation of those aspects of legislation, other than traffic laws, likely to be of practical value to the patrolling police officer. Readers wishing to avail themselves of a similar presentation of traffic legislation are referred to the 'Traffic Officer's Companion'.

The problems encountered by the present-day officer in memorising, interpreting, recalling and making decisions upon an ever-increasing field of legislation are not underestimated. The intention of this book has therefore been to provide a practical and speedy reference to those aspects likely to be of operational value.

Because the book is intended to serve merely as a guide to the operational police officer, the relevant legislation has been subjected to a practical interpretation. It has been necessary to be selective in the material used and the book should not, therefore, be regarded as a definitive work of reference. Specific technical details may require further research.

The main changes since the first edition were brought about by the Police and Criminal Evidence Act, 1984, which affected not only powers of arrest, but also many procedures. Given the 'practical' bias of the book, difficulty was encountered in deciding where to draw the line on how much of the Act to include. There was a great temptation to restrict the alterations to the powers of arrest, search and Judges Rules. However, because the duties of custody officer could be undertaken by *any* police officer in certain circumstances, those aspects relating to the detention, questioning and treatment of persons in custody were seen to be worthy of inclusion. This has necessarily meant a substantial increase in the range of policework covered but it is hoped the value of the book will be enhanced accordingly.

In this edition the main changes have been brought about by:

a) The Theft (Amendment) Act 1996 which introducd new offences of obtaining a money transfer by deception and retaining a wrongful credit. Changes were also made to the offence of obtaining a service by deception under S1 of the Theft Act 1978 by clarifying the position regarding inducement to make a loan.

b) The Sex Offenders Act 1997 and the Sexual Offences (Conspiracy and Incitement) Act 1996 which introduce offences in connection with sexual acts committed outside the UK, and make requirements for sexual offenders to notify the police of details of their abode.

c) The Firearms (Amendment) Act 1997 which prohibits possession and storage of certain weapons and tightens up on the aspect of certificates.

d) The Protection from Harassment Act 1997, which seeks to give protection from harassment and fear of violence.

e) The Knives Act 1997 which provides for further prohibition of possession and sale of knives and other offensive weapons.

In some cases, the above provisions has not been fully brought into force at the time of going to press.

Gordon Wilson
Ex-Superintendent, Warwickshire Police
November 1994

Chapter 1
Crime

Criminal Attempts

S 1 CRIMINAL ATTEMPTS ACT 1981

IF, WITH

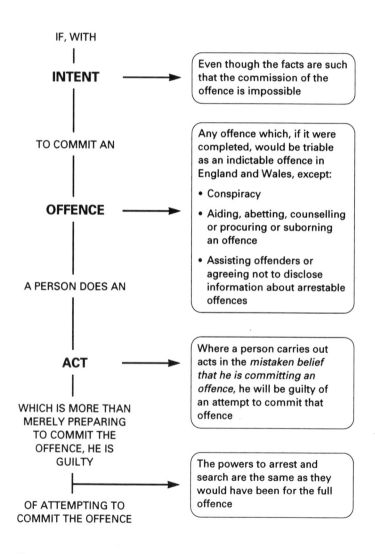

INTENT → Even though the facts are such that the commission of the offence is impossible

TO COMMIT AN

OFFENCE → Any offence which, if it were completed, would be triable as an indictable offence in England and Wales, except:

- Conspiracy
- Aiding, abetting, counselling or procuring or suborning an offence
- Assisting offenders or agreeing not to disclose information about arrestable offences

A PERSON DOES AN

ACT → Where a person carries out acts in the *mistaken belief that he is committing an offence*, he will be guilty of an attempt to commit that offence

WHICH IS MORE THAN MERELY PREPARING TO COMMIT THE OFFENCE, HE IS GUILTY

→ The powers to arrest and search are the same as they would have been for the full offence

OF ATTEMPTING TO COMMIT THE OFFENCE

Theft

S 1 Theft Act 1968

The essential ingredients of the offence of theft are outlined below and discussed in a little more depth in the following pages

A person will be guilty of theft if he:

- **DISHONESTLY**
- **APPROPRIATES**
- **PROPERTY**
- **BELONGING TO ANOTHER**
- **WITH THE INTENTION TO PERMANENTLY DEPRIVE**

THIS IS AN ARRESTABLE OFFENCE

DISHONESTLY

S 2 Theft Act 1968

The appropriation of property will not be regarded as 'dishonest' if:

- He believed he had the right in law to take it, or
- He believed he would have had the owner's consent, had the owner known about it, or
- The owner cannot be discovered by taking reasonable steps

But even if he intended to pay for it, it could amount to dishonesty.

APPROPRIATES

S 3 Theft Act 1968

An appropriation is any assumption of the rights of an owner.

This includes the case where he comes by the property without stealing it (even if he does so innocently) and later treats it as his own.

But where he gives value for the property in good faith, any later assumption by him of the rights he believed he was acquiring shall not, because of any defect in the vendor's title to the property, amount to theft.

PROPERTY

S 4 Theft Act 1968

The term 'property' includes money and all other property, real or personal (including things in action and other intangible property) – but special provisions relate to the following:

Personal property includes the printed paper on which a cheque is written or upon which an examination or other confidential information is written; and other intangible property such as debts and shares in a company.

Land and things forming part of land and severed from it cannot be stolen except:

- By a trustee, personal representative, etc.
- By a person not in possession of it who appropriates something forming part of the land by severing it
- By a person in possession who takes fixtures or structures let with the land

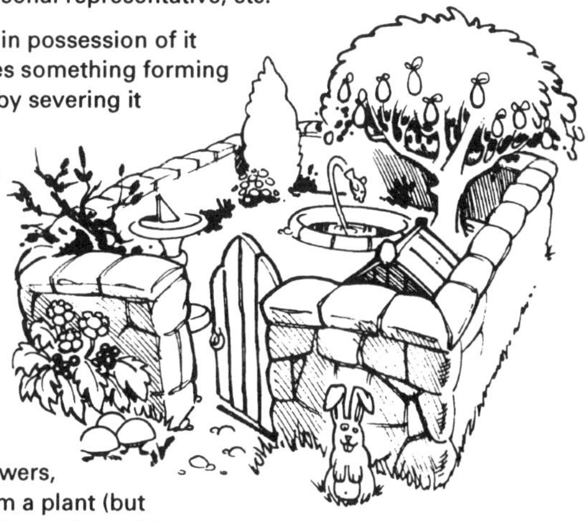

Mushrooms or flowers, fruit or foliage from a plant (but not the plant itself) *growing wild* cannot be stolen unless for reward, sale or commercial use.

Electricity cannot be stolen but see s. 13 later.

Wild creatures cannot be stolen if not tamed and not ordinarily kept in captivity unless they have been caught and not since lost or abandoned.

BELONGING TO ANOTHER

In normal situations it is obvious who is the owner of the property but sometimes there are complications. The law has therefore defined certain categories of people from whom property may be stolen:

Property belongs to any person who has possession or control of it, or who has in it any proprietary interest.

S 5 THEFT ACT 1968

Proprietary right or interest
eg The owner of a vehicle being repaired

Control
eg The garage proprietor

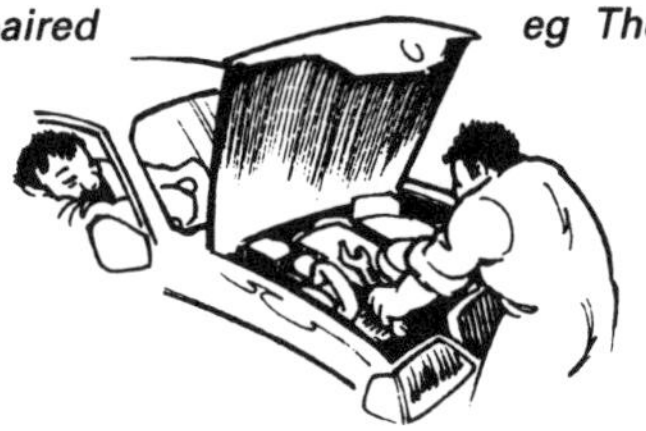

Possession
eg The person repairing the vehicle

INTENTION TO PERMANENTLY DEPRIVE

S 6 THEFT ACT 1968

If a person takes property belonging to another, but does not mean the other to be permanently deprived of it, he will still be regarded in law as having such an intention if he means to treat the property as his own to dispose of regardless of the other's rights – such as:

- Borrowing or lending in such a way that it is equivalent to an outright taking or disposal
- Parting with the property (obtained legally or not) under a condition which he may not be able to perform eg pawning
- The 'other' to whom the property belongs need not be an individual, but may be a registered company or other legal entity.

Removal of Articles from Places Open to the Public

Where the public have access to a building (or part of a building) in order to view the building or a collection housed in it, any person who without lawful authority removes from the building or its grounds any article kept for display to the public, shall be guilty of an offence.

S 11 Theft Act 1968

Collection
Includes a temporary collection, but not one intended to promote sales or commercial dealings.

Public access
May be limited to a particular period or occasion but anything removed which is not part of a permanent exhibition must be done on a day when the public have access.

Unlike theft, it is not necessary to prove an intention permanently to deprive.

THIS IS AN ARRESTABLE OFFENCE

Taking a Conveyance without Authority

Without having the consent of the owner or other lawful authority, **taking** a conveyance for his own or another's use

or

Knowing that a conveyance has been taken without the consent of the owner or other lawful authority, **drives** it or allows himself to be **carried** in or on it

S 12(1) THEFT ACT 1968

The conveyance must be moved, however short the distance may be, merely trying to start an engine will not suffice. Also, it must be taken for use as a conveyance, merely pushing it around the corner for a prank will not satisfy this offence.

CONVEYANCE

Constructed or adapted for the carriage of a person by land, water or air.

THIS IS AN ARRESTABLE OFFENCE

A similar offence exists in relation to pedal cycles but it is not an arrestable offence. S 12(5).

AGGRAVATED VEHICLE-TAKING ACT 1992 adds s 12A to the Theft Act 1968. Provides for obligatory disqualification and endorsement where the above offence under s12(1) has been committed and, before the vehicle was recovered, the vehicle was driven dangerously or was damaged or was driven in a way which led to personal injury or damage to other property.

Vehicle Interference

S 9 Criminal Attempts Act 1981

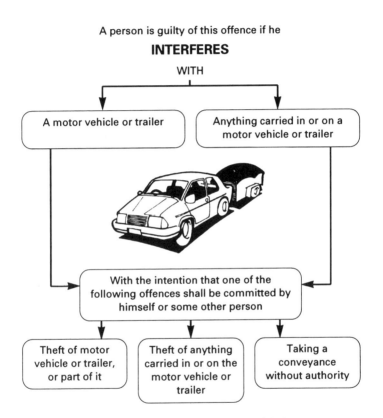

A person is guilty of this offence if he

INTERFERES

WITH

A motor vehicle or trailer

Anything carried in or on a motor vehicle or trailer

With the intention that one of the following offences shall be committed by himself or some other person

Theft of motor vehicle or trailer, or part of it

Theft of anything carried in or on the motor vehicle or trailer

Taking a conveyance without authority

Any arrest must be in accordance with the Police and Criminal Evidence Act 1984

Note: A person may still be guilty of an offence under s 25 of the Road Traffic Act 1988, if, while a motor vehicle is on a road or local authority parking place, he gets onto the vehicle or tampers with the brakes or other parts of its mechanism.

Abstracting Electricity

S 13 Theft Act 1968

This offence is committed by any person who dishonestly uses elecricity without authority, or dishonestly causes it to be wasted or diverted.

THIS IS AN ARRESTABLE OFFENCE

It is not necessary to prove that personal benefit was gained. An employee who leaves on the lights of his employer's premises throughout the night because of a grudge, would be guilty of the offence.

FRAUDULENT USE OF TELECOMMUNICATIONS SYSTEM

S 42 Telecommunications Act 1984

An offence is committed by any person who dishonestly obtains a licensed telecommunications service with intent to avoid payment of any charge for the service.

Robbery

S 8 Theft Act 1968

This offence is committed by any person who

STEALS

AND

IMMEDIATELY BEFORE

OR

AT THE TIME OF DOING SO

AND IN ORDER TO DO SO

Uses **force** on any person

or

Puts or seeks to put any person in **fear** of being then and there subjected to force

THIS IS AN ARRESTABLE OFFENCE

Burglary

S 9 Theft Act 1968, as amended by the Criminal Justice and Public Order Act 1994, Sched 10

Is committed by any person who

ENTERS ANY BUILDING
(Residential or commercial)
Includes an inhabited vehicle, eg

OR PART OF A BUILDING AS A TRESPASSER
A person who has no right to be in the building (or that particular part of it, eg behind a shop counter*)*

WITH INTENT TO

- Steal
- Inflict GBH on any person therein
- Rape any person therein
- Cause damage therein

OR HAVING ENTERED IN SUCH CIRCUMSTANCES

- Steals
- Attempts to steal
- Inflicts or attempts to inflict GBH on any person therein

THIS IS AN ARRESTABLE OFFENCE

AGGRAVATED BURGLARY

S 10 Theft Act 1968

The punishment for the above offence may be increased if, at the time of committing the offence, the offender has with him any of the following:

Explosive

Firearm
(including air guns or air pistols)

Weapon of offence
(made or adapted, or intended by the person possessing to injure or incapacitate)

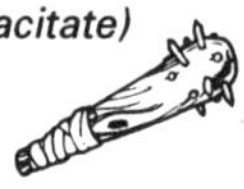

Imitation firearm
(anything having the appearance whether capable of being fired or not)

Obtaining Property by Deception

It is an offence by any deception dishonestly to obtain property belonging to another with the intention to permanently deprive the other of it.

S 15 Theft Act 1968

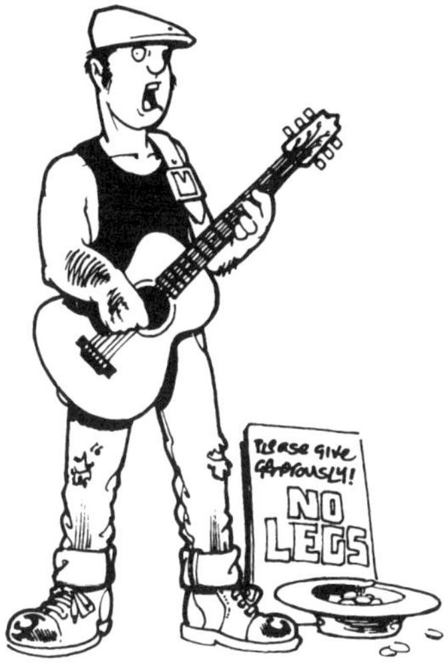

THIS IS AN ARRESTABLE OFFENCE

Deception
Means by words or conduct as to fact or law (made either deliberately or recklessly) including a deception as to the present intentions of himself or another. The deception need not be practised on the person from whom the property is obtained.

Obtaining
Means obtaining ownership, possession or control, or enabling another to do so.

Successful
If the other person did not part with the property, or was not deceived, or would have parted with it regardless of the deception, the elements of the offence have not been fulfilled.
But consider an attempt.

See also S1 1978 Act later.

OBTAINING A MONEY TRANSFER BY DECEPTION

THEFT ACT 1968, SS 15A, 15B THEFT (AMENDMENT) ACT 1996

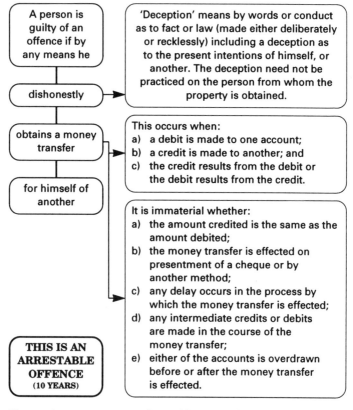

A person is guilty of an offence if by any means he

dishonestly

'Deception' means by words or conduct as to fact or law (made either deliberately or recklessly) including a deception as to the present intentions of himself, or another. The deception need not be practiced on the person from whom the property is obtained.

obtains a money transfer

This occurs when:

a) a debit is made to one account;
b) a credit is made to another; and
c) the credit results from the debit or the debit results from the credit.

It is immaterial whether:

a) the amount credited is the same as the amount debited;
b) the money transfer is effected on presentment of a cheque or by another method;
c) any delay occurs in the process by which the money transfer is effected;
d) any intermediate credits or debits are made in the course of the money transfer;
e) either of the accounts is overdrawn before or after the money transfer is effected.

for himself of another

THIS IS AN ARRESTABLE OFFENCE (10 YEARS)

'Account' means an account kept with: a) a bank; or b) a person carrying on a business of receiving deposits to lend to others or to finance other activities of the business.

Retaining a Wrongful Credit

THEFT ACT 1968, S 24A

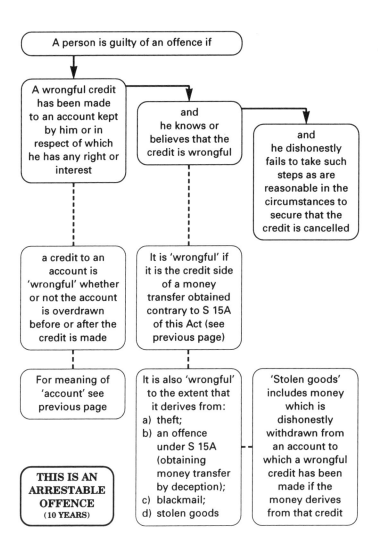

A person is guilty of an offence if

A wrongful credit has been made to an account kept by him or in respect of which he has any right or interest

and he knows or believes that the credit is wrongful

and he dishonestly fails to take such steps as are reasonable in the circumstances to secure that the credit is cancelled

a credit to an account is 'wrongful' whether or not the account is overdrawn before or after the credit is made

It is 'wrongful' if it is the credit side of a money transfer obtained contrary to S 15A of this Act (see previous page)

For meaning of 'account' see previous page

It is also 'wrongful' to the extent that it derives from:

a) theft;
b) an offence under S 15A (obtaining money transfer by deception);
c) blackmail;
d) stolen goods

'Stolen goods' includes money which is dishonestly withdrawn from an account to which a wrongful credit has been made if the money derives from that credit

THIS IS AN ARRESTABLE OFFENCE
(10 YEARS)

OBTAINING PECUNIARY ADVANTAGE

S 16 Theft Act 1968

IT IS AN OFFENCE BY ANY

DECEPTION

DISHONESTLY TO OBTAIN FOR HIMSELF OR ANOTHER ANY

PECUNIARY ADVANTAGE

A pecuniary advantage may be gained by:

Overdraft
If he is allowed to borrow by overdraft or to obtain an improvement in existing terms

Insurance
If he is allowed to take out a policy of insurance or annuity contract, or to obtain an improvement of existing terms

Remuneration
If he is given the opportunity to earn remuneration or greater remuneration in an office or employment, or to win money by betting

THIS IS AN ARRESTABLE OFFENCE

See also 1978 Act later.

BY DECEPTION

The Theft Act 1978 was introduced to cover additional areas of obtaining by deception which were not adequately dealt with by the 1968 Act.

Obtaining a Service

S 1 THEFT ACT 1978
AS AMENDED BY THE THEFT (AMENDMENT) ACT 1996, S4(1)

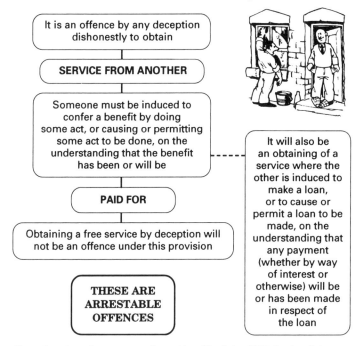

It is an offence by any deception dishonestly to obtain

SERVICE FROM ANOTHER

Someone must be induced to confer a benefit by doing some act, or causing or permitting some act to be done, on the understanding that the benefit has been or will be

PAID FOR

Obtaining a free service by deception will not be an offence under this provision

It will also be an obtaining of a service where the other is induced to make a loan, or to cause or permit a loan to be made, on the understanding that any payment (whether by way of interest or otherwise) will be or has been made in respect of the loan

THESE ARE ARRESTABLE OFFENCES

Note *that there is some overlap with s 15 of the 1968 Act but it is usually better to charge under s 1 of the 1978 Act.*

EVADING LIABILITY

S 2 THEFT ACT 1978

It is an offence by deception dishonestly to:

SECURE REMISSION
of the whole or part of an existing liability to make payment, whether his own or another's

OR

Induce the creditor to
WAIT FOR OR FOREGO
payment with intent that he or some other person may make permanent default of the whole or part of a payment

OR

obtain (for himself or another or allows another to obtain)
EXEMPTION OR ABATEMENT
of liability to make payment

***Note** that the obligation to pay must be legally enforceable, thus evading an unenforceable debt (eg a gambling debt or payment for the services of a prostitute) will not fall within the sections.*

THIS IS AN ARRESTABLE OFFENCE

Making off Without Paying

S 3 THEFT ACT 1978

A person who, knowing that payment

ON THE SPOT
for any goods supplied or service done is expected of him

Includes payment at the time of collecting goods on which work has been done or a service provided

DISHONESTLY MAKES OFF
without having paid as required or expected and

Does not apply where the supply of goods or services is contrary to law or not legally enforceable

WITH INTENT TO AVOID PAYMENT
of the amount due, shall be guilty of an offence

It must be proved that the intention was to make permanent default

Any person may arrest, without warrant, anyone who is or is reasonably suspected to be, committing or attempting to commit an offence under this section.

Handling Stolen Goods

S 22 Theft Act 1968

This offence is committed by a person who (otherwise than in the course of stealing)

KNOWING

OR

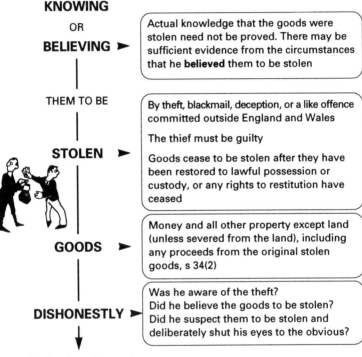

BELIEVING ► Actual knowledge that the goods were stolen need not be proved. There may be sufficient evidence from the circumstances that he **believed** them to be stolen

THEM TO BE

STOLEN ► By theft, blackmail, deception, or a like offence committed outside England and Wales

The thief must be guilty

Goods cease to be stolen after they have been restored to lawful possession or custody, or any rights to restitution have ceased

GOODS ► Money and all other property except land (unless severed from the land), including any proceeds from the original stolen goods, s 34(2)

DISHONESTLY ► Was he aware of the theft?
Did he believe the goods to be stolen?
Did he suspect them to be stolen and deliberately shut his eyes to the obvious?

A **Receives** the goods

B **Undertakes** the retention, removal, disposal or realisation of the goods by or for the benefit of another person

C **Assists** in the retention, removal, disposal or realisation of the goods by or for the benefit of another person, or

D **Arranges** to do 'A' to 'C' above

THIS IS AN ARRESTABLE OFFENCE

Going Equipped

S 25 Theft Act 1968

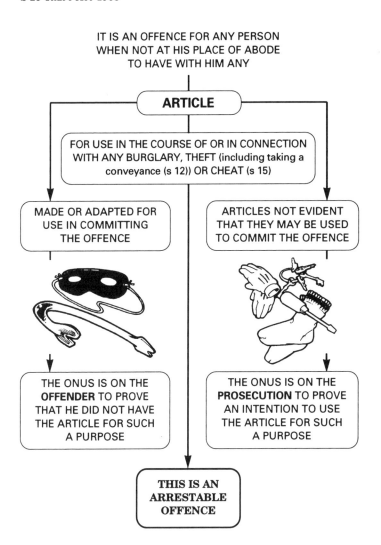

IT IS AN OFFENCE FOR ANY PERSON
WHEN NOT AT HIS PLACE OF ABODE
TO HAVE WITH HIM ANY

ARTICLE

FOR USE IN THE COURSE OF OR IN CONNECTION WITH ANY BURGLARY, THEFT (including taking a conveyance (s 12)) OR CHEAT (s 15)

MADE OR ADAPTED FOR USE IN COMMITTING THE OFFENCE

THE ONUS IS ON THE **OFFENDER** TO PROVE THAT HE DID NOT HAVE THE ARTICLE FOR SUCH A PURPOSE

ARTICLES NOT EVIDENT THAT THEY MAY BE USED TO COMMIT THE OFFENCE

THE ONUS IS ON THE **PROSECUTION** TO PROVE AN INTENTION TO USE THE ARTICLE FOR SUCH A PURPOSE

THIS IS AN ARRESTABLE OFFENCE

Assault

In the case of Fagan v Metropolitan Police Commissioner, 1968, 'assault' was defined as:

> **'Any act which intentionally or recklessly causes another person to apprehend immediate and unlawful personal violence.'**

A person is responsible for injuries which result from inducing into another's mind an immediate sense of danger which causes that person to injure himself in trying to escape.

There are varying degrees of assault which are governed by the seriousness of the injury, the harm done and the attendant circumstances.

Specific offences are discussed on the following pages and reflect the new charging standards in assault cases issued by the Crown Prosecution Service in August 1994.

COMMON ASSAULT

S 39 Criminal Justice Act 1988

An incident is referred to as being a common assault where the injury is either non-existent or of a negligible nature, eg grazes, minor bruising, black eye etc. The police do not normally institute proceedings for this type of occurrence, thus affording the aggrieved person the choice of taking proceedings either criminally or by civil action to obtain damages.

ACTUAL BODILY HARM

S 47 Offences Against the Person Act 1861

This includes any hurt or injury calculated to interfere with the health or comfort of the victim. It need not be a permanent injury but must be more than something which is only momentary and trifling, eg lost teeth, minor fractures, loss of consciousness. It may include shock which causes injury to the victim's state of mind. 'Harm' also includes psychological harm. No foresight or foreseeability of the consequences is required.

THIS IS AN ARRESTABLE OFFENCE

DEFENCES TO ASSAULT

Consent
But only a defence if:

a) An illegal purpose is not involved *eg a duel or injecting illegal drugs*

b) Violence or injury is not excessive

c) Consent is not obtained by fear, fraud or ignorance or the facts

Lawfully justified
For example:

Defence of oneself, a close relative or one's property. *But only sufficient force may be used to repel the attack*

Legal right
For example:

In the course of a lawful arrest, prevention of a breach of the peace, or serious crime.

But only such force as is necessary to achieve the result may be used

WOUNDING OR INFLICTING GRIEVOUS BODILY HARM

S 20 OFFENCES AGAINST THE PERSON ACT 1861

IT IS AN OFFENCE TO
UNLAWFULLY AND MALICIOUSLY

WOUND OR INFLICT ANY GRIEVOUS BODILY HARM

WITH OR WITHOUT ANY
WEAPON OR INSTRUMENT

These charges should be used for injuries involving permanent disability, serious permanent disfigurement, loss of sensory function, broken bones, substantial loss of blood or lengthy treatment, including psychiatric injury.

The defendant must have foreseen that his act would cause harm, even if not of the seriousness which actually resulted.

THESE ARE ARRESTABLE OFFENCES

WOUNDING OR CAUSING GRIEVOUS BODILY HARM WITH INTENT

S 18 Offences Against The Person Act 1861

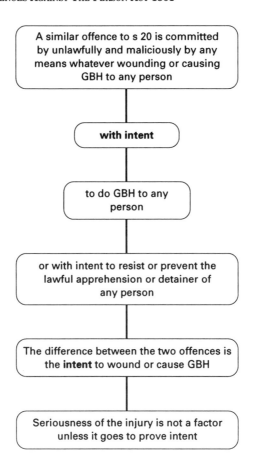

A similar offence to s 20 is committed by unlawfully and maliciously by any means whatever wounding or causing GBH to any person

with intent

to do GBH to any person

or with intent to resist or prevent the lawful apprehension or detainer of any person

The difference between the two offences is the **intent** to wound or cause GBH

Seriousness of the injury is not a factor unless it goes to prove intent

ASSAULT ON THE POLICE

S 51 Police Act 1964

IT IS AN OFFENCE TO ASSAULT
A POLICE CONSTABLE

IN THE EXECUTION OF HIS DUTY

OR A PERSON ASSISTING HIM

This covers a range of activities in which the constable may be involved, eg:

Arrest
Must be in accordance with the Police and Criminal Evidence Act 1984.

On premises
Unless specifically authorised, when on premises the constable is not acting in the execution of his duty once he has been requested to leave. (But he must be given time to leave).

Stopping vehicles
This power must be exercised lawfully
eg not just to get a lift

Disturbances
If it is believed that a breach of the peace is about to occur, a constable may use reasonable force to prevent it.

Questioning suspects
There is no power to detain short of an arrest, and any attempt forcibly to restrain cannot amount to execution of duty.

It is also an offence to assault ANY PERSON with intent to resist or prevent the lawful apprehension or detainer of himself or another for any offence (s 38 Offences Against the Person Act 1861).

Homicide

THESE ARE ARRESTABLE OFFENCES

As far as the criminal law is concerned, there are four types of unlawful killing.

MURDER COMMON LAW

This is committed when a sane person over 10 years of age, through some deliberate act or omission causes the death of a human being, either intending to kill that person or some other person, or to cause grievous bodily harm.

Threats

It is also an offence to threaten to kill some person, intending that the person to whom the threat is made will fear that the threat will be carried out.

MANSLAUGHTER COMMON LAW

This is the unlawful killing of another without the intention to kill or cause grievous bodily harm, the death taking place within a year and a day of the injury. Manslaughter is usually described as being either voluntary or involuntary:

Voluntary

Where death follows an intended injury (but if the injury is serious, then this may be murder). It normally occurs as a result of a sudden 'fraying of temper' or following some degree of provocation.

Involuntary

Where injury is not intended, but is nevertheless caused through gross negligence or an unlawful act.

INFANTICIDE S 1 INFANTICIDE ACT 1938

Committed by a mother who, by any wilful act or omission causes the death of her child (under 12 months old) whilst being mentally unbalanced through childbirth or milk fever.

CHILD DESTRUCTION S 1 INFANT LIFE (PRESERVATION) ACT 1929

Committed by any person who, by any wilful act intentionally causes the death of a child capable of being born alive (this is presumed after 28 weeks pregnancy) before it has had a life independent of its mother.

Damage

S 1(1) Criminal Damage Act 1971

THIS IS AN ARRESTABLE OFFENCE

DAMAGE
IS THE OFFENCE COMMITTED BY ANY PERSON WHO WITHOUT

LAWFUL EXCUSE ➤ He will be treated as having a lawful excuse if he believed he had consent of a person entitled to consent, or he would have consented had he known of the circumstances; or if he caused, or threatened to cause damage in protection of his own property

DESTROYS ◄ If a building: *to pull down or demolish*

If growing things: *to lay waste*

If machinery: *to break up*

If animals: *to kill*

OR

DAMAGES ◄ Nothing need be actually broken or deformed, eg uncoupling the brake pipe on a car; tampering with machinery so that it will not work; watering milk

PROPERTY ➤ Whether real of personal. Including wild animals which have been tamed or are ordinarily kept in captivity but does not include mushrooms growing wild on any land or flowers, fruit or foliage from wild plants

BELONGING TO ANOTHER ◄ Property belongs to any person having custody or control of it, having a right or interest in it, or having a charge on it

INTENDING ➤ If he intends or foresees damage to property, he may be liable where he in fact causes damage to other property which he had not intended or foreseen

TO DESTROY OR DAMAGE ANY SUCH PROPERTY OR BEING RECKLESS AS TO WHETHER ANY SUCH PROPERTY WOULD BE DESTROYED OR DAMAGED

DAMAGE WITH INTENT TO ENDANGER LIFE

S 1(2) Criminal Damage Act 1971

This offence is committed by a person who:

without lawful excuse destroys or damages any property, whether belonging to himself or another

↓

intending to destroy or damage any property or being reckless as to whether any property would be destroyed or damaged

↓

intending by the destruction or damage to endanger the life of another or being reckless as to whether the life of another would be thereby endangered

THESE ARE ARRESTABLE OFFENCES

ARSON

S 1(3) Criminal Damage Act 1971

An offence of damage or endangering life by damage, **by destroying or damaging property by fire** shall be charged as 'arson'.

THESE ARE ARRESTABLE OFFENCES

THREATS TO DAMAGE

S 2 Criminal Damage Act 1971

THIS OFFENCE IS COMMITTED BY A PERSON WHO WITHOUT LAWFUL EXCUSE MAKES TO ANOTHER A

THREAT

INTENDING THAT THE OTHER WOULD FEAR THAT IT WOULD BE CARRIED OUT

To destroy or damage any property belonging to that other or a third person

OR

To destroy or damage his own property in a way which he knows is likely to endanger the life of that other or a third person

POSSESSION WITH INTENT TO DAMAGE

S 3 Criminal Damage Act 1971

THIS OFFENCE IS COMMITTED BY A PERSON WHO HAS

ANYTHING

IN HIS CUSTODY OR CONTROL INTENDING

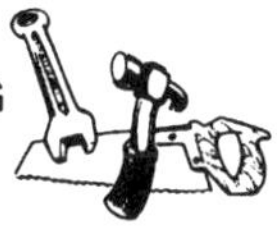

WITHOUT LAWFUL EXCUSE

TO USE OR CAUSE OR PERMIT ANOTHER TO USE IT

To destroy or damage any property belonging to some other person

OR

To destroy or damage his own or the user's property in a way which he knows is likely to endanger the life of some other person

Drugs

The Misuse of Drugs Act 1971 creates a number of offences relating to:

controlled drugs

This means any substance or product listed in one of the three classes (A, B or C) in Sched 2 to the Act.

Whilst drugs are listed in their basic form it is clear that other forms of the drug and esters or salts are also included. Both the natural substances and any substance resulting from chemical transformation are controlled drugs.

Powers to arrest are contained in the Police and Criminal Evidence Act 1984. The Misuse of Drugs Act 1971, provides wide powers of search, and contains specific defences.

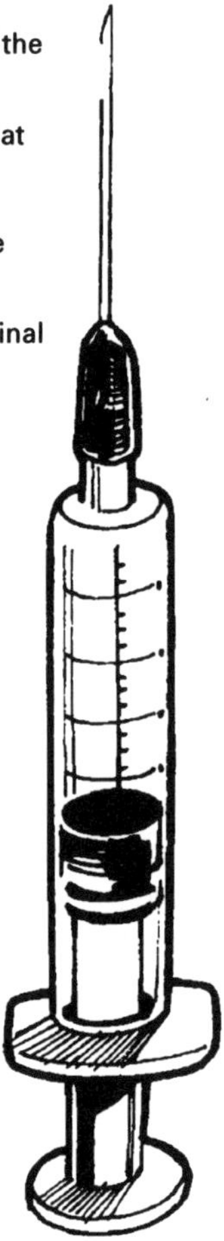

A variety of aspects are listed below and dealt with in more detail in the following pages:

IMPORT & EXPORT

S 3 Misuse of Drugs Act 1971

The import or export of controlled drugs are prohibited unless authorised under the regulations.

Being concerned with the improper import or export, or the fraudulent evasion of prohibition or restriction are all offences under the Customs and Excise Management Act 1979, s 50 and are all arrestable offences.

THESE ARE ARRESTABLE OFFENCES

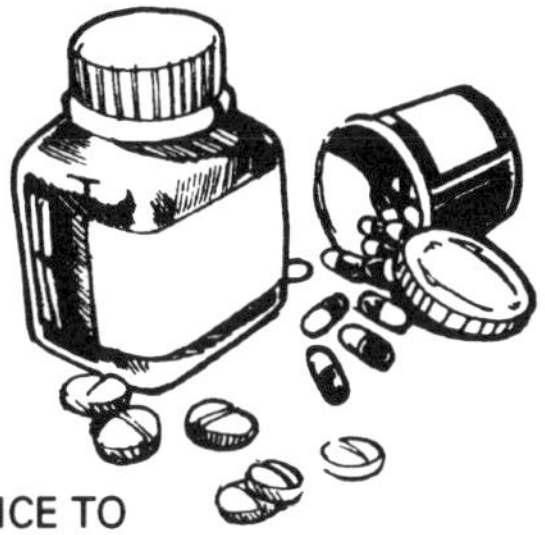

PRODUCTION

S 4(2) Misuse of Drugs Act 1971

IT IS AN OFFENCE TO

UNLAWFULLY

To be lawful it must be authorised by regulations eg manufacturers

PRODUCE

By manufacture, cultivation or any other method eg cultivating or growing

BE CONCERNED IN THE PRODUCTION OF

Actual participation is not necessary. All that needs to be proved is an interest eg hiring premises

A CONTROLLED DRUG

SUPPLY

S 4(3) Misuse of Drugs Act 1971

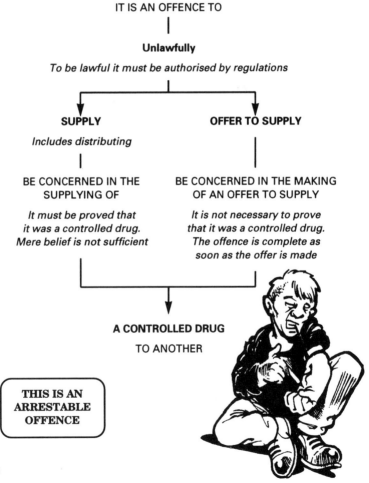

IT IS AN OFFENCE TO

Unlawfully

To be lawful it must be authorised by regulations

SUPPLY

Includes distributing

BE CONCERNED IN THE SUPPLYING OF

It must be proved that it was a controlled drug. Mere belief is not sufficient

OFFER TO SUPPLY

BE CONCERNED IN THE MAKING OF AN OFFER TO SUPPLY

It is not necessary to prove that it was a controlled drug. The offence is complete as soon as the offer is made

A CONTROLLED DRUG

TO ANOTHER

THIS IS AN ARRESTABLE OFFENCE

POSSESSION

S 5(2) Misuse of Drugs Act 1971

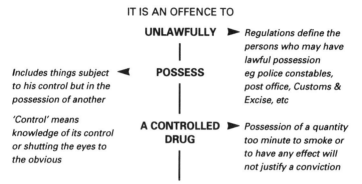

IT IS AN OFFENCE TO

UNLAWFULLY ► *Regulations define the persons who may have lawful possession eg police constables, post office, Customs & Excise, etc*

Includes things subject to his control but in the possession of another ◄ **POSSESS**

'Control' means knowledge of its control or shutting the eyes to the obvious

A CONTROLLED DRUG ► *Possession of a quantity too minute to smoke or to have any effect will not justify a conviction*

THIS IS AN ARRESTABLE OFFENCE
UNLESS THE DRUG CONCERNED IS MERELY
ONE OF THE MILDER TYPE eg MANDRAX
AND IN A SMALL QUANTITY

Defence

S 5(4) Misuse of Drugs Act 1971

It is a defence to a charge of possession to prove that, knowing or suspecting it to be a controlled drug, he took possession of it for the purpose of:

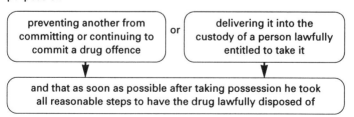

preventing another from committing or continuing to commit a drug offence

or

delivering it into the custody of a person lawfully entitled to take it

and that as soon as possible after taking possession he took all reasonable steps to have the drug lawfully disposed of

POSSESSION WITH INTENT TO SUPPLY

S 5(3) MISUSE OF DRUGS ACT 1971

IT IS AN OFFENCE FOR A PERSON

TO HAVE A CONTROLLED DRUG IN HIS POSSESSION

WHETHER LAWFULLY OR NOT ➤ *The offence may be committed by a person who has lawful possession eg a chemist*

WITH INTENT TO SUPPLY IT UNLAWFULLY TO ANOTHER

THESE ARE ARRESTABLE OFFENCES

CANNABIS – CULTIVATING

S 6(2) MISUSE OF DRUGS ACT 1971

IT IS AN OFFENCE TO

UNLAWFULLY ➤ *Cultivation may be lawful only under licence of the Secretary of State*

CULTIVATE ➤ *Knowingly tending to the plant at any stage of its maturity*

ANY PLANT OF THE GENUS 'CANNABIS'

THIS IS AN ARRESTABLE OFFENCE

USE OF PREMISES

S 8 Misuse of Drugs Act 1971

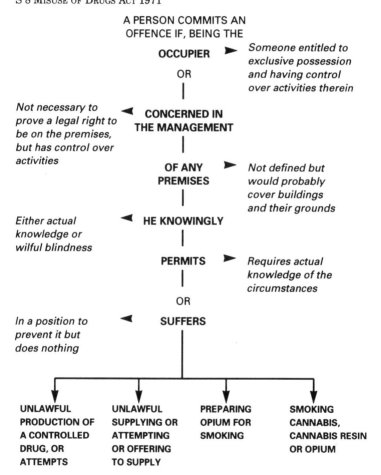

A PERSON COMMITS AN OFFENCE IF, BEING THE

OCCUPIER ➤ *Someone entitled to exclusive possession and having control over activities therein*

OR

CONCERNED IN THE MANAGEMENT ◄ *Not necessary to prove a legal right to be on the premises, but has control over activities*

OF ANY PREMISES ➤ *Not defined but would probably cover buildings and their grounds*

HE KNOWINGLY ◄ *Either actual knowledge or wilful blindness*

PERMITS ➤ *Requires actual knowledge of the circumstances*

OR

SUFFERS ◄ *In a position to prevent it but does nothing*

- **UNLAWFUL PRODUCTION OF A CONTROLLED DRUG, OR ATTEMPTS**
- **UNLAWFUL SUPPLYING OR ATTEMPTING OR OFFERING TO SUPPLY**
- **PREPARING OPIUM FOR SMOKING**
- **SMOKING CANNABIS, CANNABIS RESIN OR OPIUM**

OPIUM

S 9 MISUSE OF DRUGS ACT 1971

IT IS AN OFFENCE

TO SMOKE OR OTHERWISE USE PREPARED OPIUM

Opium prepared for smoking, including dross and any other residues remaining after opium has been smoked

TO FREQUENT A PLACE USED FOR THE PURPOSE OF OPIUM SMOKING

Not restricted to premises

TO HAVE IN POSSESSION

ANY PIPES OR OTHER UTENSILS MADE FOR USE IN CONNECTION WITH THE SMOKING OF OPIUM

BEING PIPES OR UTENSILS WHICH HAVE BEEN USED BY HIM OR WITH HIS KNOWLEDGE AND PERMISSION

OR WHICH HE INTENDS TO USE OR PERMIT OTHERS TO USE

ANY UTENSILS WHICH HAVE BEEN USED BY HIM OR WITH HIS KNOWLEDGE AND PERMISSION IN CONNECTION WITH THE PREPARATION OF OPIUM FOR SMOKING

THIS IS AN ARRESTABLE OFFENCE

POLICE POWERS

SEARCH

S 23(2) Misuse of Drugs Act 1971

If a constable has reasonable grounds to suspect that any person is unlawfully in possession of a controlled drug, he may:

Search that person
And detain him for the purpose of searching him

Search any vehicle or vessel in which the constable suspects that the drug may be found
And require the vehicle to be stopped for that purpose

And seize and detain anything found in the course of the search which appears to the constable to be evidence of an offence under this Act

Note should be made of the following provisions of the Police and Criminal Evidence Act 1984.

Where the power is exercised to search a person or vehicle without making an arrest, then **before** the search is commenced:

THE FOLLOWING INFORMATION SHOULD BE BROUGHT TO THE ATTENTION OF THE APPROPRIATE PERSON

- Constable's name and his police station. If not in uniform, documentary evidence of being a constable
- Object and grounds of proposed search
- Where a record of the search is made, his entitlement to a copy within 12 months if he asks for it

Where an unattended vehicle is searched, a notice should be left stating that it has been searched and giving the officer's name and station, the right to apply for compensation for any damage caused and his right to a copy of the search record. The notice is to be left inside the vehicle unless not practicable.

Chapter 2
Sexual Offences

THIS IS AN ARRESTABLE OFFENCE

Rape

S 1 Sexual Offences Act 1956 as amended by s 142 Criminal Justice and Public Order Act 1994

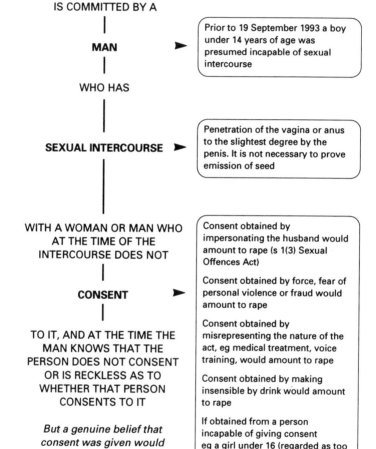

IS COMMITTED BY A

MAN

Prior to 19 September 1993 a boy under 14 years of age was presumed incapable of sexual intercourse

WHO HAS

SEXUAL INTERCOURSE

Penetration of the vagina or anus to the slightest degree by the penis. It is not necessary to prove emission of seed

WITH A WOMAN OR MAN WHO AT THE TIME OF THE INTERCOURSE DOES NOT

CONSENT

Consent obtained by impersonating the husband would amount to rape (s 1(3) Sexual Offences Act)

Consent obtained by force, fear of personal violence or fraud would amount to rape

Consent obtained by misrepresenting the nature of the act, eg medical treatment, voice training, would amount to rape

Consent obtained by making insensible by drink would amount to rape

If obtained from a person incapable of giving consent eg a girl under 16 (regarded as too young to give a valid consent) or a mental defective (depending on the severity of the condition)

TO IT, AND AT THE TIME THE MAN KNOWS THAT THE PERSON DOES NOT CONSENT OR IS RECKLESS AS TO WHETHER THAT PERSON CONSENTS TO IT

But a genuine belief that consent was given would not amount to rape

Sexual Intercourse with Girl Under Age

SEXUAL OFFENCES ACT 1956

THIS IS COMMITTED BY A

MAN

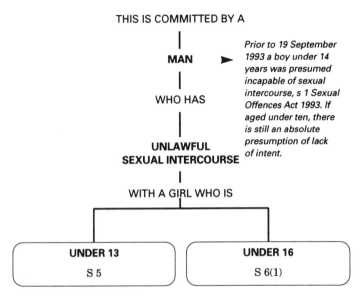

Prior to 19 September 1993 a boy under 14 years was presumed incapable of sexual intercourse, s 1 Sexual Offences Act 1993. If aged under ten, there is still an absolute presumption of lack of intent.

WHO HAS

UNLAWFUL SEXUAL INTERCOURSE

WITH A GIRL WHO IS

UNDER 13

S 5

Belief, even though reasonable, that she is not under 13 years of age is no defence

THIS IS AN ARRESTABLE OFFENCE

UNDER 16

S 6(1)

Will not be guilty if he genuinely, but mistakenly believes that the girl is his wife

or

He is under 24 years of age; has not previously been charged with an offence under this section (he is not charged until he appears before the court); and has reasonable cause to believe her to be 16 years or over

Power to arrest in accordance with the Police and Criminal Evidence Act 1984

Incest

SEXUAL OFFENCES ACT 1956

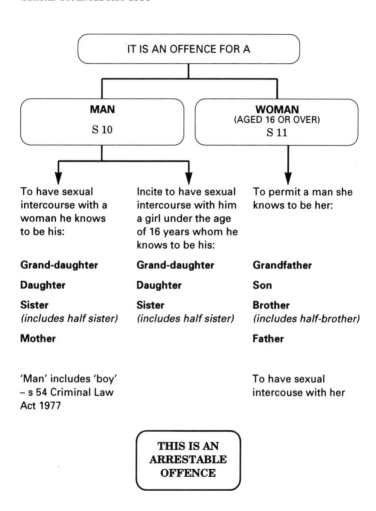

IT IS AN OFFENCE FOR A

MAN S 10		**WOMAN** (AGED 16 OR OVER) S 11
To have sexual intercourse with a woman he knows to be his:	Incite to have sexual intercourse with him a girl under the age of 16 years whom he knows to be his:	To permit a man she knows to be her:
Grand-daughter	**Grand-daughter**	**Grandfather**
Daughter	**Daughter**	**Son**
Sister *(includes half sister)*	**Sister** *(includes half sister)*	**Brother** *(includes half-brother)*
Mother		**Father**
'Man' includes 'boy' – s 54 Criminal Law Act 1977		To have sexual intercouse with her

THIS IS AN ARRESTABLE OFFENCE

Mental Patients

SEXUAL OFFENCES ACT 1956
MENTAL HEALTH ACT 1959

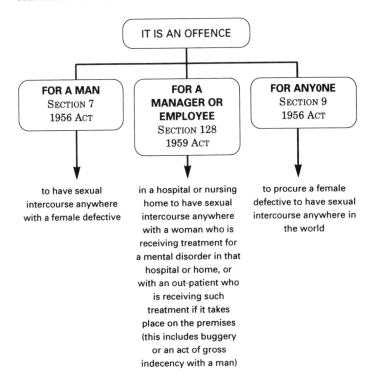

IT IS AN OFFENCE

FOR A MAN
SECTION 7
1956 ACT

to have sexual intercourse anywhere with a female defective

FOR A MANAGER OR EMPLOYEE
SECTION 128
1959 ACT

in a hospital or nursing home to have sexual intercourse anywhere with a woman who is receiving treatment for a mental disorder in that hospital or home, or with an out-patient who is receiving such treatment if it takes place on the premises (this includes buggery or an act of gross indecency with a man)

FOR ANYONE
SECTION 9
1956 ACT

to procure a female defective to have sexual intercourse anywhere in the world

Defective means a state of arrested or incomplete development of mind which includes severe impairment of intelligence and social functioning.

Consent does not provide a defence but lack of knowledge of the condition and having no reason to suspect it is a defence.

Prostitution

S 1 Street Offences Act 1959

IT IS AN OFFENCE FOR A

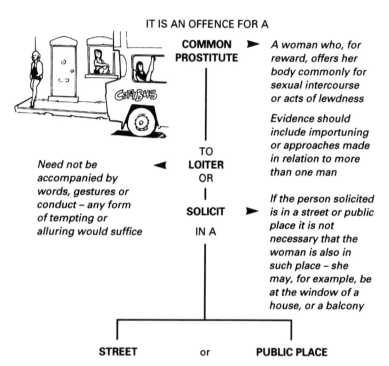

COMMON PROSTITUTE ➤ *A woman who, for reward, offers her body commonly for sexual intercourse or acts of lewdness*

Evidence should include importuning or approaches made in relation to more than one man

TO

LOITER ◄ *Need not be accompanied by words, gestures or conduct – any form of tempting or alluring would suffice*

OR

SOLICIT ➤ *If the person solicited is in a street or public place it is not necessary that the woman is also in such place – she may, for example, be at the window of a house, or a balcony*

IN A

STREET or **PUBLIC PLACE**

(Roads, lanes, alleys, subways, squares and other similar places open to the public. Also includes doorways, entrances to premises and any ground adjoining a street)

(Any highway and any other premises or place to which at the material time the public are permitted to have access whether on payment or otherwise, eg parks, libraries, railway stations, buses, etc)

FOR THE PURPOSE OF PROSTITUTION

A constable may arrest without warrant anyone he finds in a public place and suspects, with reasonable cause, to be committing this offence.

Kerb-Crawling

S 1 Sexual Offences Act 1985

An offence is committed by a

MAN if he — *includes 'boy'*

SOLICITS — *or persistently solicits (s 2)*

*for the purpose of obtaining **her** services, therefore does not apply to male prostitutes soliciting*

A WOMAN for the purpose of — *includes 'girl'*

PROSTITUTION

FROM A **MOTOR VEHICLE** *(has the same meaning as in the Road Traffic Act)* WHILE IT IS IN A **STREET OR PUBLIC PLACE** *(has the same meaning as in the Street Offences Act (see previous page))*

IN A STREET OR PUBLIC PLACE WHILE IN THE **IMMEDIATE VICINITY** OF A **MOTOR VEHICLE** WHICH HE HAS JUST GOT OUT OF OR OFF

- persistently
- being likely to cause annoyance to the woman solicited, or nuisance to other persons in the neighbourhood

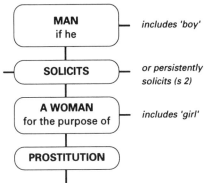

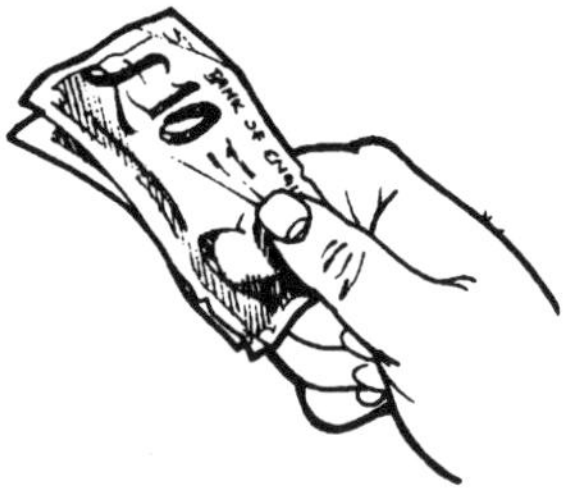

TRADING IN PROSTITUTION

S 30(1) Sexual Offences Act 1956
S 31 Sexual Offences Act 1956
S 5(1) Sexual Offences Act 1967

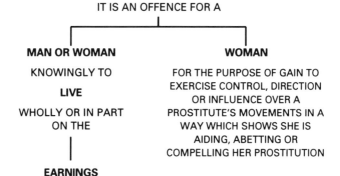

IT IS AN OFFENCE FOR A

MAN OR WOMAN

KNOWINGLY TO

LIVE

WHOLLY OR IN PART ON THE

EARNINGS

A man who lives with or is habitually in the company of a prostitute, or who exercises control, direction or influence over a prostitute's movements in a way which shows he is aiding, abetting or compelling her prostitution with others, shall be presumed to be living on the earnings of prostitution unless he proves to the contrary.

OF PROSTITUTION

WOMAN

FOR THE PURPOSE OF GAIN TO EXERCISE CONTROL, DIRECTION OR INFLUENCE OVER A PROSTITUTE'S MOVEMENTS IN A WAY WHICH SHOWS SHE IS AIDING, ABETTING OR COMPELLING HER PROSTITUTION

THESE ARE ARRESTABLE OFFENCES

PROCURING PROSTITUTION

S 22 Sexual Offences Act 1956

It is an offence to procure or attempt to procure a woman to become a prostitute or to leave the UK to become an inmate of, or frequent, a brothel for prostitution abroad.

Brothels

SEXUAL OFFENCES ACT 1956

IT IS AN OFFENCE FOR

S 34

Landlord or Agent
To let premises (in whole or in part) knowing that they are to be used as, or wilfully to be a party to them being used as, a brothel

Where one prostitute is the tenant and occupier, it is necessary only to show that the premises are being used by ***one*** *other prostitute in this case*

A house occupied by one woman and used by her for prostitution but not allowed by her to be used by other women will not be a regarded as a brothel

S 35 AND 36

Tenant or occupier
Knowingly to permit anyone to use any part of any premises for use or habitual use as a brothel

S 33

Anyone
To keep, or act or assist in the management of, a brothel

The porter of a block of flats where women habitually brought different men nightly for prostitution, was held to have committed the offence

A block of flats inhabited by different women and used by them for prostitution may be a brothel

A BROTHEL IS ANY PREMISES OR PART OF PREMISES, HABITUALLY USED OR RESORTED TO BY PERSONS OF BOTH SEXES FOR THE PURPOSES OF PROSTITUTION OR LEWD HOMOSEXUAL PRACTICES

SEXUAL INTERCOURSE NEED NOT BE PROVED – LEWD PRACTICES WILL SUFFICE

EXTENDED TO INCLUDE LEWD HOMOSEXUAL PRACTICES BY THE SEXUAL OFFENCES ACT 1967, S 6

THESE ARE ARRESTABLE OFFENCES

Buggery and Gross Indecency

When committed in private by a man of any age with a consenting man over 18 years, or when committed by a man under 18 with a consenting man over 16. **Not arrestable**

S 12 Sexual Offences Act 1956 as amended by s 143 Criminal Justice and Public Order Act 1994

It is an offence for a person to commit **buggery** with another person (otherwise than in lawful circumstances) or with an animal.

Buggery consists of intercourse per anum by a man with a man or woman; or intercourse per anum or per vaginum by a man or a woman with an animal.

An act of buggery takes place in lawful circumstances if it takes place in private and both parties have attained the age of 18. It will not take place in private if it takes place between men:
(a) When more than 2 persons take part or are present, or
(b) in a lavatory to which the public have access.

S 13 Sexual Offences Act 1956

It is an offence for a person to commit **gross indecency** with another man, whether in public or private, or to be a party to it, or to procure such an act.

'Indecency' may occur, for example, where two men kiss each other, but this would not amount to 'gross indecency'.

The offence is usually: i) Mutual masturbation ii) Oral-genital contact

It is an offence for any person to commit gross indecency with a child under 14 (A child under 14 cannot be convicted of the principal offence)

But it shall not be an offence for a man to commit gross indecency with another man provided that the act is done:

(a) **In private**
An act is not done in private if:
i) More than 2 persons take part or are present
ii) The act is done in a lavatory to which the public have access, whether on payment or otherwise

(b) If the parties **consent**. A person suffering from severe subnormality cannot consent (see pages 51 & 57).

(c) If the parties have attained the **age of 18** S 1 Sexual Offences Act 1967 (as amended by s 143 Criminal Justice and Public Order Act 1994)
It would probably not be a defence to show that a party was believed to be over 18 if, in fact, he was not

IMPORTUNING S 32

It is an offence for a man persistently to solicit or importune in a public place for an immoral purpose (see also 'kerb crawling').

Indecent Assault

Ss 14 & 15 Sexual Offences Act 1956

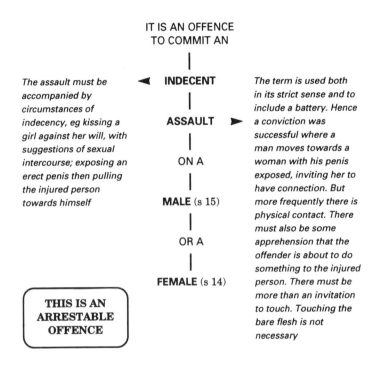

IT IS AN OFFENCE
TO COMMIT AN

INDECENT

The assault must be accompanied by circumstances of indecency, eg kissing a girl against her will, with suggestions of sexual intercourse; exposing an erect penis then pulling the injured person towards himself

ASSAULT

The term is used both in its strict sense and to include a battery. Hence a conviction was successful where a man moves towards a woman with his penis exposed, inviting her to have connection. But more frequently there is physical contact. There must also be some apprehension that the offender is about to do something to the injured person. There must be more than an invitation to touch. Touching the bare flesh is not necessary

ON A

MALE (s 15)

OR A

FEMALE (s 14)

THIS IS AN ARRESTABLE OFFENCE

Consent is a complete defence, but not if:

- assault on a person under 16 unless the man has reasonable cause to believe the woman to be his wife
- assault on a mental defective if the offender knew or had reasonable grounds to suspect her to be a defective
- obtained by misrepresenting the act
- intended or is likely to cause bodily harm

Indecent Photographs

S 1 Protection of Children Act 1978 as amended by s 84 Criminal Justice and Public Order Act 1994

IT IS AN OFFENCE TO

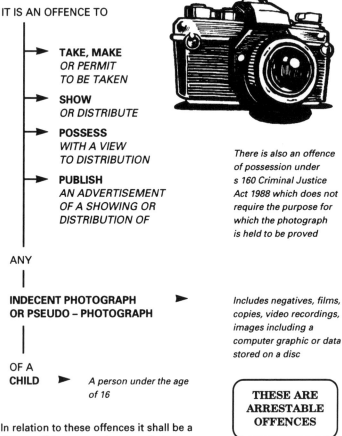

- **TAKE, MAKE** *OR PERMIT TO BE TAKEN*
- **SHOW** *OR DISTRIBUTE*
- **POSSESS** *WITH A VIEW TO DISTRIBUTION*
- **PUBLISH** *AN ADVERTISEMENT OF A SHOWING OR DISTRIBUTION OF*

There is also an offence of possession under s 160 Criminal Justice Act 1988 which does not require the purpose for which the photograph is held to be proved

ANY

INDECENT PHOTOGRAPH OR PSEUDO - PHOTOGRAPH ➤ *Includes negatives, films, copies, video recordings, images including a computer graphic or data stored on a disc*

OF A

CHILD ➤ *A person under the age of 16*

THESE ARE ARRESTABLE OFFENCES

In relation to these offences it shall be a **defence** if the accused proves that:

- There is a legitimate reason for distribution or possession, or
- He had not seen the photographs and neither knew nor suspected they were indecent

Indecent Displays

S 1 Indecent Displays (Control) Act 1981

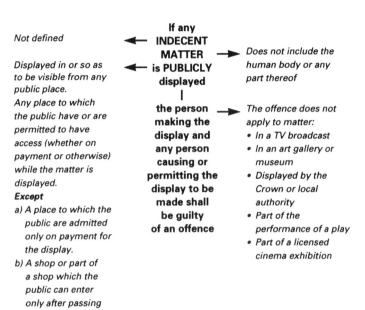

If any INDECENT MATTER is PUBLICLY displayed the person making the display and any person causing or permitting the display to be made shall be guilty of an offence

INDECENT MATTER ← *Not defined*

INDECENT MATTER → *Does not include the human body or any part thereof*

PUBLICLY displayed ← *Displayed in or so as to be visible from any public place.*

Any place to which the public have or are permitted to have access (whether on payment or otherwise) while the matter is displayed.

Except

a) A place to which the public are admitted only on payment for the display.

b) A shop or part of a shop which the public can enter only after passing a warning notice.

If in either case persons under 18 are not permitted during the display.

the person → *The offence does not apply to matter:*

- *In a TV broadcast*
- *In an art gallery or museum*
- *Displayed by the Crown or local authority*
- *Part of the performance of a play*
- *Part of a licensed cinema exhibition*

POLICE POWERS

If a constable has reasonable cause to suspect that a person has committed an offence:

- He may require him to give his name and address, and may arrest him if he fails to do so in accordance with the provisions of the Police and Criminal Evidence Act 1984.
- A constable may seize any article which he has reasonable grounds for believing to be indecent matter used in the commission of an offence.

Obscene Publications

OBSCENE PUBLICATIONS ACTS 1959 & 1964

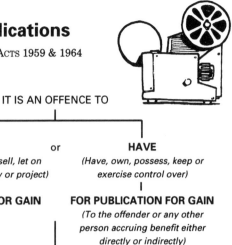

IT IS AN OFFENCE TO

PUBLISH or **HAVE**

PUBLISH
(To distribute, circulate, sell, let on hire, give, lend, show, play or project)
WHETHER OR NOT FOR GAIN

HAVE
(Have, own, possess, keep or exercise control over)
FOR PUBLICATION FOR GAIN
(To the offender or any other person accruing benefit either directly or indirectly)

THESE ARE ARRESTABLE OFFENCES

ANY

OBSCENE → *A tendency to deprave or corrupt those who are likely to read, see or hear the matter contained in it.*

ARTICLE → *Anything containing matter to be read or looked at; any sound, record, film, or other record of a picture or pictures, whether intended to be used alone or as one of a set, or for the reproduction or manufacture of such articles, eg negatives, printing blocks, etc.*

DEFENCES

The offender had not examined the article and had no reasonable cause to suspect that his having it was an offence, or

Its publication was justifiable as being for the public good in the interests of science, literature or art.

HARMFUL PUBLICATIONS

CHILDREN AND YOUNG PERSONS (HARMFUL PUBLICATIONS) ACT 1955

it is an offence to

PRINT **PUBLISH** **SELL** **HIRE**

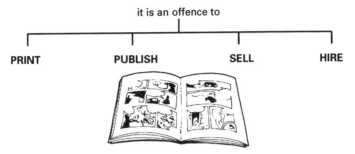

Any book, magazine or other like work which is likely to fall into the hands of juveniles and which consists wholly or mainly of stories told in pictures (with or without written material)

PORTRAYING

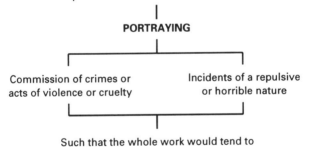

Commission of crimes or acts of violence or cruelty

Incidents of a repulsive or horrible nature

Such that the whole work would tend to

CORRUPT

A JUVENILE

who might read it

DEFENCE

That the accused had not examined the work and had no reasonable cause to suspect that it constituted an offence.

Indecent Exposure

The offence of indecent exposure is covered by three separate authorities, each of which must be considered to ensure that the offence charged is appropriate to the circumstances under which the offence was committed.

	Common law	Vagrancy Act 1824, s 4	Town Police Clauses Act 1847, s 28
How	Outraging public decency by exposing the person or engaging in or simulating a sexual act	Wilfully, openly, lewdly & obscenely with intent to insult a female	Wilfully and indecently to the annoyance of residents or passengers
Where	In public, or seen from a public place	In either a public or private place	In a street
What	Any part of the body	Penis	The person
By whom	Male or female	Male	Male or female
To whom	Male or female	Female	Male or female

Sexual Offences Committed Outside the UK Sex Offenders Act 1997, S7

An act done by a person in a country or territory outside the U.K. which constituted an offence under the law in force in that country or territory, and would constitute one of the following offences if it has been done in England and Wales, or in Northern Ireland (including attempts, conspiracies, incitements, aiding, abetting, counselling or procuring such an offence):

ENGLAND AND WALES

Sexual Offences Act 1956

S1 Rape (victim under 16)
S5 Intercourse with girl under 13
S6 Intercourse with girl between 13 and 16
S12 Buggery (victim under 16)
S14 Indecent assault on girl (under 16)
S15 Indecent assault on boy (under 16)
S16 Assault with intent to commit buggery (victim under 16)

Indecency with Children Act 1960

S1 Indecent conduct with young child

Protection of Children Act 1978

S1 Indecent photographs of children

NORTHERN IRELAND

Rape (victim under 16) Offences Against the Person Act 1861

S52 Indecent Assault on girl (under 16)
S61 Buggery (victim under 16)
S62 Assault with intent to commit buggery or indecent assault on male person (victim under 16)

Criminal Law Amendment Act 1885

S4 Unlawful carnal knowledge of a girl under 14
S5 Unlawful carnal knowledge of girl under 16

Children and Young Persons Act (Northern Ireland) 1968

S22 Indecent conduct towards a child

Protection of Children (Northern Ireland) Order 1978

Act 3 Indecent photographs of children

The offender must have been at the commencement of this section coming into force, or subsequently became a British citizen or resident in the U.K.

Shall constitute that sexual offence under the law of that parts of the U.K.

Note: At the time of going to press this section had not been brought into force.

Conspiracy or Incitement to Commit Sexual Offences Outside the UK

SEXUAL OFFENCES (CONSPIRACY AND INCITEMENT) ACT 1996

A person will be guilty of conspiracy (or incitement) if each of the following conditions is satisfied:

1. The agreed course of action would involve:
   a) an act by one or more of the parties, or
   b) the happening of some other event,
   intended to take place outside the UK.
2. The act or other event (or what he had in view) is an offence in that other country.
3. The agreement (or what he had in view) would otherwise have been an offence of conspiracy under s1 of the Criminal Law Act 1977 (or of incitement) relating to one of the offences in the list below.
4. (does not apply to an offence of incitement)
   A party to the agreement (or his agent):
   a) did anything in England and Wales relating to the agreement before its formation, or
   b) became a party in England and Wales, or
   c) did or omitted anything in England and Wales in pursuance of the agreement.

Listed Sexual Offences

Sexual Offences Act 1956:
- S1 rape (victim under 16)
- S5 intercourse with girl under 13
- S6 intercourse with girl under 16
- S12 buggery (victim under 16)
- S14 indecent assault on girl (victim under 16)
- S15 indecent assault on boy (victim under 16)

Indecency with Children Act 1960:
- S1 indecent conduct towards young child

Notification of Details to the Police of Sexual Offenders SEX OFFENDERS ACT 1997

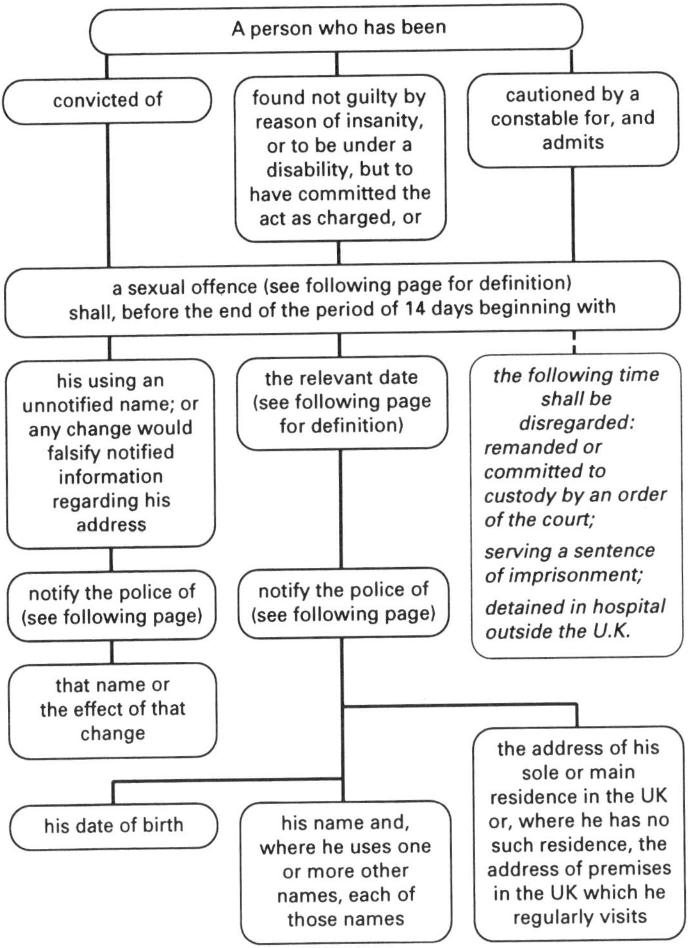
A person who has been
convicted of
found not guilty by reason of insanity, or to be under a disability, but to have committed the act as charged, or
cautioned by a constable for, and admits
a sexual offence (see following page for definition) shall, before the end of the period of 14 days beginning with
his using an unnotified name; or any change would falsify notified information regarding his address
the relevant date (see following page for definition)
the following time shall be disregarded: remanded or committed to custody by an order of the court; serving a sentence of imprisonment; detained in hospital outside the U.K.
notify the police of (see following page)
notify the police of (see following page)
that name or the effect of that change
the address of his sole or main residence in the UK or, where he has no such residence, the address of premises in the UK which he regularly visits
his date of birth
his name and, where he uses one or more other names, each of those names

Failure, without reasonable excuse, to notify the police: or to give false information is an offence.

'Sexual Offence' means

Offences under the Sexual Offenders Act 1956:

S1 Rape.
S5 Intercourse with girl under 13.
S6 Intercourse with girl between 13 and 16.
S10 Incest by a man (unless the other party is over 18).
S12 Buggery (unless the offender is under 20 or the other party is over 18).
S13 Indecency between men (unless the offender is under 20 or the other party is over 18).
S14 Indecent assault on a woman (unless the woman is over 18).
S15 Indecent assault on a man (unless the victim is over 18).
S16 Assault with intent to commit buggery (unless the victim is over 18).
S28 Causing or encouraging prostitution of intercourse with, or indecent assault on, a girl under 16.

An offence under S1 Indecency with Children Act 1960:
indecent conduct towards a young child.

An offence under S54 Criminal Law Act 1977:
inciting a girl under 16 to have incestuous sexual intercourse.

An offence under S1 Protection of Children Act 1978:
indecent photographs of children.

The Act also includes similar offences in Scotland, Northern Ireland and under service law. It also includes attempts, conspiracy, incitement aiding abetting, counselling or procuring such offences.

An offence under S170 of the Customs and Excise Management Act 1979:
fraudulent evasion of duty in relation to goods prohibited to be imported and which include indecent photographs of persons under 16.

An offence under S160 Criminal Justice Act 1988:
possessing indecent photographs of children.

'Relevant Date' means

Where a person has been convicted: *The date of conviction.*
If guilty but insane: *The date of such finding.*
If cautioned by a constable: *The date of the caution.*

'Notification' means

May be given by attending any police station and giving notification orally; or by sending written notification to any police station.

Chapter 3
Firearms and Explosives

Firearms – Definitions

S 57 Firearms Act 1968

The term 'firearm' includes any:

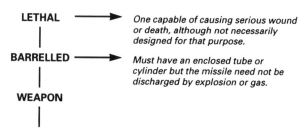

LETHAL → *One capable of causing serious wound or death, although not necessarily designed for that purpose.*

BARRELLED → *Must have an enclosed tube or cylinder but the missile need not be discharged by explosion or gas.*

WEAPON

of any description from which any shot, bullet or other missile can be discharged and including any:

- **Prohibited weapon** whether it is lethal or not.
- **Component part** of such lethal or prohibited weapon.
- **Accessory** to such weapons designed or adapted to diminish the noise or flash caused by firing the weapon.

The term 'small calibre pistol':

See following page.

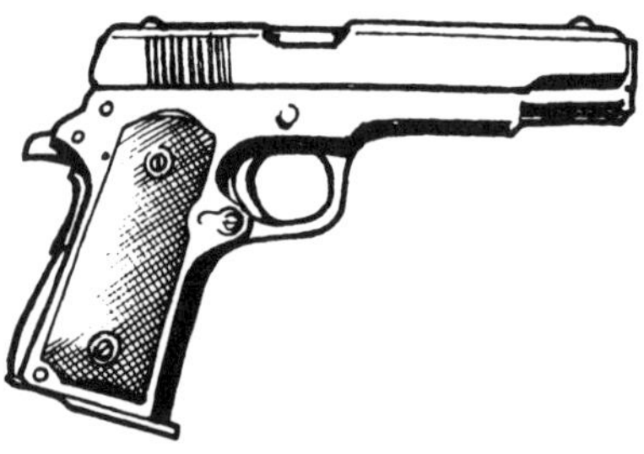

The term 'imitation firearm' means:

Anything which has the appearance of being a firearm whether or not it is capable of discharging any shot, bullet or other missile.

PROHIBITED WEAPONS

S 5(1) FIREARMS ACT 1968 AS AMENDED BY THE FIREARMS (AMENDMENT) ACTS 1988 AND 1997, AND THE FIREARMS (AMENDMENT) REGULATIONS 1992

A person commits an offence if, without the authority of the Secretary of State, he has in his possession, or purchases or acquires, or manufactures, sells or transfers:

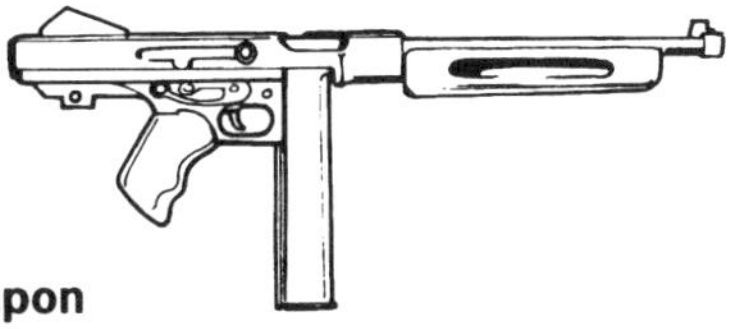

A prohibited weapon

- Any firearm which is so designed or adapted that two or more missiles can be successively discharged without repeated pressure on the trigger.
- Any self-loading or pump-action rifle gun other than one which is chambered for .22 rim-fire cartridges.
- Any firearm which either has a barrel less than 30cm or less than 60cm overall (disregarding any detachable, folding, retractable or other moveable butt-stock) other than an air weapon, a small calibre pistol, a muzzle-loading gun or a firearm designed as signalling apparatus.

  A 'small calibre pistol' means:
  a) A pistol chambered for .22 or smaller rim-fire cartridges; or
  b) An air pistol to which S1 applied and which is designed to fire .22 or smaller diameter ammunition.
- Any self-loading or pump action smooth-bore gun which is not an air weapon or chambered for .22 rim-fire cartridges and either:
  a) has a barrel less than 24" in length, or
  b) is less than 40" in overall length.
- Any smooth-bore revolver gun other than one which is chambered for 9mm rim-fire cartridges or a muzzle loading gun.

Prohibited weapons continued...

- Any rocket-launcher, or any mortar, for projecting a stabilised missile, other than a launcher or mortar designed for line-throwing or pyrotechnic purposes or as signalling apparatus.
- Any weapon of whatever description designed or adapted for the discharge of any noxious liquid, gas or other thing.

Prohibited ammunition

- Any cartridge with a bullet designed to explode on or immediately before impact, any ammunition containing or designed or adapted to contain any such noxious thing mentioned above and, if capable of being used with a firearm of any description, any grenade, bomb (or other like missile), or rocket or shell designed to explode on or immediately before impact.

Exemptions

Exemptions exist (but Firearm Certificate is still required) in relation to slaughtering instruments, humane killing of animals, starting pistols, trophies of war acquired before 1.1.46, part of a collection and manufactured before 1.1.19, rare or historic importance, shooting vermin or treating animals.

Prohibited weapons continued...

S5(1A) FIREARMS ACT 1968 AS AMENDED BY THE FIREARMS (AMENDMENT) ACTS 1988 AND 1997, AND THE FIREARMS (AMENDMENT) REGULATIONS 1992

A person commits an offence if, without the authority of the Secretary of State he has in his possession, or purchases or acquires, or sells or transfers:

- Any firearm which is disguised as another object.
- Any rocket or ammunition which consists in or incorporates a missile designed to explode on or immediately before impact and is for military use.
- Any launcher or other projecting apparatus designed to be used with any rocket or ammunition.
- Any ammunition for military use which consists in or incorporates a missile designed so that a substance contained in the missile will ignite on or immediately before impact, or which is designed, on account of its having a jacket or hardcore, to penetrate armour plating, armour screening or body armour.
- Any ammunition which incorporates a missile designed or adapted to expand on impact.
- Anything which is designed to be projected as a missile from any weapon and is designed to be, or had been, incorporated in any ammunition.

Exemptions

Exemptions exist in relation to holders of certificates or authority, firearms collectors, bodies concerned in cultural or historical aspects of firearms, slaughtering instruments, and registered firearms dealers.

Firearms Certificates

S 1(1) FIREARMS ACT 1968
AS AMENDED BY THE FIREARMS (AMENDMENT) ACT 1988

Subject to any exemption under the act, it is an offence for a person to **purchase**, or **acquire** (to hire, accept as a gift or borrow), or **possess** (to have ultimate control over it, and not necessarily in physical possession):

1) Any AMMUNITION except:

- **Cartridges** containing 5 or more shot, none of which exceeds .36" diameter.
- Ammunition for an **air weapon.**
- **Blank cartridges** not more than 1" diameter.

2) A FIREARM except:

- A **shotgun** (not being an air gun) which is a smooth-bore gun:
  - having a barrel not less than 24" in length nor more than 2" in diameter;
  - having either no magazine or a non-detachable magazine incapable of holding more than 2 cartridges; and
  - not being a revolver gun.

- An **air weapon** (air rifle, air gun, air pistol not declared by the Secretary of State to be specially dangerous).

WITHOUT holding an in force firearm certificate, or otherwise than as authorised by such a certificate (in certain circumstance an imitation firearm (see later)).

In relation to small-calibre pistols conditions are normally attached requiring the pistol only to be used for target shooting; membership of a licenced club; and the pistol to be kept at the club. The police may, in exceptional circumstances, grant a permit authorising the possession of the pistol elsewhere, eg. recognised target shooting competitions.

THIS IS AN ARRESTABLE OFFENCE

EXEMPTIONS

In addition to registered firearms dealers, operators of miniature rifle ranges, and persons in the service of the Crown, who may be authorised to possess, purchase and acquire firearms, shotguns and ammunition, provision is made for the following exemptions:

- **Police permit**: The holder of a **police permit** may possess a firearm and ammunition in accordance with the terms of his permit (s 7(1)).
- **Auctioneer**: An **auctioneer, carrier** or **warehouseman**, or servant of such may possess a firearm and ammunition in the course of his business (s 9(1)). The auctioneer may also **sell** if he holds a police permit (s 9(2)).
- **Slaughterman**: A **licensed slaughterman** may possess a slaughtering instrument and ammunition in a slaughterhouse or knackers yard where he is employed, (Also applies to the **proprietor**), (s 10(1) & (2)).
- **Sport**: A person may **carry for another** a firearm or ammunition, under instruction from, and for the use of, that other person for sporting purposes only (s 11(1)).
- **Starter: A starter at an athletic** meeting may possess a firearm for starting races (s 11(2)).
- **Cadet corps**: A member of a **cadet corps** approved by the Secretary of State may possess a firearm and ammunition when engaged in drill or target practice (s 11(3)).
- **Ranges**: User of air rifles and miniature rifles at a **miniature rifle range** or shooting gallery may possess such weapons (s 11(4)).
- **Clubs**: A **member of a rifle club**, miniature rifle club or pistol club approved by the Secretary of State (certain types of weapons may be specified in the approval), (s 15 1988 act).

...continued on next page

EXEMPTIONS continued...

- **Private premises:** A person may borrow a **shotgun** from the occupier of **private premises** and use it on those premises in the occupier's presence (s 11(5)).
  A person over 17 years of age may borrow a **rifle** from the occupier of **private premises** if the occupier holds a certificate and he or his servant is present (s 16 1988 Act).
- **Approved:** A person may use a shotgun at police-approved meetings for **shooting at artificial targets** (s 11(6)).
- **Theatres:** Persons taking part in **theatrical performances** or rehearsals, or production of films, may possess firearms and, if approved by the Secretary of State, prohibited weapons (s 12(1) & (2)).
- **Signalling equipment: Signalling apparatus** on an aircraft or at an aerodrome, or firearms or ammunition on board a ship, as equipment of such (s 13(1)).
- **Northern ireland:** The holder of a **Northern Ireland firearm certificate** (s 15).
- **Crown service:** Persons in the **service of the Crown** (includes police officers in their capacity as such) (s 54).
- **Proof houses:** Possession of a firearm going to, at, or coming from a specified **proof house** where they are tested (s 58).
- **Visitor's permit:** The holder of a **visitor's firearms or shotgun permit** (s 17 1988 Act).
- **Antique firearms:** See appropriate page.

Licenced Pistol Clubs

FIREARMS (AMENDMENT) ACT 1997 SS 19 – 31

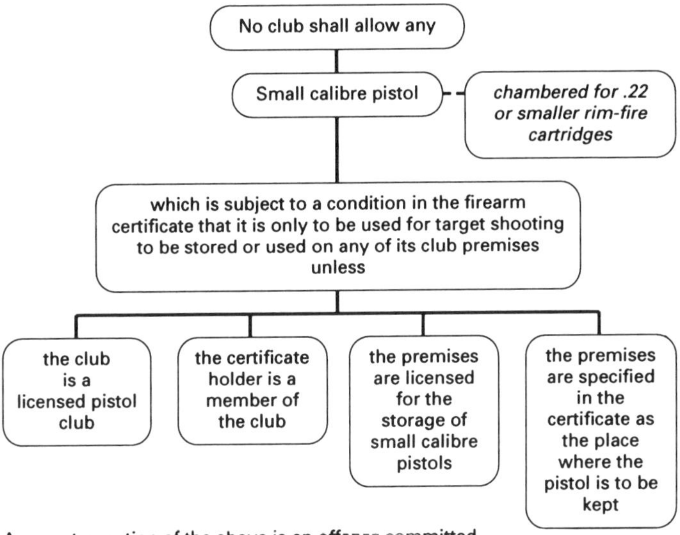

Any contravention of the above is an offence committed by the persons responsible for the management of the club.

Registers (S26)

- Must be kept at all licensed premises.
- Must contain particulars of:
  a) weapons stored;
  b) name and address of certificate holder;
  c) dates of storage, removal and return.
- Dates to be entered within 24 hours of the event.
- To be available for inspection for 5 years.

A constable or civilian officer authorisedby the chief constable may, on producing his authority enter and inspect the premises and anything on them.

It is an offence to fail to keep a register, make false entries, or obstruct entry/inspection.

Shotguns

S 2(1) Firearms Act 1968

IT IS AN OFFENCE FOR A PERSON TO

Means to have ultimate control over it ◄ **POSSESS**

PURCHASE

Means to hire, accept as a gift or borrow ◄ **ACQUIRE**

THIS IS AN ARRESTABLE OFFENCE

A SHOTGUN

(A smooth-bore gun with a barrel not less than 24" in length, not being an air gun. But component parts and sound moderators are not included. It must be a complete shotgun. A certificate would not be required for a part, eg a barrel)

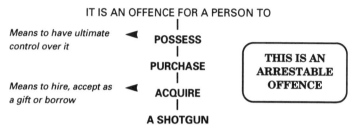

WITHOUT HOLDING A CERTIFICATE AUTHORISING HIM TO POSSESS SHOTGUNS

ANTIQUES

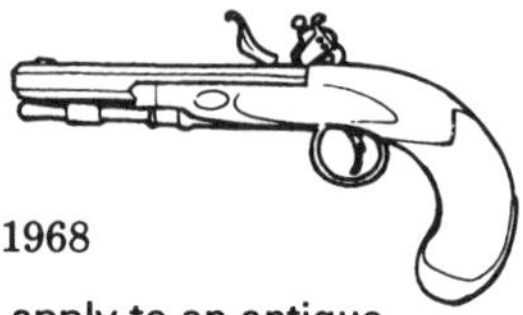

S 58(2) Firearms Act 1968

Nothing in the Act relating to firearms shall apply to an antique rifle or shotgun which is sold, transferred, purchased, acquired or possessed as a curiosity or ornament.

The term 'antique' is not defined. But for practical purposes, a breach-loading weapon capable of firing a metallic cartridge would probably not be an antique.

A genuine antique used for target practice would not be possessed as a curio and, therefore, would require a certificate.

Criminal Use of Firearms

FIREARMS ACT, 1968 AS AMENDED BY THE FIREARMS (AMENDMENT) ACT 1994

The law attempts to prevent the criminal use and possession of firearms and imitation firearms in the following provisions, **all of which are arrestable offences**:

THESE ARE ARRESTABLE OFFENCES

SECTION 16

Possession of a firearm or ammunition with **intent to endanger life** or enable another to do so (injury not essential)

SECTION 16A

Possession of a firearm or imitation firearm with intent by means thereof, or to enable another by means thereof, to cause any person to believe that **unlawful violence** will be used against him or another person.

SECTION 17(1)

Making use or attempting to make use of a firearm or imitation firearm with **intent to resist or prevent arrest** of self or another

SECTION 17(2)

Possession of a firearm or imitation firearm **at time of committing or of arrest for schedule 1 offence** (see following page)

SECTION 18(1)

Having with him a firearm or imitation firearm with **intent to commit an indictable offence** or to resist or prevent arrest of self or another

SCHEDULE 1 TO THE FIREARMS ACT 1968

The list of offences below are those referred to in section 17(2) of the Firearms Act 1968

1 Offences under s 1 of the Criminal Damage Act 1971

2 Offences under any of the following provisions of the Offences Against the Person Act 1861:
   - Ss 20-22 (Inflicting bodily injury; garrotting; criminal use of stupefying drugs)
   - S 30 (Laying explosive to building, etc)
   - S 32 (Endangering railway passengers by tampering with track)
   - S 38 (Assault with intent to resist arrest)
   - S 47 (Criminal assaults)

3 Offences under the Child Abduction Act 1984, Pt 1

4 Theft, robbery, burglary, blackmail and any offence under s 12(1) (taking of motor vehicle or other conveyance without the owner's consent) of the Theft Act 1968

5 Offences under s 51(1) of the Police Act 1964 (Assaulting a constable in the execution of his duty)

6 An offence under s 90(1) of the Criminal Justice Act 1991 (assaulting a prisoner custody officer)

7 An offence under s 13(1) of the Criminal Justice and Public Order Act 1994 (assaulting a secure training centre custody officer)

8 Offences under any of the following provisions of the Sexual Offences Act 1956
   - S 1 (rape)
   - Ss 17, 18 and 20 (abduction of women)

9 Aiding and abetting the commission of any offence specified in the foregoing sections, and attempts to commit them

Firearms Dealers

S 3(1) FIREARMS ACT 1968

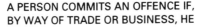

A PERSON COMMITS AN OFFENCE IF, BY WAY OF TRADE OR BUSINESS, HE

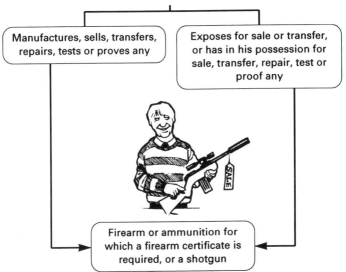

Manufactures, sells, transfers, repairs, tests or proves any

Exposes for sale or transfer, or has in his possession for sale, transfer, repair, test or proof any

Firearm or ammunition for which a firearm certificate is required, or a shotgun

*Does not include air weapons, cartridges containing 5 or more shot, none of which exceeds .36" dia. But **does** include ammunition capable of being fired from a shotgun or smooth-bore gun for which a firearms certificate is required* (S 5 FIREARMS (AMENDMENT) ACT 1988)

Unless he is registered as a firearms dealer

He must keep a register in which the prescribed particulars are recorded within 24 hours of the transaction. Inspection of the register must be allowed by a police officer authorised in writing by the chief constable

The main exemptions cover auctioneers, miniature rifle ranges and proof houses.

Possession of Firearms

FIREARMS ACT 1968, AS AMENDED BY THE FIREARMS (AMENDMENT) ACT 1994

A person commits an offence if, without lawful authority or reasonable excuse (the proof whereof lies on him), he has with him in a **public place**:

- A **loaded** shotgun.
- A **loaded** air weapon.
- Any firearm, **loaded or not**, together with ammunition suitable for use in that firearm. S 19

It is an offence for a person to have a small-calibre pistol with him **outside licenced premises** of a licenced pistol club unless he possess a police permit or has a firearms certificate which is not subject to a condition requiring it to be kept at a licenced pistol club. S 19A

A person commits an offence if, while he has a firearm or imitation firearm with him, he enters or is in any building or part of a **building** as a **trespasser** and without reasonable excuse (the proof whereof lies on him). S 20(1)

A person commits an offence if, while he has a firearm or imitation firearm with him, he enters or is on any **land** as a **trespasser** and without reasonable excuse (the proof whereof lies on him) S 20(2)

A person who has been sentenced to serve 3 years or more **imprisonment** or detention, shall not have a firearm or ammunition in his possession **at any time.** A person who has been sentenced to borstal training, to corrective training for less than 3 years, or to imprisonment for 3 months or more but less than 3 years, shall not have a firearm or ammunition in his possession for **5 years** from the date of his release. S 21

Miscellaneous Offences

DRUNKENNESS

S 12 Licensing Act 1872

It is an offence to be drunk when in possession of any **loaded** firearm, and such a person may be apprehended. Includes air guns

HIGHWAYS

S 161(2) Highways Act 1980

It is an offence, without lawful authority or excuse, to discharge any firearm within 50 feet of the centre of a highway if a user of the highway is injured, interrupted or endangered.

A constable may arrest without warrant any person who, within his view, wantonly discharges any firearm in any street to the obstruction, annoyance or danger of the residents or passengers.

SHORTENING BARRELS, ETC

S 4(1) Firearms Act 1968

It is an offence to shorten the barrel of a shotgun to a length less than 24" (except registered dealers). When less than 24" the shortened shotgun becomes a firearm for which a certificate is required – but there is no way one will be possessed because the police would never issue one for a sawn-off shotgun. Possession of a Section 1 firearm without a certificate is already an arrestable offence (5 years), but when it arises from shortening a shotgun, it is committed in 'aggravated' form and carries a maximum of 7 years.' It is also an offence to possess, purchase or acquire such a weapon. S 6 of the Firearms (Amendment) Act 1988 creates an offence (unless a dealer) to shorten to less than 24" the barrel of a smooth-bore gun for which a firearm certificate is required (other than one with bore exceeding 2").

It is an offence (other than as a registered dealer) to convert into a firearm anything which, though having the appearance of being a firearm, is so constructed as to be incapable of discharging any missile through its barrel, s 4(3).

It is also an offence to possess, purchase or acquire such a weapon, s 4(4).

Ages

FIREARMS ACT 1968

	Under 17 but over 14	Under 15	Under 14
Firearms and ammunition	• May not purchase or hire • Offence to sell or let on hire to, s 22(1), s 24(1) • May accept as a gift or loan if both parties have firearms certificates		• May not possess except as gun bearer, member of rifle club or cadet corps etc, miniature rifle range or shooting gallery, s 22(2) • Offence to make a gift to, lend to, or part with possession to, s 24(4)
Shotguns	• May not purchase or hire • Offence to sell or let on hire to, s 22(1)	• May not have with him an assembled shotgun except: i) Under supervision of a person over 21, or ii) When so covered with a securely fastened gun cover that it cannot be fired, s 22(3) • Offence to make a gift to, s 24(3)	
Air weapons	• May not possess **air pistol** in a public place • May not purchase or hire, s 22(1) • Offence to sell or let on hire to, s 24(1) • May not have with him in a public place except when securely fastened in a gun cover so that it cannot be fired (but no such exemption is given for **pistols**) • Offence not committed if member of rifle club or shooting gallery, s 22(5)		• May not have with him (nor ammunition) except under supervision of person over 21, s 22(4) • If in a public place must also be securely fastened in a gun cover so that it cannot be fired • If on premises may not fire any missile beyond those premises, s 23(1) • Offence not committed if member of rifle club or shooting gallery, s 23(2) • May not make a gift or part with possession, s 24(4)

Police Powers

FIREARMS ACT 1968

Production of certificate

S 48(1)

A constable may demand from any person whom he believes to be in possession of a firearm or ammunition for which a certificate is required, or of a shotgun, the production of his firearm certificate or, as the case may be, his shotgun certificate.

Seizure of weapon

S 48(2)

If he fails to produce the certificate or to permit the constable to read it, or to show that he is exempt from the requirement to hold one, the constable may seize and detain the firearm, ammunition or shotgun, and demand the person to declare to him immediately his name and address.

It is an offence for a person having a firearm or ammunition with him to fail to hand it over when required to do so by a constable, s 47(2).

Arrest

Where the person fails to satisfy the constable as to his identity, consider arrest under s 25 of the Police and Criminal Evidence Act 1984 (see later).

Chapter 4

Licensing

Betting

BETTING, GAMING AND LOTTERIES ACT 1963

Although 'betting' is not defined in the statutes it is commonly taken to mean:

The staking of money or other value on the event of a doubtful issue

Betting is not in itself unlawful but becomes so in any one of four ways:

Unauthorised business S 2

A bookmaker is a person who carries on a business of betting and he must hold a bookmaker's permit.

The permit must be produced at the request of a constable.

A person acting as a servant or agent of a bookmaker must:

- *Be over 21*
- *Be authorised in writing by the bookmaker*

unless he acts only on the bookmaker's premises.

The bookmaker must keep a register of persons authorised to act as his servant or agent.

Unauthorised premises S 1

Otherwise than on horse racecourses and dog tracks, premises may not be used for betting transactions.
(See betting offices on following page)

But premises may be used if all persons involved in the transaction either reside or work there.

An offence is committed by any person who resorts to unauthorised premises for the purpose of betting (proof that he was on the premises will be sufficient until he proves otherwise).

With young persons S 21

It is an offence to have a betting transaction with; to employ to effect betting transactions; or to receive or negotiate a bet through – a person under the age of 18.

In a street or public place S 8

It is an offence to frequent or loiter in a street or public place for betting except on a racecourse.

BETTING OFFICES

S 10 & Sched 4 Betting, Gaming and Lotteries Act 1963,
Licensed Betting Office Regulations 1986
Licensed Betting Office (Amendment) Regs 1993
Betting, Gaming and Lotteries Act 1963 (Schedule 4) (Amendment) Order 1995

Under 18s Not permitted. A notice to this effect must be displayed.

Licence The betting office licence must be displayed on the premises.

Hours Must remain closed Good Friday, Christmas Day, and daily between 6.30pm and 7am (10pm and 7am from April to August).

Access Except for the licensee and his servant, no access must be available to premises used for other purposes.

Refreshments The only refreshments allowed are non-alcoholic drinks, pre-packaged sandwiches, snacks, confectionery, biscuits and cakes.

Notice A notice must be displayed setting out the terms of betting (including deductions from winnings, maximum amount of bets and the procedure for resolving disputes).

Apparatus Sound or visual apparatus may only provide information about betting on sporting events and incidental advertisements. Any screen must be not more than 30" wide and not capable of being seen from outside. Images received must be intended for the general public or other licensees generally. If video recordings are used, they must be available to other licensees generally.

Advertisements No advertisement may be published indicating that the premises are a licensed betting office, its location or the facilities offered except (a) inside the office, or (b) outside the office (but only the words 'licensed betting office' or similar expression eg 'bookmaker' or 'turf accountant' (limited to 3 words), the name of the licensee, directions to the office if those premises give access only, and opening hours).

Entertainment No music, dancing or other entertainment may be provided or allowed except as authorised above.

ENFORCEMENT

Betting, Gaming and Lotteries Act 1963

Licensee, etc S 10(1)

The licensee, his servant or agent, may refuse to admit to, or may expel from premises any person who is:

- Drunk
- Violent
- Quarrelsome
- Disorderly
- Likely to subject the licensee to a penalty.

Any person who fails to leave when requested commits an offence.

Constable S 10(3)

A constable may, at the request of the licensee, his servant or agent, help to expel from the premises any person whom the constable has reasonable cause to suspect to be liable to be expelled, and such force as may be required may be used for that purpose.

Power of Entry S 10(4)

A constable may enter a licensed betting office for the purpose of ascertaining whether provisions are being complied with, and any person who obstructs the constable commits an offence.

ADVERTISEMENTS AND NOTICES

S 10(5) Betting, Gaming and Lotteries Act 1963, Licensed Betting Office Regulations 1986

Betting office licence to be displayed on the premises.

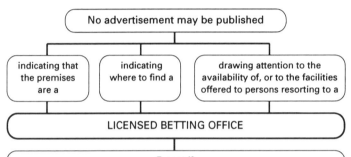

No advertisement may be published

- indicating that the premises are a
- indicating where to find a
- drawing attention to the availability of, or to the facilities offered to persons resorting to a

LICENSED BETTING OFFICE

Except if

(a) it is published inside but not outside the licensed betting office; or

(b) it is published outside the office:

(i) from a place inside the office; or
(ii) in premises giving access to the office; or
(iii) by being painted on or otherwise attached to the outside of the office or premises in which the office is situated

And is restricted to text which does not exceed three words in length stating "LICENSED BETTING OFFICE" or similar words, included in the name of the licensee, indicating where the premises may be found (where premises give access) and the hours of opening.

A conspicuous notice must be displayed inside the premises, but not so that it can be read from the outside, setting out the terms on which persons are invited to bet on the premises including the amount of deductions made from winnings, the maximum limit on the amount of winnings and the procedure for the resolution of disputed bets.

Gaming

S 52(1) GAMING ACT 1968

MEANS THE PLAYING OF A GAME OF CHANCE FOR WINNINGS IN MONEY OR MONEY'S WORTH, WHETHER ANY PERSON PLAYING THE GAME IS AT RISK OF LOSING ANY MONEY OR MONEY'S WORTH OR NOT

GAME OF CHANCE

DOES NOT INCLUDE ANY ATHLETIC GAME OR SPORT BUT, WITH THAT EXCEPTION, INCLUDES A GAME OF CHANCE AND SKILL COMBINED AND A PRETENDED GAME OF CHANCE OR OF CHANCE AND SKILL COMBINED

Bingo, card games and dominoes are all gaming because they all involve an element of chance

Any money staked would be gaming

Darts would not be gaming because it is pure skill

Any money staked would be betting

The Gaming Act 1968 controls gaming

The four parts into which the Act is divided are as follows:

Part 1 Gaming other than on premises licensed or registered under the Act.

Part 2 Gaming on premises which have been licensed or registered.

Part 3 Gaming machines.

Part 4 Gaming at small parties, etc.

These are now discussed in turn on the following pages.

GAMING ELSEWHERE THAN ON PREMISES LICENSED OR REGISTERED UNDER THE ACT

GAMING ACT 1968

Certain restrictions are imposed on the gaming which is allowed:

THE NATURE OF THE GAME S 2

This restriction does not apply to domestic occasions in a private dwelling, in a hostel, hall of residence or similar place not used as a business, and the players are all inmates or residents

The game shall not involve playing or staking against a bank, whether or not a player holds the bank

The chances must be equally favourable to all players

Where the players are playing against some other person, the chances must not be more favourable to the other person than the players

CHARGES FOR TAKING PART S 3

Other than any stakes hazarded, no charge, in money or money's worth, may be made to take part (this would include an admission charge) but this restriction would not apply to members clubs

LEVY ON STAKES OR WINNINGS S 4

A levy may not be charged on any of the stakes or winnings, whether by direct payment, deduction, exchange or tokens at a lower rate than of issue, or any other means

Public places S 5

No person may take part in gaming in a street or any place to which the public have access on payment or otherwise.

Street includes any bridge, road, lane, footway, etc, which is open to the public, and the doorways and entrances of premises abutting upon, and any ground adjoining and open to, a street.

Licensed premises S 6

Dominoes and cribbage, and any other game authorised by the licensing justices may be played on premises for which a justices' on-licence is in force (other than a restaurant or guest house licence).

GAMING S 12 GAMING ACT 1968

The following restrictions apply to premises which are either licensed under the Act, or which consist of a club or miners' welfare institute registered under the Act. But not in respect of gaming machines.

Who may take part?

- Only persons who are present on the premises at the time gaming takes place.
- They must be members of the club in question, or bona fide guests of such a member.
- Neither the licence holder nor any other person acting on his behalf may take part in the gaming except holding the bank.
- At least 48 hours must have elapsed since application being made for membership and taking part in the gaming.
- No person under 18 years shall be present whilst gaming is taking place (except on premises restricted to the playing of bingo). S 17.

A constable may at any reasonable time enter any premises LICENSED under the Act and may inspect the premises, machines or other equipment, and any book or other document on the premises, for the purpose of ascertaining whether any contravention has been committed. S 43

GAMING MACHINES GAMING ACT 1968

For practical purposes, machines are of two types:

JACKPOT MACHINES S31

- May only be used on premises which are either licensed or registered under the Act for the purpose of gaming or gaming machines.
- There is a limit to the charge for playing the machines (20p).
- There is no limit to the maximum prize which may be won, but it must be by way of coins from the machine.
- There must be a statement on the machines specifying the prize(s) which may be won and the percentage of payout.
- The machines may not be used on the premises on any occasion when the public are admitted whether on payment or otherwise.
- Not more than two machines may be available on the premises unless authorised under s 32, in which case the provisions of s 34 (below) must be complied with instead of those above.

AMUSEMENTS WITH PRIZES S 34

- May only be used on premises for which a permit has been granted; on licensed or registered premises where this type of machine has been opted for instead of jackpot machines; on premises used a a pleasure fair for which a permit has been granted; or at a travelling showmen's pleasure fair.
- There is a 20p limit to the charge for playing the machine.
- Prizes are restricted to one of the following:
  - Money prize not exceeding £3.00 or tokens exchangeable for such amount;
  - Non-money prize not exceeding £6.00 or tokens exchangeable for such non-money prize.
  - A mixture of money and non-money prizes which do not exceed the above amounts;
  - Tokens which can be either used to play further games or be exchanged as above.

But jackpot machines, amusement with prizes machines, or any other type of machine may be used at non-commercial entertainment if not on premises licensed or registered under the Act, without further authority and without limits on numbers or prizes. This would apply to bazaars, fêtes, dinners, dances, etc, whether limited to one day or extended over two or more days. In these cases the whole of the proceeds after deducting expenses must be devoted to other than private gain. S 33

GAMING - ADVERTISEMENTS

S 42 GAMING ACT 1968 (AS AMENDED)

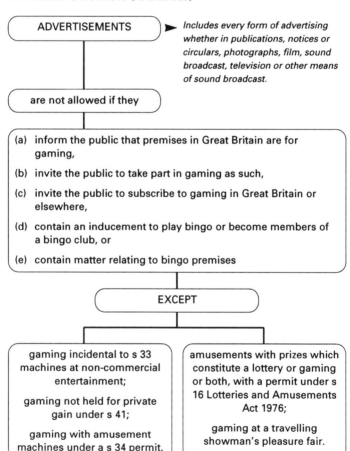

ADVERTISEMENTS

Includes every form of advertising whether in publications, notices or circulars, photographs, film, sound broadcast, television or other means of sound broadcast.

are not allowed if they

(a) inform the public that premises in Great Britain are for gaming,

(b) invite the public to take part in gaming as such,

(c) invite the public to subscribe to gaming in Great Britain or elsewhere,

(d) contain an inducement to play bingo or become members of a bingo club, or

(e) contain matter relating to bingo premises

EXCEPT

gaming incidental to s 33 machines at non-commercial entertainment;

gaming not held for private gain under s 41;

gaming with amusement machines under a s 34 permit.

amusements with prizes which constitute a lottery or gaming or both, with a permit under s 16 Lotteries and Amusements Act 1976;

gaming at a travelling showman's pleasure fair.

GAMING AT SMALL PARTIES, ETC

S 41 GAMING ACT 1968 (AS AMENDED)

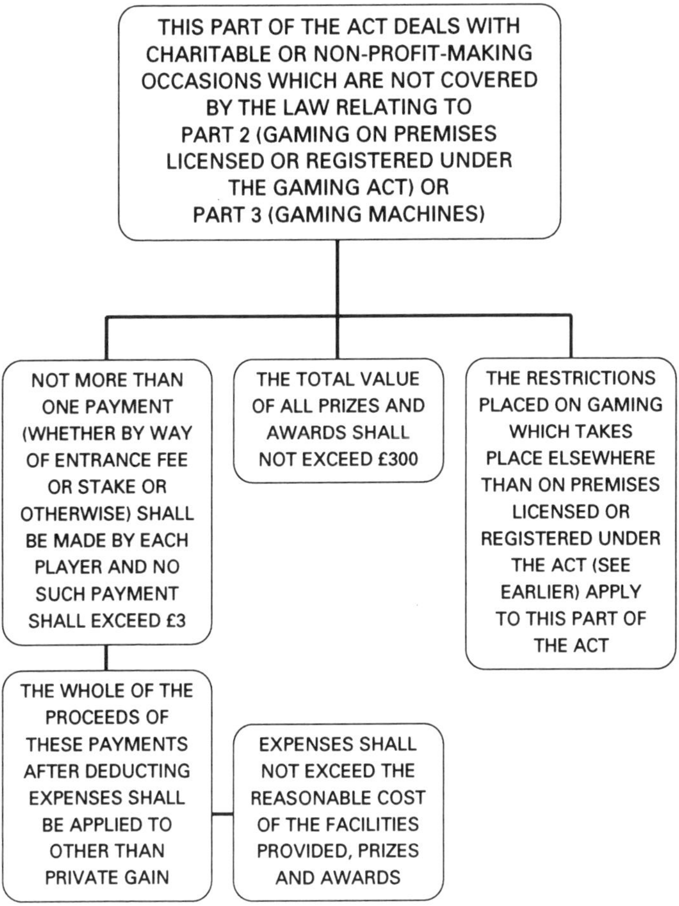
THIS PART OF THE ACT DEALS WITH CHARITABLE OR NON-PROFIT-MAKING OCCASIONS WHICH ARE NOT COVERED BY THE LAW RELATING TO PART 2 (GAMING ON PREMISES LICENSED OR REGISTERED UNDER THE GAMING ACT) OR PART 3 (GAMING MACHINES)
NOT MORE THAN ONE PAYMENT (WHETHER BY WAY OF ENTRANCE FEE OR STAKE OR OTHERWISE) SHALL BE MADE BY EACH PLAYER AND NO SUCH PAYMENT SHALL EXCEED £3
THE TOTAL VALUE OF ALL PRIZES AND AWARDS SHALL NOT EXCEED £300
THE RESTRICTIONS PLACED ON GAMING WHICH TAKES PLACE ELSEWHERE THAN ON PREMISES LICENSED OR REGISTERED UNDER THE ACT (SEE EARLIER) APPLY TO THIS PART OF THE ACT
THE WHOLE OF THE PROCEEDS OF THESE PAYMENTS AFTER DEDUCTING EXPENSES SHALL BE APPLIED TO OTHER THAN PRIVATE GAIN
EXPENSES SHALL NOT EXCEED THE REASONABLE COST OF THE FACILITIES PROVIDED, PRIZES AND AWARDS

Lotteries

S 1 Lotteries and Amusements Act 1976
Readers Digest Ass v Williams [1976]
3 All ER 737

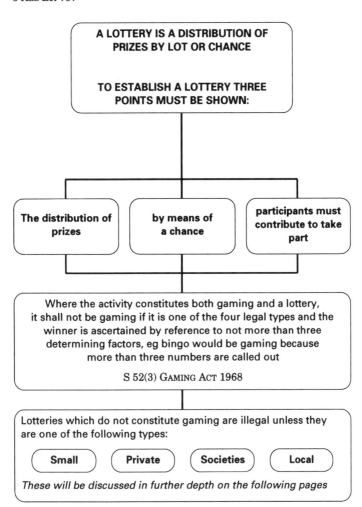

A LOTTERY IS A DISTRIBUTION OF PRIZES BY LOT OR CHANCE

TO ESTABLISH A LOTTERY THREE POINTS MUST BE SHOWN:

- **The distribution of prizes**
- **by means of a chance**
- **participants must contribute to take part**

Where the activity constitutes both gaming and a lottery, it shall not be gaming if it is one of the four legal types and the winner is ascertained by reference to not more than three determining factors, eg bingo would be gaming because more than three numbers are called out

S 52(3) Gaming Act 1968

Lotteries which do not constitute gaming are illegal unless they are one of the following types:

Small | **Private** | **Societies** | **Local**

These will be discussed in further depth on the following pages

SMALL LOTTERIES

S 3 Lotteries & Amusements Act 1976

These take place at a bazaar, sale of work, fête, dinner, dance, sporting or athletic event, or other entertainment of similar character, whether for one day or for two or more days.

Certain conditions must be complied with:

- All proceeds less expenses must be devoted to other than private gain.
- Prizes must not be money.
- Sale of tickets etc, and declaration or result must take place at the entertainment.
- The lottery shall not be the only or substantial inducement to attend.

PRIVATE LOTTERIES

S 4 Lotteries & Amusements Act 1976

The lottery is confined to members of one society, established and conducted for purposes not connected with gaming, betting or lotteries; persons who work on the same premises, or persons who reside on the same premises and which is promoted by such persons (and in the case of a lottery, authorised in writing to do so by the governing body of the society).

A private lottery is not unlawful but must comply with the following conditions:

- All proceeds less expenses must be devoted to the purpose of the society and/or prizes to the members.
- No advertising of the lottery except a notice exhibited on the society's premises or, if applicable, where the participants work or reside, or on the tickets etc.
- Prices of all tickets to be the same, and stated on the ticket.
- Tickets to bear the name and address of the promoter, the persons to whom the sale of tickets is restricted, and that the prize will only be given to the person to whom the ticket was sold.
- Tickets shall be issued only upon receipt of the full price, which is not refundable.
- No tickets to be sent through the post.

'Society' includes any club, institution, organisation or association of persons by whatever name called.

LOTTERIES & AMUSEMENTS ACT 1976 AND
LOTTERIES REGULATIONS ACT 1977

SOCIETIES' LOTTERIES S 5

Promoted by a society established for: Charitable purposes, Athletic sports or games or culture, Other purposes which are not for private gain or commercial

A society's lottery is not unlawful if the following conditions are met:
- Promoted in GB
- Society is registered under the Act
- Scheme approved by the society
- Total value of tickets etc sold is £10,000 or less, otherwise scheme to be registered with the Board before sale of tickets
- All proceeds less expenses to be applied to purposes of the society

LOCAL LOTTERIES S 6

These are lotteries promoted by the local authority

A local lottery is not unlawful if the following conditions are met:
- Promoted in GB
- Promoted in accordance with a scheme approved by the local authority
- Scheme registered with the Board before sale of tickets
- Publicity must be given to the objects of the lottery. S 7
- All money accruing must be applied to the objects of the lottery unless the Secretary of State consents otherwise. S 7

AND

- No more than 50% of proceeds to be spent on prizes. S 11
- No ticket to exceed £1.00. S 11
- Full price must be paid for tickets and no refunds. S 11
- Tickets etc may not be sold by or to persons under 16 or by machine. REGS 4&7
- Tickets not to be sold in a street except from a kiosk or shop front. REG 5
- Not to be sold in premises being a licensed betting office, amusement arcade or bingo or gaming club. REG 6
- Not to be sold by a person during the discharge of official duties not connected with the lottery. REG 8
- Tickets must bear name and address of promoter (in the case of societies) and the name of the society. S 11
- The price of every ticket shall be the same and shall be stated on the ticket. S 11
- The promoter of the lottery must be authorised in writing by the governing body.

'Society' – see previous page
'Board' – the Gaming Board of Great Britain

LIABILITY

S 2 LOTTERIES & AMUSEMENTS ACT 1976

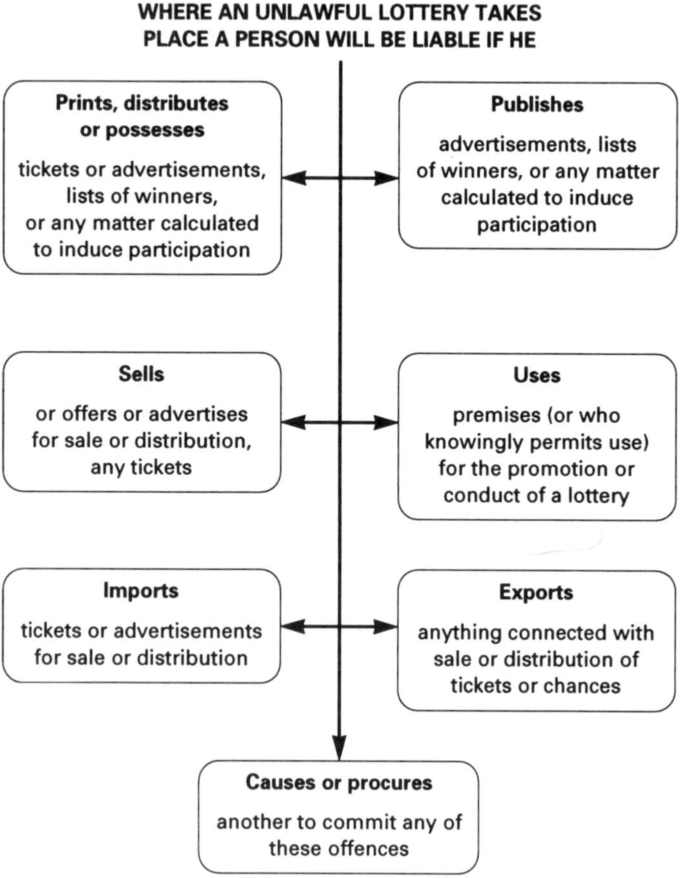
WHERE AN UNLAWFUL LOTTERY TAKES PLACE A PERSON WILL BE LIABLE IF HE
Prints, distributes or possesses
tickets or advertisements, lists of winners, or any matter calculated to induce participation
Publishes
advertisements, lists of winners, or any matter calculated to induce participation
Sells
or offers or advertises for sale or distribution, any tickets
Uses
premises (or who knowingly permits use) for the promotion or conduct of a lottery
Imports
tickets or advertisements for sale or distribution
Exports
anything connected with sale or distribution of tickets or chances
Causes or procures
another to commit any of these offences

Intoxicating Liquor

Ss 160 and 167 Licensing Act 1964,
s 1 Licensing (Low Alcohol Drinks) Act 1990

It is an offence to sell or expose for sale any intoxicating liquor unless authorised to do so by a justices' licence, or canteen licence or occasional permission.

Means spirits, wine, beer, cider and any fermented, distilled or spiritous liquor but does not include:
(a) any liquor which is of a strength not exceeding 0.5 per cent;
(b) perfumes;
(c) flavouring essences not intended for consumption as or with dutiable liquor;
(d) spirits, wine or made–wine intended for use as a medicine and not as a beverage.

A licence is not required for the sale, supply or purchase of **liqueur chocolates** provided that their alcoholic content is not more than 1/50 gall of liquor (spirit) per pound of confectionery and either consists of separate pieces weighing not more than 1.5 oz or designed to be broken into such pieces. But this chocolate must not be sold to a person **under the age of 16 years.**

Beer Includes ale, porter, stout and all other description of beer exceeding 2° proof. Shandy (a mixture of beer and lemonade) is intoxication liquor.

Wine Any liquor obtained from the alcoholic fermentations of fresh grapes or the must of fresh grapes whether or not the liquor is fortified with spirits.

THERE ARE TWO TYPES OF LICENCE (S 1):

'OFF'
Authorises the sale of intoxicating liquor for consumption off the premises only, and may authorise the sale of:

- Intoxicating liquor of all descriptions, or
- Beer, cider and wine only

'ON'
Authorises the sale of intoxicating liquor for consumption either on or off the premises for which the licence is granted, and may authorise the sale of:

- Intoxicating liquor of all descriptions, or
- Beer, cider and wine only, or
- Beer and cider only, or
- Cider only, or
- Wine only

Permitted Hours

S 60 Licensing Act 1964 as amended by the Licensing Act 1988 and the Licensing (Sunday Hours) Act 1995

WEEKDAY

'ON' licence

On weekdays, other than Christmas day or Good Friday, the hours from 11am to 11pm.

If the licensing justices are satisfied that the requirements of the district make it desirable, may by order modify the hours so that they begin earlier than 11am but not earlier than 10am.

'OFF' licence

8am to the end of permitted hours for that locality. There need be no afternoon break.

SUNDAY, CHRISTMAS DAY AND GOOD FRIDAY

For 'ON' or 'OFF' premises

ENGLAND

On Sundays and Good Friday from 12 noon to 10.30pm. On Christmas Day from 12 noon to 10.30pm with a break of 4 hours beginning at 3pm.

For 'OFF' licences, on Sundays other that Christmas Day permitted hours begin at 10 am.

WALES

Christmas Day and Good Friday are the same as England. Sundays have the same hours if open at all. A local poll is held to decide whether opening will be allowed. S 66

SALES ETC OUTSIDE PERMITTED HOURS

S 59(1) Licensing Act 1964

Subject to the exceptions on the following page, it is an offence to:

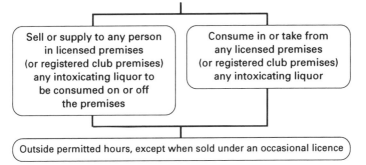

Sell or supply to any person in licensed premises (or registered club premises) any intoxicating liquor to be consumed on or off the premises

Consume in or take from any licensed premises (or registered club premises) any intoxicating liquor

Outside permitted hours, except when sold under an occasional licence

REGISTERED CLUBS S 62(1)

The permitted hours in respect of a registered club are fixed by the rules of the club in accordance with the following:

Weekdays
Other than Christmas Day – the general licensing hours

Christmas Day
- No more than 6.5 hours beginning no earlier than 12 noon nor ending later than 10.30 pm.
- Must be a break of not less than 2 hours in the afternoon including the hours from 3 pm to 5 pm.
- There shall not be more than 3.5 hours after 5 pm.

EXCEPTIONS

S 63 Licensing Act 1964

Normal permitted hours will not apply to:

'Drinking-up time'
During the first twenty minutes after the end of permitted hours, consumption may take place and liquor may be removed from the premises, unless supplied or taken away in an open vessel.

After meals
During the first half hour following permitted hours, consumption of liquor is allowed by persons taking meals if the drink is ancillary to the meal.

Residents
Sale or supply to, or consumption by, any person who is residing in the premises (this also includes persons not residing there but in charge of or carrying on the business on the premises).

Off sales
The ordering or drinks for consumption off the premises, and the despatch of liquor so ordered.

Traders
Sale to a trader for the purposes of his trade, or to a registered club, canteen or mess.

Employees
Supply of drink for consumption on the premises to persons employed there if it is supplied at the expense of the employer.

Private friends
Supply for consumption on the premises to any private friends of a person residing there who are bona fide entertained by him at his own expense, (This would include the licensee, but the persons entertained must be real personal friends and not merely customers).

Extension of hours, special hours certificate, extended hours, general order of exemption, special order of exemption – see later.

PERMITTED HOURS – RESTRICTIONS

LICENSING ACT 1964 (AS AMENDED BY THE LICENSING ACT 1988)

SEASONAL LICENCES (S 64)

These are conditions inserted in the licence on application by the person applying for the grant of a licence, that during certain parts of the year there shall be **no** permitted hours on the premises. These variations are to cater for the requirements of the district.

SIX DAY AND EARLY CLOSING LICENCES (S 65)

On application by the licensee the justices shall insert in the licence a condition that on **Sundays** there shall be no permitted hours; or that the **permitted hours** shall end one hour earlier than general licensing hours.

RESTRICTION ORDERS (S 67A)

These orders are made in relation to 'on' licences and registered clubs on application by the police, persons living in the neighbourhood, business people in the neighbourhood, or the head teacher of an **educational establishment** in the neighbourhood. Orders may be made in order to avoid or reduce disturbance or annoyance due to the use of the premises. The order may specify any time between 2.30 pm and 5.30 pm on weekdays other than Good Friday, and between 3pm and 7pm on Sunday and Good Friday.

Extensions to Permitted Hours

S 68 LICENSING ACT 1964, AS AMENDED BY THE LICENSING (RESTAURANT MEALS) ACT 1987 AND THE LICENSING ACT 1988

Granted to the holder of a justices' **'on'** licence or to a registered club in respect of premises which are structurally adapted and bona fide used for the purpose of **habitually** providing for customers **substantial refreshment** to which the sale and supply of intoxicating liquor is ancillary.

Hours
The effect of the grant of this certificate is to extend general permitted hours by one hour in the evening and on Christmas Day, between the first and second parts of the general licensing hours.

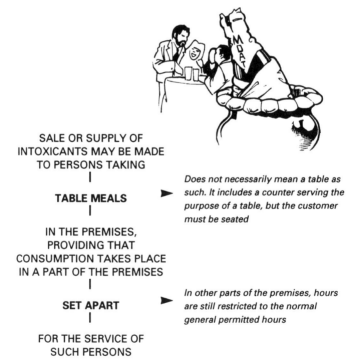

SALE OR SUPPLY OF INTOXICANTS MAY BE MADE TO PERSONS TAKING

TABLE MEALS ► *Does not necessarily mean a table as such. It includes a counter serving the purpose of a table, but the customer must be seated*

IN THE PREMISES, PROVIDING THAT CONSUMPTION TAKES PLACE IN A PART OF THE PREMISES

SET APART ► *In other parts of the premises, hours are still restricted to the normal general permitted hours*

FOR THE SERVICE OF SUCH PERSONS

SPECIAL HOURS CERTIFICATE

SS 76, 77, 78 AND 78A LICENSING ACT 1964, AS AMENDED BY THE LOCAL GOVERNMENT (MISCELLANEOUS PROVISIONS) ACT 1982 AND THE LICENSING ACT 1988

This may be granted where a **music and dancing** licence is in force in relation to any licensed premises or to a registered club and the whole or part of the premises is **structurally adapted** and bona fide used, or intended to be used for the purpose of providing **music, dancing and substantial refreshments** to which the sale of intoxicating liquor is ancillary.

HOURS

WEEKDAYS
This includes any day or the week except Sunday.

Permitted hours extend until 2am

If the licensing justices think fit, they may rule that the hours must end before 2am.

Half an hour is allowed for 'drinking up'.

SUNDAYS
If the music, singing and dancing licence allows the hours to continue after midnight on Saturdays, the special hours certificate will continue into Sunday for a like period.

VARIATIONS

But the hours shall end at midnight on any day when music and dancing is not provided after midnight.
In the Metropolis (outside the City of London) permitted hours end at 3am instead of 2am if the premises are specified in an order by the Secretary of State.
On any day that the music and dancing ends between 12mn and 2am the permitted hours shall cease when the music and dancing ends.
If the music, singing and dancing licence ends at any time earlier than the closing time authorised by the special hours certificate, then the latter will also cease at the earlier time.
The licensing justices may limit the certificate to particular times of the day, days of the week or periods of the year in which case the permitted hours may not extend beyond the limitations.

EXTENDED HOURS IN RESTAURANTS ETC PROVIDING ENTERTAINMENT

S 70 LICCENSING ACT 1964 AS AMENDED BY THE LICENSING (AMENDMENT) ACT 1985

This type of order allows premises in areas where music and dancing licences cannot be granted, to apply for additional permitted hours.

There must be in force in relation to the premises a:

SUPPER HOUR EXTENSION see s 68

THE PREMISES MUST BE

STRUCTURALLY ADAPTED AND BONA FIDE USED

OR INTENDED TO BE USED FOR THE PURPOSE OF **HABITUALLY** PROVIDING

LIVE ENTERTAINMENT
(musical or otherwise)

AND

SUBSTANTIAL REFRESHMENT

AND THE SALE OR SUPPLY OF INTOXICATING LIQUOR IS ANCILLARY TO THE REFRESHMENT AND ENTERTAINMENT

PERMITTED HOURS SHALL BE UNTIL 1.00am for the purpose of sale and supply of intoxicating liquor **before the entertainment or refreshment has ended** and the consumption of drinks so supplied.

Half an hour 'drinking-up' time allowed
S 70 LICENSING ACT 1964

Persons may not be served if admitted to the premises after midnight or less than half an hour before the entertainment is due to end (except when admitted for the purpose of taking a table meal under the provisions of the 'supper hours extension').

Orders of Exemption

S 74 LICENSING ACT 1964 AS AMENDED BY THE LICENSING ACT 1988

GENERAL ORDER

This may be granted to the holder of a justices 'on' licence, or to the secretary of a club, if the premises are situated in the immediate vicinity of a public market or place where people follow a lawful trade or calling, if the justices are satisfied that it is desirable to do so for the accommodation of a considerable number of persons attending the market, etc

SPECIAL ORDER

This may be granted to the holder of a justices 'on' licence on a specified **special occasion.** The order applies not only to the room in which the function is being held, but to the entire premises. The licence holder may, however, be requested to give an undertaking limiting the exemption to a particular room

In the City of London or the Metropolitan Police district the order may be made by the Commissioner of Police with the approval of the Lord Mayor (in the City of London) or the Secretary of State (in the Metropolitan district)

If granted, such hours as may be specified are added to permitted hours

In Martin v Spalding 1979 the Divisional Court gave guidance on interpreting a 'special occasion':

> *The occasion must not be too frequent. The more often a thing takes place, the less special it becomes. It must be special in the local or national sense. The licensee may not make a special occasion in order to claim the benefit of an exemption order.*

Occasional Licences

S 180 LICENSING ACT 1964

Granted to the holder of a justices' 'ON' licence to sell in some place other than his licensed premises such intoxicants as his justices' licence empowers him to sell between such hours as may be specified in the order

Such premises need not be licensed, or may have a restricted licence which does not cater for the needs of a particular function

The police have the same powers of entry as they have in relation to 'licensed premises'

There is no offence of children under 14 being present

Permitted hours applicable to the premises of the licensee do not apply

There is no offence of selling outside of permitted hours where there is an occasional licence

But consider an offence of selling without a licence if the occasional licence has expired

The licence cannot be granted for Xmas Day, Good Friday or any day of public fast or thanksgiving

The licence may not extend over more than three consecutive weeks at a time

Restaurants and Residential Licences

Licensing Act 1964 as amended by the Licensing (Restaurant Meals) Act 1987 and the Licensing Act 1988

The following licences may be granted:

RESTAURANT S 94(1)

This is granted for premises **structurally adapted and bona fide used** or intended to be used for the purpose of **habitually** providing a main meal at midday or in the evening, or both. But intoxicating liquor may not be sold or supplied on the premises other than to persons taking table meals where the drink is ancillary to the meal.

RESIDENTIAL S 94(2)

This is granted for premises **bona fide used** or intended to be used for the purpose of **habitually** providing, for reward, **board and lodging** including breakfast and one other main meal. But intoxicating liquor shall not be sold or supplied other than to persons residing there or their bona fide friends entertained by them at their own expense.

RESTAURANT AND RESIDENTIAL S 94(3)

This is granted for premises falling within the conditions of both restaurant and residential licence, but intoxicating liquor may only be sold or supplied as permitted by the conditions of both licences.

Permitted hours

These are general permitted hours and the break between the first and second part of general licensing hours on Christmas Day (s 95).

CHILDREN IN BARS

S 168 LICENSING ACT 1964 (AS AMENDED)

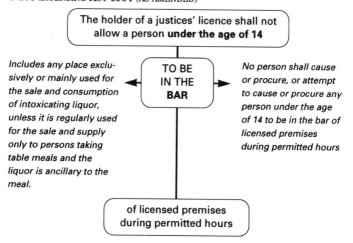

The holder of a justices' licence shall not allow a person **under the age of 14**

TO BE IN THE **BAR**

Includes any place exclusively or mainly used for the sale and consumption of intoxicating liquor, unless it is regularly used for the sale and supply only to persons taking table meals and the liquor is ancillary to the meal.

No person shall cause or procure, or attempt to cause or procure any person under the age of 14 to be in the bar of licensed premises during permitted hours

of licensed premises during permitted hours

But no offence will be committed if:

- The person under 14 was in the bar solely for the purpose of passing through to another part of the premises which was not a bar and there was no other convenient means of access
- The bar was part of a railway refreshment room or other premises for which the holding of a justice' licence was merely ancillary
- The licensee used due diligence to prevent under 14s being admitted
- The person under 14 had apparently attained that age
- The person under 14 was the licensee's child
- The person under 14 resided there but was not employed there, or
- The person under 14 was accompanied by an adult and a 'Children's Certificate' was in force for that part of the premises.

Persons Under 18

S 169 LICENSING ACT 1964

In relation to a person under 18

THE LICENSEE OR HIS SERVANT

- Shall not, in licensed premises, sell to him/her intoxicating liquor.
- Shall not knowingly allow him to consume intoxicating liquor in a bar.
- The licensee shall not knowingly allow any person to sell intoxicating liquor to him.
- Shall not knowingly deliver (or the licensee allow) to him intoxicating liquor sold in licensed premises for consumption off the premises (except where delivery is made at the residence or place or work of the purchaser).
- Must not employ him in any bar when it is open for the sale or consumption of intoxicating liquor. S 170

ANY PERSON

- Shall not buy or attempt to buy intoxicating liquor for consumption by a person under 18 in a bar.
- Shall not knowingly send a person under 18 to licensed premises to obtain intoxicating liquor for consumption off the premises (this includes 'OFF' licensed premises).

HE / SHE

- Shall not, in licensed premises, buy or attempt to buy intoxicating liquor, nor consume intoxicating liquor in a bar.

  But if he is 16 years of age he can buy beer, porter, cider or perry for consumption with a meal in a room set apart for such purpose. If in a bar, it must be a table meal.

Drunks in Licensed Premises

LICENSING ACT 1964

PERMITTING DRUNKENNESS S 172

The holder of a justices' licence shall not permit drunkenness or any violent, quarrelsome or riotous conduct to take place in the licensed premises.

SELLING TO DRUNKS S 172

The holder of a justices' licence shall not sell intoxicating liquor to a drunken person.

PROCURING ALCOHOL S 173

No person in licensed premises may procure or attempt to procure intoxicating liquor for consumption by a drunken person, nor aid a drunken person to obtain or consume it.

POWER TO EXPEL S 174

The holder of a justices' licence may refuse to admit to, or may expel from, the premises any person who is drunk, violent, quarrelsome or disorderly, or whose presence is in breach of an exclusion order or may subject the licensee to a penalty.

A constable is required to assist to expel any person as above on the request of the licensee, his servant or agent. He may use such force as is necessary for this purpose.

See also:
S 3 LICENSED PREMISES (EXCLUSION OF CERTAIN PERSONS) ACT 1980

Prostitutes in Licenced Premises

S 175(1) LICENSING ACT 1964

The licence holder shall not knowingly allow the premises to be the habitual resort or place of meeting of reputed prostitutes

The object of their so resorting need not be prostitution (but they may be allowed for the purpose of obtaining reasonable refreshment)

Neither shall the licensee allow his premises to be used as a brothel (s 176)

Gaming in Licenced Premises

S 177 LICENSING ACT 1964

The licensee shall not allow any game to be played on the premises in such circumstances that an offence under the Gaming Act 1968 is committed (see earlier).

Constables in Licenced Premises

S 178 LICENSING ACT 1964

It is an offence for the licence holder to:

- knowingly allow a constable to remain on the premises whilst on duty, except for the purposes of the execution of his duty
- bribe or attempt to bribe any constable
- supply any liquor or refreshment to any constable on duty except by authority of a superior officer of the constable

Power of Entry

S 186 LICENSING ACT 1964

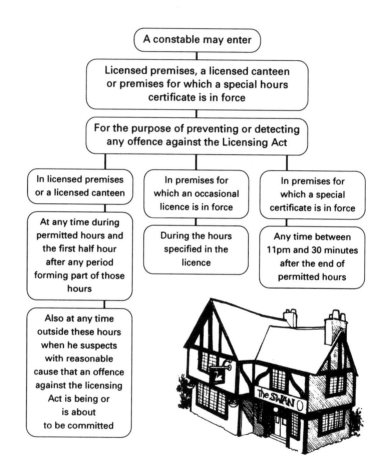

A constable may enter

Licensed premises, a licensed canteen or premises for which a special hours certificate is in force

For the purpose of preventing or detecting any offence against the Licensing Act

- In licensed premises or a licensed canteen
  - At any time during permitted hours and the first half hour after any period forming part of those hours
  - Also at any time outside these hours when he suspects with reasonable cause that an offence against the licensing Act is being or is about to be committed
- In premises for which an occasional licence is in force
  - During the hours specified in the licence
- In premises for which a special certificate is in force
  - Any time between 11pm and 30 minutes after the end of permitted hours

An offence is committed by any person who fails to admit a constable who demands entry to the premises under the authority of this section.

Drunks in Public Places

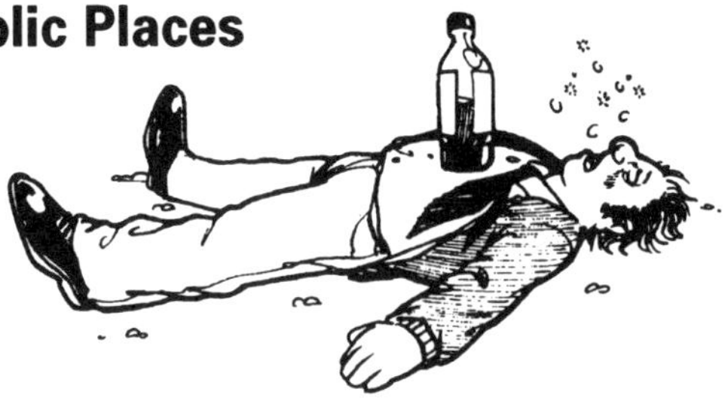

DRUNKENNESS

S 12 Licensing Act 1872

It is an offence to be found drunk in any highway or other public place. (Public place includes all places where the public have access whether on payment or otherwise).

CARRIAGE, ETC

S 12 Licensing Act 1872
It is an offence to be drunk whilst in charge on any highway or other public place of any horse, cattle, pig, sheep, carriage, motor vehicle, trailer, bicycle or steam engine.
The offender may be arrested.

FIREARMS

S 12 Licensing Act 1872
It is an offence, whilst drunk, to be in possession of any loaded firearm (including an airgun).
The offender may be arrested.

CHILDREN

S 2 Licensing Act 1902
It is an offence to be drunk in a highway or other public place, whether a building or not, or any licensed premises, while having the charge of a child apparently under the age of 7 years.

DISORDERLY

S 91(1) Criminal Justice Act 1967
It is an offence in a public place to be guilty, whilst drunk, of disorderly behaviour. (Public place includes any highway and any other premises or place to which at the material time the public have, or are permitted to have, access whether on payment or otherwise).
The offender may be arrested without warrant by any person.

Public Charitable Collections

S 66 Charities Act 1992

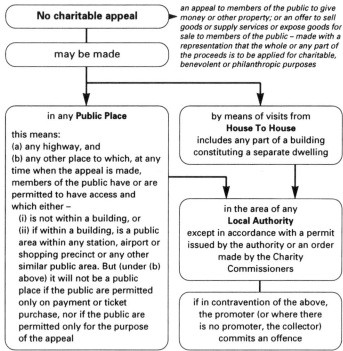

No charitable appeal – *an appeal to members of the public to give money or other property; or an offer to sell goods or supply services or expose goods for sale to members of the public – made with a representation that the whole or any part of the proceeds is to be applied for charitable, benevolent or philanthropic purposes*

may be made

in any **Public Place**

this means:
(a) any highway, and
(b) any other place to which, at any time when the appeal is made, members of the public have or are permitted to have access and which either –
 (i) is not within a building, or
 (ii) if within a building, is a public area within any station, airport or shopping precinct or any other similar public area. But (under (b) above) it will not be a public place if the public are permitted only on payment or ticket purchase, nor if the public are permitted only for the purpose of the appeal

by means of visits from **House To House**
includes any part of a building constituting a separate dwelling

in the area of any **Local Authority**
except in accordance with a permit issued by the authority or an order made by the Charity Commissioners

if in contravention of the above, the promoter (or where there is no promoter, the collector) commits an offence

Exceptions

Does not apply to a charitable appeal which:
(a) is made in the course of a public meeting; or
(b) is made –
 (i) on land within a churchyard or burial ground contiguous or adjacent to a place or public worship, or
 (ii) on other land occupied for the purposes of a place of public worship and contiguous or adjacent to it, being in each case land which is enclosed, or substantially enclosed; or
 (c) is an appeal to the public to give money or other property by placing it in a receptacle

Chapter 5
Animals

Cruelty to Animals

S 1 Protection of Animals Act 1911

Means to cause, permit or in any way to be concerned with:

PHYSICAL CRUELTY

To cruelly beat, kick, ill-treat, over-ride, over-drive, over-load, torture, infuriate or terrify any animal, or in any way to cause unnecessary suffering to any animal.

CONVEYANCE

To convey or carry any animal in such a manner or position as to cause any unnecessary suffering.

ABANDONING

S 1 Abandonment of Animals Act 1960 S 1

Without reasonable cause or excuse, whether temporarily or not, in circumstances likely to cause unnecessary suffering, eg leaving animals at home whilst on holiday.

FIGHTING

The fighting or baiting of any animal.

DRUGS

The administration of any poisonous or injurious drug or substance to any animal without reasonable cause or excuse.

OPERATIONS

To subject the animal to any operation which is performed without due care and humanity.

TETHERING

To tether any horse, ass or mule under such conditions or in such a manner as to cause that animal unnecessary suffering.

POLICE POWERS

A police constable may arrest without warrant any person whom he has reason to believe to be guilty of this offence either upon his own view or that of a third person.

He may take charge of any animal or vehicle. S 12

S 15 PROTECTION OF ANIMALS ACT 1911

For the purposes of the offence of cruelty to animals,

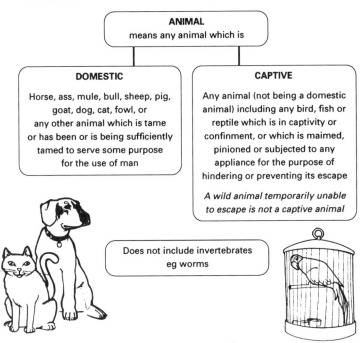

ANIMAL
means any animal which is

DOMESTIC

Horse, ass, mule, bull, sheep, pig, goat, dog, cat, fowl, or any other animal which is tame or has been or is being sufficiently tamed to serve some purpose for the use of man

CAPTIVE

Any animal (not being a domestic animal) including any bird, fish or reptile which is in captivity or confinement, or which is maimed, pinioned or subjected to any appliance for the purpose of hindering or preventing its escape

A wild animal temporarily unable to escape is not a captive animal

Does not include invertebrates eg worms

The offences created by this Act do not apply:

To anything done in the course of destruction, or preparation for destruction, of any animal as food for mankind unless unnecessary suffering is inflicted. S 1(3)

To the coursing or hunting of any captive animal, unless such animal is liberated in an injured, mutilated or exhausted condition, or if it is done in an enclosed space from which it has no reasonable chance of escape.

Animal Fights

Ss 5A, 5B Protection of Animals Act 1911
added by the Protection of Animals (Amendment) Act 1988
S 1 Cockfighting Act 1952

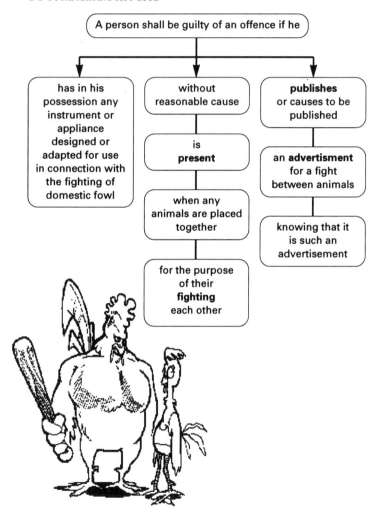

A person shall be guilty of an offence if he

- has in his possession any instrument or appliance designed or adapted for use in connection with the fighting of domestic fowl
- without reasonable cause
  - is **present**
  - when any animals are placed together
  - for the purpose of their **fighting** each other
- **publishes** or causes to be published
  - an **advertisment** for a fight between animals
  - knowing that it is such an advertisement

Injured Animals

S 11 PROTECTION OF ANIMALS ACT 1911

If a police constable finds any animal

Horse, mule, ass, bull, sheep, goat or pig

So diseased or so severely injured or in such a physical condition that in his opinion the animal cannot be removed without cruelty

Then if the owner is absent or refuses to consent to its destruction the constable may summon a veterinary surgeon, if one resides within a reasonable distance

Does not include dogs or cats

But although not included in this enactment, the main consideration should be the welfare of the animal

If the veterinary surgeon certifies that it is cruel to keep the animal alive the constable may, without the consent of the owner, cause the animal to be slaughtered in such a manner as to inflict as little suffering as possible and, if on a highway, cause the carcase to be removed

If the veterinary surgeon certifies that the animal **can** be removed, the person in charge of the animal shall forthwith cause it to be removed with as little suffering as possible and, if that person fails to do so, the constable may, without his consent, cause it to be removed

A veterinary surgeon should still be called and if the owner is not present or fails to meet his expenses it is usual for the police to seek the aid of a local voluntary organisation, or for the police authority to pay them

Pets

PET ANIMALS ACT 1951
AS AMENDED BY THE PET ANIMALS (AMENDMENT) ACT 1983

No person shall keep a pet shop except under the authority of a licence granted by the local authority. S 1

If any person carries on a business of selling animals as pets in any part of a street or public place, except at a stall or barrow in a market, he shall be guilty of an offence. S 2

If any person sells an animal as a pet to a person who he has reasonable cause to believe to be under the age of 12 years, the seller shall be guilty of an offence. S 3

Dogs

DOG COLLARS

ARTICLE 1 CONTROL OF DOGS ORDER 1992

Every dog while in a highway or in a place of public resort, shall wear a collar with the name and address of the owner inscribed on the collar or on a plate or badge attached thereto.

Exceptions

- Dogs used on official duties by the armed forces, HM Customs & Excise or the police.
- Dogs used for sporting purposes and packs of hounds
- Dogs used for the capture or destruction of vermin
- Dogs used for driving or tending cattle or sheep
- Guide dogs for the blind
- Dogs used for emergency rescue work

The owner of the dog and any person in charge of it, who, without lawful authority or excuse causes or permits the dog to be on the highway or place of public resort shall each be guilty of an offence. Dogs not wearing a collar may be seized as a stray dog. This order will be executed and enforced by officers of a local authority and not by the police.

DOGS WORRYING LIVESTOCK

S 1 DOGS (PROTECTION OF LIVESTOCK) ACT 1953 AS AMENDED

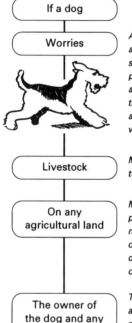

If a dog

Worries

Attacking livestock, chasing livestock in such a way as may reasonably be expected to cause injury or suffering, or abortion or loss or diminution of their produce. It is sufficient to prove that the dog ran among the livestock and alarmed them, provided the result is achieved. Also, being at large (not on a lead or under close control) in a field or enclosure where there are sheep

Livestock

Means cattle, sheep, goats, swine, horses, fowl, turkeys, geese and ducks

On any agricultural land

Means land used as arable meadow or grazing land, poultry land, pig land, market gardens, allotments, nursery grounds or orchards. It will not be an offence if is the livestock are 'trespassing' and the dog belongs to, is in charge of, the owner/occupier of the land, unless he causes it to attack the livestock

The owner of the dog and any other person in charge of it

The owner shall not be convicted if he proves that at the material time the dog was in the charge of some other person whom he reasonably believed to be a fit and proper person

Shall be guilty of an offence

A PC who believes that a dog has been worrying livestock as above may seize the dog if no person admits to being the owner or person in charge of it

It is a defence to a civil claim arising from killing, or injuring a dog, to prove that it was done to protect the livestock and the police were informed with 48 hours

ORDERS FOR CONTROLLING DANGEROUS DOGS

S 2 Dogs Act 1871

Where a dog is regarded as being dangerous, either because it has attacked someone, or because it has worried livestock and is not kept under proper control, application may be made to the court for an order to be made for the dog to kept by the owner under proper control or destroyed. It is an offence to fail to comply with such an order.

S 28 Town Police Clauses Act 1847

Where the Town Police Clauses Act applies, an offence is committed by any person who in any street, to the obstruction, annoyance or danger of residents or passengers, suffers to be at large any unmuzzled ferocious dog, or sets on or urges any dog or other animal to attack, worry or put in fear any person or animal.

DANGEROUS DOGS

S 1 Dangerous Dogs Act 1991

This section applies to:

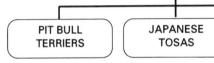

- PIT BULL TERRIERS
- JAPANESE TOSAS
- DOGS DESIGNATED BY THE SECRETARY OF STATE
  At the time of going to press, this includes the Dogo Argentina and the Fila Braziliero
  Dangerous Dogs (Designated Types) Order 1991

A person commits an offence if he:

BREEDS
or breeds from, any of the above.

SELLS
or exchanges such a dog or offers, advertises or exposes such a dog for sale or exchange.

MAKES A GIFT
(or offers to do so) of such a dog or advertises or exposes such a dog as a gift.

ALLOWS
such a dog of which he is the owner or of which he is for the time being in charge to be in a **PUBLIC PLACE** without being **MUZZLED** and **KEPT ON A LEAD**.
('Muzzled' means sufficient to prevent it biting someone, and 'kept on a lead' means securely held by a person not less than 16 years. S 7)

ABANDONS
such a dog of which he is the owner.

Allows such a dog to **STRAY**, being the owner or for the time being in charge.

Have such a dog in his **POSSESSION** or **CUSTODY** except under a power of seizure or in accordance with an order for its destruction.

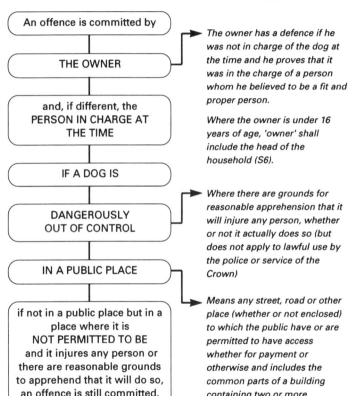

CONTROL OF DOGS

S 3 Dangerous Dogs Act 1991

An offence is committed by

THE OWNER

The owner has a defence if he was not in charge of the dog at the time and he proves that it was in the charge of a person whom he believed to be a fit and proper person.

Where the owner is under 16 years of age, 'owner' shall include the head of the household (S6).

and, if different, the PERSON IN CHARGE AT THE TIME

IF A DOG IS

DANGEROUSLY OUT OF CONTROL

Where there are grounds for reasonable apprehension that it will injure any person, whether or not it actually does so (but does not apply to lawful use by the police or service of the Crown)

IN A PUBLIC PLACE

Means any street, road or other place (whether or not enclosed) to which the public have or are permitted to have access whether for payment or otherwise and includes the common parts of a building containing two or more separate dwellings. S 10

if not in a public place but in a place where it is NOT PERMITTED TO BE and it injures any person or there are reasonable grounds to apprehend that it will do so, an offence is still committed.

IF THE DOG **INJURES SOMEONE** WHILST OUT OF CONTROL AN AGGRAVATED OFFENCE IS COMMITTED FOR WHICH HEAVIER PENALTIES ARE LIABLE

POLICE POWERS

S 5 Dangerous Dogs Act 1991

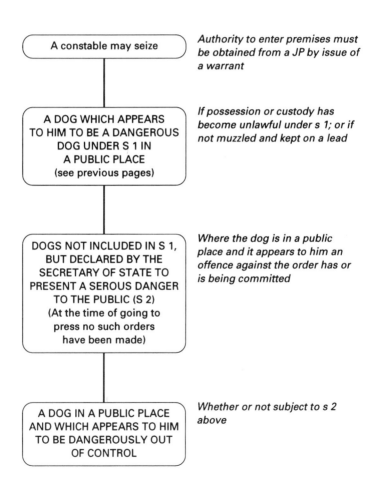

A constable may seize

Authority to enter premises must be obtained from a JP by issue of a warrant

A DOG WHICH APPEARS TO HIM TO BE A DANGEROUS DOG UNDER S 1 IN A PUBLIC PLACE (see previous pages)

If possession or custody has become unlawful under s 1; or if not muzzled and kept on a lead

DOGS NOT INCLUDED IN S 1, BUT DECLARED BY THE SECRETARY OF STATE TO PRESENT A SEROUS DANGER TO THE PUBLIC (S 2) (At the time of going to press no such orders have been made)

Where the dog is in a public place and it appears to him an offence against the order has or is being committed

A DOG IN A PUBLIC PLACE AND WHICH APPEARS TO HIM TO BE DANGEROUSLY OUT OF CONTROL

Whether or not subject to s 2 above

GUARD DOGS

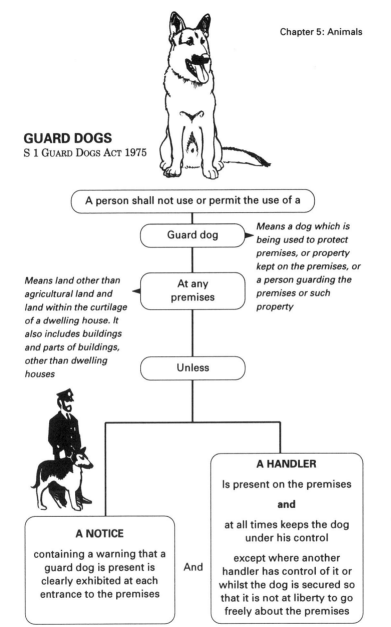

S 1 Guard Dogs Act 1975

A person shall not use or permit the use of a

Guard dog

Means a dog which is being used to protect premises, or property kept on the premises, or a person guarding the premises or such property

At any premises

Means land other than agricultural land and land within the curtilage of a dwelling house. It also includes buildings and parts of buildings, other than dwelling houses

Unless

A NOTICE

containing a warning that a guard dog is present is clearly exhibited at each entrance to the premises

And

A HANDLER

Is present on the premises

and

at all times keeps the dog under his control

except where another handler has control of it or whilst the dog is secured so that it is not at liberty to go freely about the premises

Dangerous Wild Animals

S 1 DANGEROUS WILD ANIMALS ACT 1976

No person is allowed to keep a dangerous wild animal unless he has been granted a licence to do so by the local authority. S 1

A 'dangerous wild animal' is one which is specifically mentioned in the Act. Many animals are mentioned but the following list gives a guide to the type of animal referred to:

Alligators, crocodiles, ostriches, apes, poisonous snakes, lions, tigers, leopards, bears, wild dogs and wolves.

The provisions of this Act do not apply to:

- Zoos
- Circuses
- Licensed pet shops
- Premises authorised to be used for experiments. S 5

Animals on Highways

S 155 Highways Act 1980

If any animal (or animals)

Horses, cattle, sheep, goats or swine

Are at at any time found straying or lying on or at the side of a highway their keeper is guilty of an offence

'Keeper' means the person in whose possession they are

Does not apply to part of a highway passing over any common, waste or unenclosed ground

A person guilty of this offence is liable for the expenses incurred in the removal and impounding of the animal

Where a local authority has designated a road upon which dogs must be kept on a lead, a person who causes or permits a dog to be on the road in contravention of the order shall be guilty of an offence

Diseases of Animals

Animal Health Act 1981

NOTIFICATION S 15(1)
Any person having possession or charge of a diseased animal shall keep it separate from unaffected animals and notify the police with all practicable speed.

'INFECTED AREAS'
If necessary, the veterinary inspector who is called to visit the infected place declares the premises and the area surrounding the premises to be an infected area.

MOVEMENT
Movement of animals from and to infected areas is then restricted to those authorised by licence. Various powers are then given to the minister and the local authority to make orders and regulations to control the situation.

POWER OF ARREST S 60
If a person is seen or found committing, or is reasonably suspected of being engaged in committing, an act which has been declared to be an offence against the Act or an order of the minister or a regulation of the local authority, a constable may stop and detain him and if his name and address is not given to the satisfaction of the constable, he **may be apprehended in accordance with** the provisions of the Police and Criminal Evidence Act 1984.

ANIMALS AND PROPERTY
Irrespective of the stopping or apprehension of the person the constable may stop, detain and examine any animal, vehicle, boat or thing to which the offence relates, and require the same to be returned to any place from which it was unlawfully removed, and he may execute and enforce that requisition.

OBSTRUCTION S 60
A person who obstructs or impedes or assists to obstruct or impede a constable or other officer in the execution of this Act or of orders or regulations made in consequence of it, may be arrested by the constable or officer.

POWERS OF ENTRY
In areas where constables are appointed as local authority inspectors, they also have power to enter land and buildings where they suspect that diseased animals are or have been kept or where provisions of the Act are not being complied with.

RABIES

Ss 15, 61 & 62 Animal Health Act 1981

The powers conferred by this Act are without prejudice to powers given on the previous page.

Offences specific to this disease involve landing or attempting to land or importing animals in contravention of the order introduced to prevent the introduction of rabies into GB and the unlawful movement of any animal into, within or out of an infected area or place.

Any person who knows or suspects that an animal is affected with rabies shall give notice of that fact to a constable. S 15

POLICE POWERS

A constable may arrest without warrant any person whom he, with reasonable cause, suspects to be in the act of committing or to have committed an offence against this section.

For the purpose of arresting a person a constable may enter (if need be by force) and search any vessel, boat, hovercraft, aircraft or vehicle of any other description in which that person is or where the constable reasonably suspects him to be. The prohibition extends to the Channel Tunnel.

The above power of entry also applies in exercising the power to seize any animal.

Game Licence

S 1 Hares Act 1848, S 4 Game Licences Act 1860, s 4 Ground Game Act 1880

It is an offence, without having a

GAME LICENCE 1860 Act

To take, kill or pursue by any means whatever, or to use any dog, gun, net or other engine for the purpose of taking, killing or pursuing any

Hare, pheasant, partridge, grouse, heath or moor game, black game, woodcock, snipe, rabbit or deer

Except

A game licence is not required for any of the following purposes:

- taking woodcock or snipe with nets or snares
- taking or destroying rabbits by the proprietor of a warren or grounds, or the tenant of land, or by his permission
- pursuing hares by coursing with greyhounds, or killing hares by hunting with beagles or other hounds
- pursuing and killing of deer by hunting with hounds
- taking and killing of deer in enclosed lands by the owner or occupier of lands or by his permission

The following persons are exempt from the requirement to hold a licence:

- the Royal Family
- any person appointed as game-keeper on behalf of Her Majesty
- a person aiding or assisting the holder of a licence
- a person authorised to kill hares under the Hares Act 1848
- the occupier of the land upon which the game is taken or killed, and persons authorised by him.

A police officer may demand production of the licence and, if not produced, require the person's name and address. Failure to produce the licence or, in default, to give the correct name and address, is an offence. S 31A

GAME – OUT OF SEASON

GAME ACT 1831

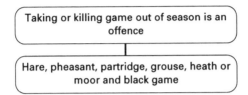

Taking or killing game out of season is an offence

Hare, pheasant, partridge, grouse, heath or moor and black game

Close Season

Sundays

Christmas Day

Partridge	1st February	to	1st September
Pheasant	1st February	to	1st October
Black Game	10th December	to	20th August
Grouse	10th December	to	12th August
Bustard	1st March	to	1st September

EGGS

S 24 GAME ACT 1831

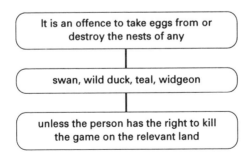

It is an offence to take eggs from or destroy the nests of any

swan, wild duck, teal, widgeon

unless the person has the right to kill the game on the relevant land

Havings such eggs in one's possession or control is also an offence (see further restrictions under 'birds')

Poaching

POACHING (BY DAY)

Ss 30, 31, 32 & 35 Game Act 1831

It is an offence by day

'Day' begins 1 hour before sunrise until 1 hour afer sunset

To trespass on any land in search or pursuit of

Hares, pheasants, partridges, grouse, heath and moor game, black game, woodcocks, snipe or rabbits

An additional penalty is payable if 5 or more persons together are found on any land for the purpose of poaching

A further offence is comitted if five or more together trespass to search for the above mentioned, any one of them being armed with a gun, and any of them, with intent to prevent an authorised person from exercising his powers under s 31, uses violence, intimidation or menace (s 32)

Exception The offence of trespassing in pursuit of game does not extend to hunting or coursing with hounds and being in fresh pursuit of any deer, hare or fox already started on other land. S 35

POACHING (BY NIGHT)

S 1 NIGHT POACHING ACT 1828 AS AMENDED

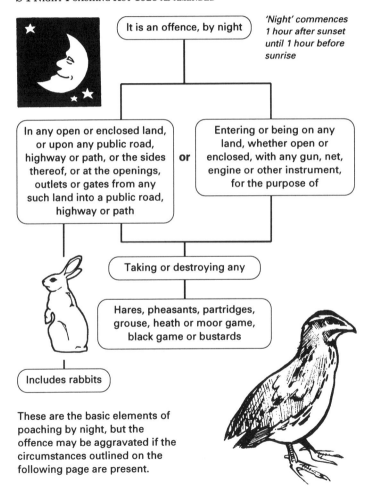

It is an offence, by night

'Night' commences 1 hour after sunset until 1 hour before sunrise

In any open or enclosed land, or upon any public road, highway or path, or the sides thereof, or at the openings, outlets or gates from any such land into a public road, highway or path

or

Entering or being on any land, whether open or enclosed, with any gun, net, engine or other instrument, for the purpose of

Taking or destroying any

Hares, pheasants, partridges, grouse, heath or moor game, black game or bustards

Includes rabbits

These are the basic elements of poaching by night, but the offence may be aggravated if the circumstances outlined on the following page are present.

Ss 2 & 9 Night Poaching Act 1828

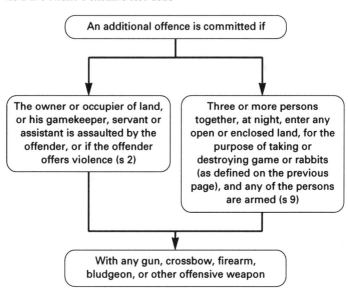

An additional offence is committed if

The owner or occupier of land, or his gamekeeper, servant or assistant is assaulted by the offender, or if the offender offers violence (s 2)

Three or more persons together, at night, enter any open or enclosed land, for the purpose of taking or destroying game or rabbits (as defined on the previous page), and any of the persons are armed (s 9)

With any gun, crossbow, firearm, bludgeon, or other offensive weapon

POLICE POWERS

On Land S 2 Game Laws (Amendment) Act 1960

A constable may enter land if he has reasonable grounds for suspecting that a person is trespassing on the land, by day or night, for the purpose of taking or destroying game or rabbits.

Night S 2 Game Laws (Amendment) Act 1960

Where a constable has reasonable grounds for suspecting that a person is committing an offence on any land under Ss 1 or 9 of the Night Poaching Act 1828, he may enter the land for the purpose of requiring him to quit and to give his name and address.

Daytime Ss 31 & 31A Game Act 1831

A constable may require any person he finds on any land in search or pursuit of game, woodcocks, snipe or rabbits, to quit the land and give his name and address. Any subsequent arrest must be in accordance with the Police and Criminal Evidence Act 1984. There is also power to enter the land for the above purpose under s 2 Game Laws (Amendment) Act, 1960.
s 31 also applies to anyone having the right to kill game on the land, occupiers, persons authorised by the aforementioned, gamekeepers or servants, and wardens, rangers and others employed in a similar capacity in royal forests and parks, etc.

Street or Public Place

A constable may, in any public place, **search** any person whom he has good cause to **suspect** of coming from any land where he has been unlawfully in pursuit of game, and having in his possession any game, gun, ammunition, nets, snares, traps or other device for killing or taking game, and also to **stop** and **search** any cart or other conveyance which the constable has good cause to suspect is carrying any game or article mentioned above, and the constable may **seize** and detain any game or article found on the person or in the conveyance. Proceedings are then taken by **summons**. There is no power of arrest.
S 2 Poaching Prevention Act 1862

A similar power to search and seize property and game is provided under s 4, Game Laws (Amendment) Act 1960, where the constable is arresting an offender under s 25, Police and Criminal Evidence Act 1984.

Deer

S 1 Deer Act 1991

POACHING OF DEER

S 1 Deer Act 1991

It is an offence

without the consent of the

OWNER
or
OCCUPIER
or
OTHER LAWFUL AUTHORITY

to ENTER any land in search or pursuit of any deer with the intention of TAKING, KILLING OR INJURING IT

- to intentionally take, kill or injure, or attempt to take, kill or injure any deer
- to search for or pursue any deer with the intention of taking, killing or injuring any deer, or
- to remove the carcass of any deer

WHILST ON ANY LAND

it shall be a defence if the person believed that

- he would have the consent of the owner or occupier of the land if they knew of it, or
- he has other lawful authority to do it

Land includes buildings and other structures, land covered with water, and any interest, etc., over the land

If an offence is suspected by the owner or occupier or any person authorised by him or having the right to kill deer on the land, he may require the offender to give his name and address and to quit the land forthwith. Failure to comply is an offence.

CLOSE SEASON

S 2 AND SCHED 1 DEER ACT 1991

It is an offence to intentionally take or kill any deer in the close season:

RED DEER (Cervus elaphus)

Stags	1st May to 31st July inclusive
Hinds	1st March to 31st October inclusive

FALLOW DEER (Dama dama)

Buck	1st May to 31st July inclusive
Doe	1st March to 31st October inclusive

ROE DEER (Capreolus capreolus)

Buck	1st November to 31st March inclusive
Doe	1st March to 31st October inclusive

SIKA DEER (Cervus nippon)

Stags	1st May to 31st July inclusive
Hinds	1st March to 31st October inclusive

There is an exemption for businessmen keeping marked deer on enclosed land for meat, other foodstuffs, skin or other by-products, or breeding stock.

Night

It is an offence to take or intentionally kill any deer between the expiry of the first hour after sunset and the beginning of the last hour before sunrise (s 3).

USE OF WEAPONS, ETC

S 4 DEER ACT 1991

It is an offence:

- To set any **traps, snare, or poisoned or stupefying bait** calculated to **cause bodily injury** to any deer.
- To use any **trap, snare, or poisoned or stupefying bait, or any net** for the purpose of **taking or killing** any deer.
- To use, for the purpose of **taking, killing or injuring** any deer:
  1. *Any smooth-bore gun.*
  2. *Any rifle having a calibre of less than .240 inches or a muzzle energy of less than 2,305 joules (1,700 foot pounds).*
  3. *Any air gun, air rifle or air pistol.*
  4. *Any cartridge for use in a smooth-bore gun.*
  5. *Any bullet for use in a rifle other than a soft-nosed or hollow-nosed bullet.*
  6. *Any arrow, spear or similar missile.*
  7. *Any missile, whether discharged from a firearm or otherwise, carrying or containing any poison, stupefying drug or muscle-relaxing agent.*
- To **discharge any firearm**, or project any missile, from any **mechanically propelled vehicle** at any deer.
- To use any **mechanically propelled vehicle** for the purpose of **driving deer.**

It shall be a defence to either of the last two offences if the act is done with the written authority of the occupier of any enclosed land in relation to deer usually kept on that land.

Other miscellaneous defences to this and previous sections are contained in ss 6, 7 and 8 (eg to prevent suffering, causing damage to crops, and for nature conservancy).

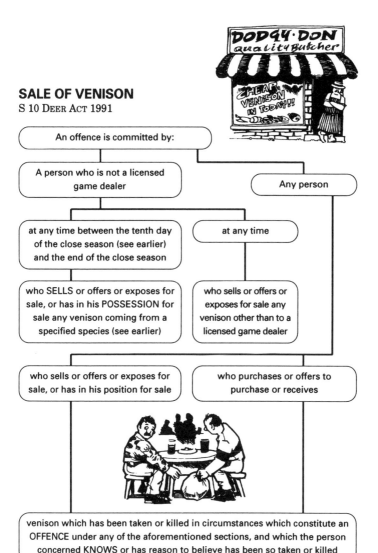

SALE OF VENISON

S 10 Deer Act 1991

An offence is committed by:

A person who is not a licensed game dealer

- at any time between the tenth day of the close season (see earlier) and the end of the close season
  - who SELLS or offers or exposes for sale, or has in his POSSESSION for sale any venison coming from a specified species (see earlier)
- at any time
  - who sells or offers or exposes for sale any venison other than to a licensed game dealer

Any person

- who sells or offers or exposes for sale, or has in his position for sale
- who purchases or offers to purchase or receives

venison which has been taken or killed in circumstances which constitute an OFFENCE under any of the aforementioned sections, and which the person concerned KNOWS or has reason to believe has been so taken or killed

Sale includes barter and exchange

POLICE POWERS

S 12 Deer Act 1991

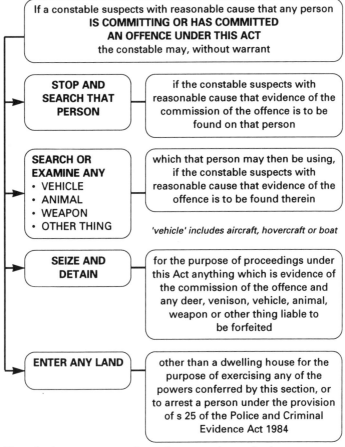

If a constable suspects with reasonable cause that any person **IS COMMITTING OR HAS COMMITTED AN OFFENCE UNDER THIS ACT** the constable may, without warrant

STOP AND SEARCH THAT PERSON — if the constable suspects with reasonable cause that evidence of the commission of the offence is to be found on that person

SEARCH OR EXAMINE ANY
- VEHICLE
- ANIMAL
- WEAPON
- OTHER THING

— which that person may then be using, if the constable suspects with reasonable cause that evidence of the offence is to be found therein

'vehicle' includes aircraft, hovercraft or boat

SEIZE AND DETAIN — for the purpose of proceedings under this Act anything which is evidence of the commission of the offence and any deer, venison, vehicle, animal, weapon or other thing liable to be forfeited

ENTER ANY LAND — other than a dwelling house for the purpose of exercising any of the powers conferred by this section, or to arrest a person under the provision of s 25 of the Police and Criminal Evidence Act 1984

There is also a power to sell any deer or venison seized.

Badgers

PROTECTION OF BADGERS ACT 1992

Killing etc S 1(1)
It is an offence to wilfully kill, injure, take or attempt to kill, injure or take a badger.
See next page for exceptions

Firearms S 2
It is an offence to use for killing a badger any firearm except: a smooth bore weapon of not less than 20 bore, or a rifle using ammunition of muzzle energy not less than 160ft/lbs or bullet weighing not less than 38 grains. See next page for exceptions

Sale, possession, etc S 4
It is an offence to sell, offer for sale, or have in possession or under control, any live badger. *See next page for exceptions*

Possession etc S 1(3)
It is an offence to have in possession or under control any dead badger or any part of, or anything derived from a dead badger unless it was not killed in contravention of this Act
See next page for exceptions

Cruelty etc
It is an offence to:
- Cruelly ill-treat a badger. S 2
- Use any badger tongs in the course of taking or killing a badger. S 2
- Dig for a badger. S 2
- Mark or ring a badger, unless authorised by a licence. S 5
- Interfere with a badger sett by:
  a) damaging a sett or part of it;
  b) destroying a sett;
  c) obstructing access to any entrance of a sett;
  d) causing a dog to enter a badger sett; or
  e) disturbing a badger when it is occupying a sett

Except: if necessary to prevent serious damage to crops, land or poultry (but licence must have been applied for); obstructing for fox hunting purposes (but only if done by hand); or incidental and unavoidable result of a lawful operation.

EXCEPTIONS

A person will not be guilty of the offences of killing, etc if:

- He is a 'licensed person' s 10, or
- A badger is found disabled and it is taken for the purpose of tending it s 6, or
- A badger is so seriously injured or in such a condition that to kill it would be an act of mercy s 6, or
- Where the killing or injuring was an unavoidable result of a lawful action. S 6
- Authorised under the Animals (Scientific Procedures) Act 1986. S 6
- The act was necessary to prevent serious damage to land, crops or poultry (but if such damage foreseeable then a licence must have been applied for).

A person shall not be guilty of having a live badger in his possession under s 4 if:

- He has possession of it in the course of his business as a carrier.
- He is a licensed person, or
- It is necessary to keep it in possession fo the purpose of tending to its disability.

Police powers

Where a police constable has reasonable cause to suspect that an offence against the Act has been or is being committed he may:

Stop and search that person and search any vehicle or article he may have with him. Order the person to quit the land and to give his name and address. Failure to do so is an offence.

Seize and detain anything which may be evidence, any badger, whether dead or alive, and any weapon or article in that person's possession.

Birds

WILDLIFE AND COUNTRYSIDE ACT 1981

The law relating to birds broadly covers restrictions on killing and taking wild birds; the prohibition of certain methods of killing or taking them; restrictions on the sale of birds and their eggs; and the prevention of disturbance to nesting birds. The various aspects are discussed in the following pages but for ease of reference the four categories into which birds are placed may be exemplified at this point.

Schedule 1

These are birds which are protected by special penalties

Part 1 At all times – eg barn owl, eagle, purple heron, osprey, stone curlew.

Part 2 During the close season – eg wild duck, wild geese.

Schedule 2

These are birds which may be killed or taken

Part 1 Outside the close season – eg moorhen, wild duck, wild geese, woodcock.

Part 2 At any time by authorised persons – eg crow, magpie, pigeon, sparrow, starling, wood pigeon.

Schedule 3

These are birds which may be sold

Part 1 Alive at all times – eg blackbird, chaffinch, magpie, barn owl, starling.

Part 2 Dead at all times – eg feral pigeon, wood pigeon.

Part 3 Dead from 1st Sept to 28th Feb – eg tufted duck, mallard, snipe, woodcock.

Schedule 4

These are birds which must be registered and ringed if kept in captivity – eg stone curlew, falcon, hawks, kingfisher, osprey, crested tit.

BIRDS

WILDLIFE AND COUNTRYSIDE ACT 1981

'Wild bird' means one which is ordinarily resident in or is a visitor to GB in a wild state but does not include poultry or game.

If the bird in question is listed in the first schedule, a greater penalty may be imposed.

S 1

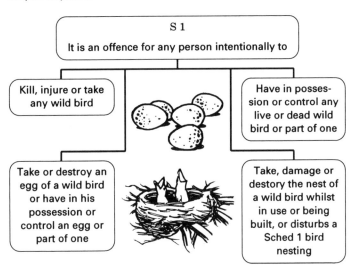

It is an offence for any person intentionally to

- Kill, injure or take any wild bird
- Have in possession or control any live or dead wild bird or part of one
- Take or destroy an egg of a wild bird or have in his possession or control an egg or part of one
- Take, damage or destory the nest of a wild bird whilst in use or being built, or disturbs a Sched 1 bird nesting

'Poultry' means domestic fowl, geese, ducks, guinea fowl, pigeons, quails and turkeys.

'Game bird' means pheasant, partridge, grouse (or game), black (or heath) game or ptarmigan.

EXCEPT →

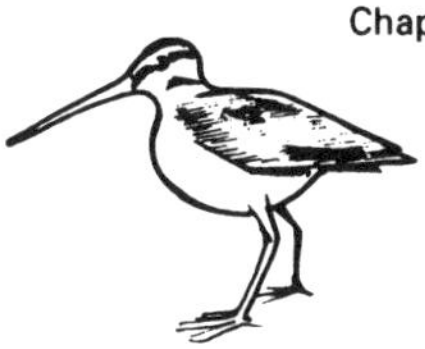

EXCEPTIONS S 2

KILLING, etc

A person shall not be guilty of an offence under s1 by reason of the killing or taking of a bird included in part 2 of Sched 2 (see earlier) or the taking, damaging or destruction of a nest of such a bird, or the taking or destruction of an egg of such a bird, when done in any case by an authorised person.

A person shall not be guilty of an offence under s1 by reason of the killing, injuring or taking of a bird included in part 1 of Sched 2 (see earlier) outside the close season for that bird.

CLOSE SEASON

CAPERCAILLIE AND (except Scotland) WOODCOCK
1st February to 30th September

SNIPE *1st February to 11th August*

WILD DUCK OR WILD GEESE (in any area below high water mark of ordinary spring tides) *21st February to 31st August*

ANY OTHER CASE *1st February to 31st August*

AUTHORISED PERSONS

An authorised person will not be guilty of an offence of killing or injuring a wild bird, other than a bird included in Sched 1, if he shows that it was necessary:

- For preserving public health or public or air safety;
- For preventing the spread of disease; or
- Preventing serious damage to livestock, foodstuffs for livestock, crops, vegetables, fruit, growing timber, or fisheries.

GENERAL

A person shall not be guilty of an offence by reason of:

- Taking a wild bird which has been disabled and which was taken to tend it and release when no longer disabled
- Killing a wild bird so seriously disabled that it would not rcover, or
- Any act which was the incidential result of a lawful operation and could not have been avoided. S 4

PROHIBITED METHODS OF KILLING, etc S 5

WILDLIFE AND COUNTRYSIDE ACT 1981

Unless authorised by licence, it is an offence for any person to:

Set in position any article to cause bodily injury to any wild bird coming into contact with it, ie springs; traps; snares; net; hook and line; any poisoned, poisonous or stupefying substance; floating container holding explosives; or any electrical device to frighten birds (except when done in the interests of public health, agriculture, forestry, fisheries or nature conservation for the purpose of lawful killing of wild animals when all reasonable precautions were taken to prevent injury to wild birds)

Use for the purpose of taking or killing any wild bird any article as aforesaid, or any net, baited board, gas, bird-lime or other like substance

Use as a decoy, for the purpose of killing or taking a wild bird, any sound recording or any live bird or other animal which is tethered or similarly secured, or which is blind, maimed or injured

Use for the purpose of killing or taking any wild bird

- A bow or crossbow
- Explosive other than ammunition
- An automatic weapon
- Shotgun over 1 ¾" dia. barrel
- An illuminating or night sighting device
- A lighting or dazzling device
- Gas or smoke
- A chemical wetting agent

Use any mechanically propelled vehicle in immediate pursuit of a wild bird for the purpose of killing or taking it.

But it shall not be unlawful – a) for an authorised person to use a cage-trap or net to take a bird included in part 2 of Sched 2; b) to use nets for taking wild duck in a duck decoy which was in use immediately before the passing of the Protection of Birds Act 1954; or c) to use a cage-trap or net for taking any game bird for the purpose of breeding.

But it will not be lawful to use a net for taking birds in flight, or a projected or propelled net for taking birds on the ground.

RESTRICTIONS ON SALE

S 6 Wildlife and Countryside Act 1981

It is an offence to sell, offer or expose for sale, or have in possession or transport for the purpose of sale, or advertise the buying or selling of

Live birds

Other than a bird included in part 1 of Sched 3 *(see earlier)*

Dead birds

Other than a bird included in part 2 or 3 of Sched 3, or any part of, or anything derived from, such a wild bird

Unless he is for the time being registered so to do

Eggs

Of a wild bird or any part of such an egg

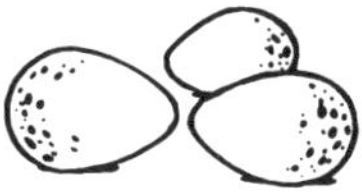

It is an offence to show or cause or permit to be shown in a competition any live bird other than a bird included in part 1 of Sched 3; or a bird one of whose parents was such a wild bird.

SPECIFIC OFFENCES

WILDLIFE AND COUNTRYSIDE ACT 1981

DISTURBING NESTING BIRDS (S 1)

It is an offence to intentionally disturb any wild bird included in Sched 1 while it is building a nest or is in, on or near a nest containing eggs or young; or to disturb dependant young of such a bird.

CONFINING (S 8)

It is an offence to keep or confine any bird in any cage or receptacle which does not allow sufficient room for the bird to stretch its wings freely.

But this offence does not apply to:

- Domestic fowl, ducks, geese, guinea fowl, pigeons and turkeys;
- Any bird whilst being conveyed, publicly exhibited (provided the time does not exceed 72 hours), or whilst undergoing veterinary treatment.

SHOOTING EVENTS (S 8)

It is an offence to be in any way involved in any event in which captive birds are liberated for the purpose of being shot immediately after their liberation.

POLICE POWERS

S 19 Wildlife and Countryside Act 1981

In relation to any offence against the Act (this includes taking or killing birds or eggs; using illegal methods of taking or killing, etc; unlawful selling etc; confining; and disturbing nesting birds) a constable may without warrant

STOP AND SEARCH

That person if the constable suspects that evidence of the commission of the offence is to be found on that person

And examine anything which that person may then be using or have in his possession if the constable suspects that evidence of the commission of the offence is to be found on that thing. The constable may, for the purpose of exercising these powers or arresting a person under s 25 Police and Criminal Evidence Act 1984, enter any land other than a dwelling house. A warrant to enter and search premises may be granted by a justice of the peace if the offence attracts a special penalty

SEIZE AND DETAIN

For the purpose of proceedings, any thing which may be evidence of the commission of the offence or may be liable to be forfeited under this Act

Fish

S 32 and Sched 1 Theft Act 1968

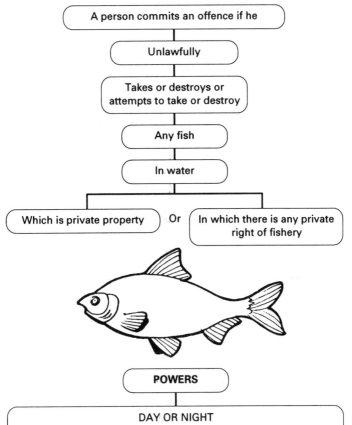

A person commits an offence if he

Unlawfully

Takes or destroys or attempts to take or destroy

Any fish

In water

Which is private property

Or

In which there is any private right of fishery

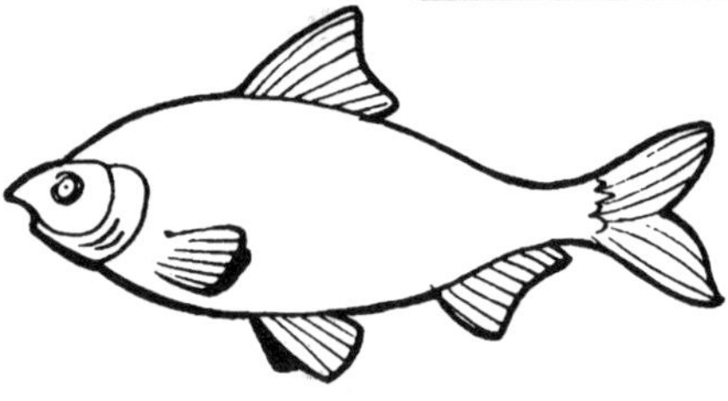

POWERS

DAY OR NIGHT
Any person may arrest without warrant anyone who is, or whom he, with reasonable cause, suspects to be committing this offence and may seize from any person who is, or whom he, with reasonable cause, suspects to be, committing the offence, anything which he has with him for use for taking or destroying fish

OFFENCES

SALMON AND FRESHWATER FISHERIES ACT 1975

The following are offences connected with salmon, trout or freshwater fish:

Nets

To use nets with meshes smaller than 2" between knots, or to use two nets of requisite mesh close together, or to work a draft net across more than ¾ of the width of any waters for salmon or migatory trout. S 3

Poison, etc

To cause or knowingly permit any poisonous or injurious substances to flow in, or be put into, any waters containing fish. S 4

Damage/Explosives

To use in or near any waters any explosive substance, any poison or other noxious substance, or any electrical device, with intent to take or destroy fish; or without lawful excuse destroy or damage any dam, flood-gate or sluice with intent to take or destroy fish. S 5

Instruments

Using any firearm; otter lath or jack, wire or snare; a crossline or setline; a spear, gaff, stroke-haul, snatch or other like instrument; or a light; or to have same in possession with intent to use for taking fish or throw or discharge any stone or other missile for the purpose of taking or killing salmon, trout or freshwater fish. S 1

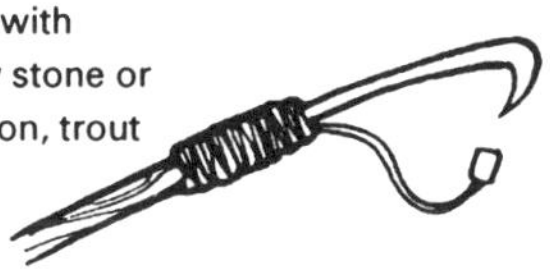

Roe

To use fish roe for fishing, or to buy, sell or have salmon or trout roe for that purpose. S 2

Young fish

To wilfully disturb any spawn or spawning fish.

To knowingly take, buy, sell or have in possession any unclean or immature fish. S 2

Weirs

No unauthorised fishing weir may be used – it must have a free gap. S 7

FISHING LICENCES

SS 25, 27 & 35 SALMON AND FRESHWATER FISHERIES ACT 1975

Water authorities are required to control fishing for

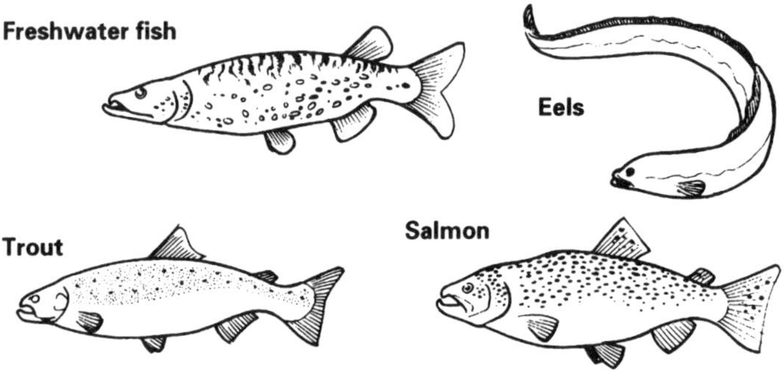
Freshwater fish
Eels
Trout
Salmon

by means of a licensing system. S 25

It is an offence to fish for or take fish otherwise than by means of an instrument authorised in the licence. S 27

Production

A constable, water bailiff, or person producing his authority may require any person found fishing to produce his licence and give his name and address. Failure to comply is an offence but if the person produces his licence within 7 days of the request at the water authority office he will not be convicted of the offence. S 35

CLOSE SEASON (fish)

S 19 & SCHED 1 SALMON AND FRESHWATER FISHERIES ACT 1975

Unless there is a bylaw to the contrary, it is an offence to fish for, take, kill or attempt to take or kill at the following times:

Salmon
By rod & line *31st Oct - 1st Feb*
By any other method *31st Aug - 1st Feb*

The weekly close time is from
6 am Saturday to 6 am Monday

Trout
By rod & line *30th Sep - 1st March*
By any other method *31st Aug - 1st March*

The weekly close time is from
6 am Saturday to 6 am Monday

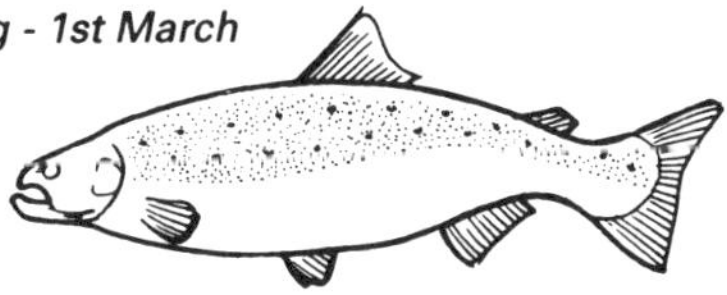

Freshwater fish
(other than salmon, trout, eels & migratory fish)
14th March - 16th June

Rainbow trout
The close season is fixed by byelaws.

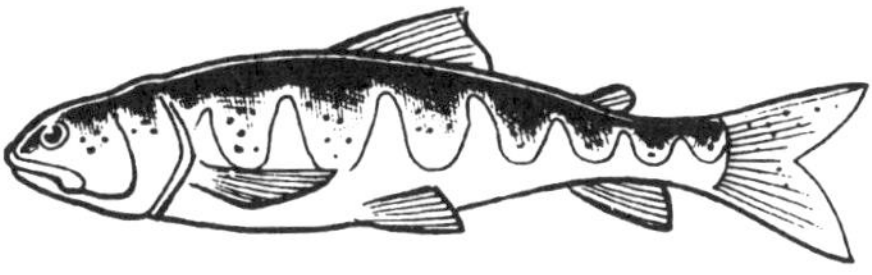

Chapter 6

People

Children and Young Persons

S 107 Children and Young Persons Act 1933

TERMS

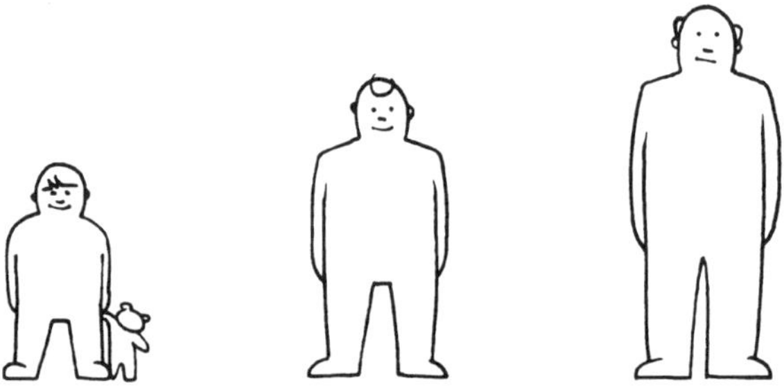

Child
Under the age of 14 years

Young person
Attained the age of 14 yrs but under 18 years

Guardian
Any person who has, for the time being, charge of or control over the child or young person

Street
Any highway and any public bridge, road, lane, footway, square, court, alley, or passage, whether a thoroughfare or not

Public place
Any public park, garden, sea, beach, railway station, and any ground to which the public have or are permitted to have access, whether on payment or otherwise

CRUELTY

S 1 CHILDRN & YOUNG PERSONS ACT 1933, AS AMENDED BY THE CHILDREN ACT 1989

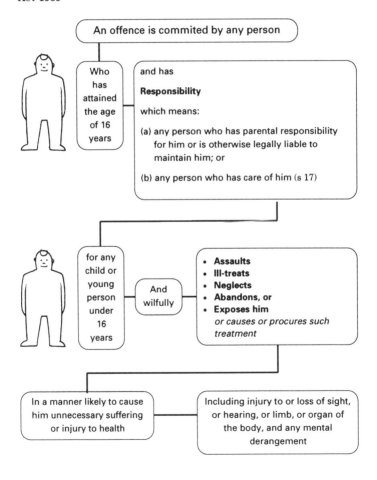

An offence is commited by any person

Who has attained the age of 16 years

and has

Responsibility

which means:

(a) any person who has parental responsibility for him or is otherwise legally liable to maintain him; or

(b) any person who has care of him (s 17)

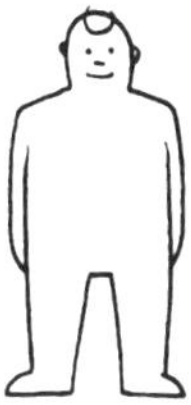

for any child or young person under 16 years

And wilfully

- **Assaults**
- **Ill-treats**
- **Neglects**
- **Abandons, or**
- **Exposes him**

or causes or procures such treatment

In a manner likely to cause him unnecessary suffering or injury to health

Including injury to or loss of sight, or hearing, or limb, or organ of the body, and any mental derangement

EMPLOYMENT

S 18 CHILDREN AND YOUNG PERSONS ACT 1933

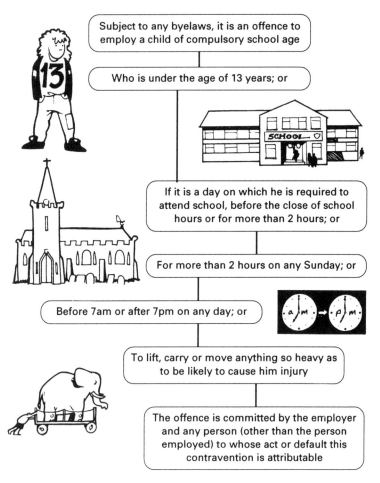

Subject to any byelaws, it is an offence to employ a child of compulsory school age

Who is under the age of 13 years; or

If it is a day on which he is required to attend school, before the close of school hours or for more than 2 hours; or

For more than 2 hours on any Sunday; or

Before 7am or after 7pm on any day; or

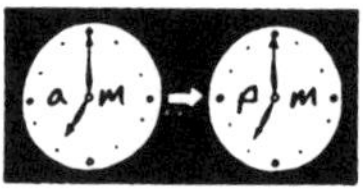

To lift, carry or move anything so heavy as to be likely to cause him injury

The offence is committed by the employer and any person (other than the person employed) to whose act or default this contravention is attributable

TOBACCO

S 7 Children and Young Persons Act 1933

It is an offence for a person to sell to a person **apparently** under the age of 16 years any tobacco or cigarette papers, whether for his own use or not

It is the duty of a constable in uniform to seize any tobacco or cigarette papers from persons apparently under 16 years found smoking in a street or public place

An order may be made by a court for the removal of any automatic cigarette machine which has been used by any person under 16 years

ALCOHOL S 5

It is an offence for any person to give or cause to be given to any child under the age of 5 years any intoxicating liquor (except under the order of a doctor or in a case of sickness or apprehended sickness, or other urgent case)

EDUCATION

S 10 Children and Young Persons Act 1933

If a person habitually wanders from place to place and takes with him any child who has attained the age of 5 years, or any young person who is of compulsory school age, he will commit an offence unless he can prove that the child or young person is not being deprived of suitable full-time education.

BEGGING S 4

It is an offence for any person to cause or procure any child or young person under 16 years, or having responsibility for such a child or young person, to allow him to be in any street, premises or place for the purpose of begging or receiving or inducing the giving of alms (whether or not there is any singing etc)

BURNING

S 11 Children and Young Persons Act 1933

If a person who has attained the age of 16 years, having responsibility for any child under the age of 12 years

allows the child to be in any room containing an open fire grate or any heating appliance liable to cause injury to any person

not sufficiently protected to guard against the risk of being burnt or scalded, without taking reasonable precautions against the risk

and by reason thereof the child is killed or suffers serious injury

then that person commits an offence

BROTHELS

S 3 CHILDREN AND YOUNG PERSONS ACT 1933

It is an offence for a person having the responsibility for a person

Who has attained the age of 4 years and is under the age of 16 years

To allow that person to reside in or frequent a brothel

POLICE PROTECTION

S 46 CHILDREN ACT 1989

Where a constable has reasonable cause to believe that a **child** would otherwise be likely to

SUFFER SIGNIFICANT HARM

he may

remove the child to **suitable accomodation** and keep him there	or	take such steps as are reasonable to ensure that the child's removal from any hospital or other place in which he is then being accomodated is prevented

The child is then referred to as having been taken into

POLICE PROTECTION ➤ *No child may be kept in police protection for more than 72 hours*

As soon as reasonably practicable thereafter the constable shall:

- Inform the local authority of the reasons for the steps taken or to be taken and give details of the place where the child is being accomodated
- Inform the child (if he can understand) of the reasons for the steps taken or to be taken
- take steps to discover the wishes and feelings of the child
- secure that the case is enquired into by a designated officer
- where the place to which the child was taken was not provided by a local authority or an official refuge, secure that he is moved to such accommodation
- take such steps as are reasonably practicable to inform:
  - (a) the child's parents;
  - (b) every person who is not a parent of his but who has parental responsibility for him; and
  - (c) any other person with whom the child was living immediately before being taken into police protection.

Armed Forces

ABSENTEES AND DESERTERS

S 186 Army Act 1955; s 186 Air Force Act 1955; s 105 Naval Discipline Act 1957

A constable may arrest without warrant any person whom he has reasonable cause to suspect of being a member of the regular forces who has deserted or is absent without leave. This provision also applies to **visiting forces** but only where a request is made by the appropriate authority of the country to which he belongs. S 13 Visiting Forces Act 1952

UNIFORMS

S 3 Uniforms Act 1894

It is an offence for any person not serving in Her Majesty's forces to wear without Her Majesty's permission any dress having the appearance, or bearing any of the regimental or other distinctive marks of any such uniform

But there is an exemption in the case of stage plays in properly authorised places for public performances, music halls, circus performances or any bona fide military representation

DECORATIONS AND BADGES etc

S 197 Army and Air Force Acts 1955

An offence is committed by any person who:

Uses or wears any military decoration or badge, wound stripe or emblem supplied or authorised by the Defence Council; or any decoration, etc. so nearly resembling an official one as to be calculated to deceive; or falsely represents himself to be a person who is or has been entitled to wear any official decoration etc

But this does not prohibit the use or wearing of ordinary regimental badges or of brooches or ornaments representing them

and

A person shall be guilty of an offence if he

Purchases, takes in pawn, solicits or procures any person to sell or pledge,

or

acts for any person in the sale or pledging of

Medals, medal ribbons, clasps and good conduct badges

Any naval, military or air forces decoration awarded to any member of Her Majesty's forces. But it shall be a defence to prove that at the time of the alleged offence the person to whom the decoration was awarded was dead or had ceased to be a member of those forces.

Aliens

IMMIGRATION ACT 1971, SS 1–3

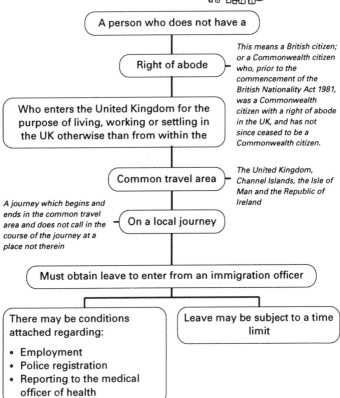

A person who does not have a

Right of abode

This means a British citizen; or a Commonwealth citizen who, prior to the commencement of the British Nationality Act 1981, was a Commonwealth citizen with a right of abode in the UK, and has not since ceased to be a Commonwealth citizen.

Who enters the United Kingdom for the purpose of living, working or settling in the UK otherwise than from within the

Common travel area

The United Kingdom, Channel Islands, the Isle of Man and the Republic of Ireland

On a local journey

A journey which begins and ends in the common travel area and does not call in the course of the journey at a place not therein

Must obtain leave to enter from an immigration officer

There may be conditions attached regarding:

- Employment
- Police registration
- Reporting to the medical officer of health

Leave may be subject to a time limit

Except that persons exercising **European Community** rights and nationals of Member States
(currently Austria, Belgium, Denmark, Finland, France, Germany, Greece, Italy, Luxembourg, Netherlands, Portugal, Spain and Sweden - plus Ireland and the UK) do not require leave to enter or remain.

ALIENS – OFFENCES

SS 24 & 25 IMMIGRATION ACT 1971 AS AMENDED BY THE ASYLUM AND IMMIGRATION ACT 1996

A person will commit an offence if he

Is knowingly concerned with making or carrying out arrangements for securing or facilitating entry by illegal entrants, asylum claimants (unless for gain or in the course of employment of assisting refugees) or obtaining leave to remain in the UK by deception

knowingly harbours anyone whom he knows or has reasonable cause for believing to be an illegal entrant or to have exceeded his time limit or failed to observe a condition of entry

enters the UK without leave, remains beyond any time limit, fails to comply with any conditions

A constable or immigration officer may arrest without warrant anyone who has, or whom he, with reasonable cause, suspects to have, committed or attempted to commit any of the above offences (except for failing to report to a medical officer of health or harbouring)

Hotels etc

ARTS 3 & 4 IMMIGRATION (HOTEL RECORDS) ORDER 1972

When a person over 16 who has no right of abode in this country stays in an hotel or other premises where lodging or sleeping accomodation is provided for reward

then upon arrival at the premises he shall furnish the keeper with

his full name and nationality, the number and place of issue of his passport or identity document

before his departure he shall inform the keeper of his next destination and, if known, full address there

The keeper is required to obtain this information and keep the record of such for 12 months

The records shall be at all times open to inspection by any constable

Mental Health

S 136 Mental Health Act 1983

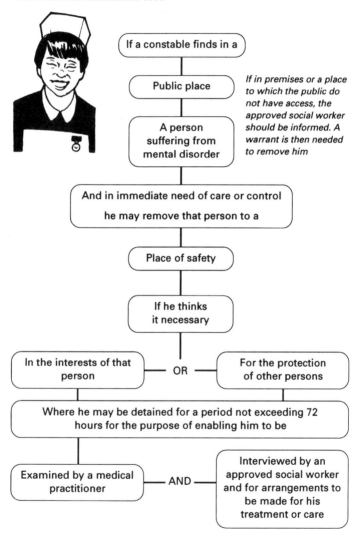

If a constable finds in a

Public place

If in premises or a place to which the public do not have access, the approved social worker should be informed. A warrant is then needed to remove him

A person suffering from mental disorder

And in immediate need of care or control

he may remove that person to a

Place of safety

If he thinks it necessary

In the interests of that person — OR — For the protection of other persons

Where he may be detained for a period not exceeding 72 hours for the purpose of enabling him to be

Examined by a medical practitioner — AND — Interviewed by an approved social worker and for arrangements to be made for his treatment or care

Pedlars

PEDLARS ACT 1871

A 'pedlar' is defined as:

Any pedlar, hawker, petty chapman, tinker caster of metals, mender of chairs, or other persons who, without any horse or other beast bearing or drawing burden

travels and trades on foot

and goes from town to town or to other mens' houses, carrying to sell, or exposing for sale any goods, wares or merchandise, or procuring orders for goods immediately to be delivered, or selling or offering for sale his skill in handicrafts. S 3

The Act does not apply to commercial travellers or other persons selling or seeking orders for goods to or from dealers for resale; or to agents authorised by publishers selling or seeking orders for books; or sellers of vegetables, fish, fruit or victuals; or persons selling at any public market, etc. S 23

Any person who acts as a pedlar must obtain a certificate. It is an offence to act without one. S 4

It is an offence to fail to produce the certificate to a justice, police officer, person to whom he offers goods, or a person on whose private grounds or premises he is found. S 17

It is also an offence to lend, borrow, forge or fail to produce a certificate. S 10

A constable may open and inspect any pack, box, bag, trunk or case in which a pedlar carries his goods. It is an offence to refuse or prevent him from doing so. S 19

Scrap Metal Dealers

SCRAP METAL DEALERS ACT 1964

A scrap metal dealer is defined as:

A person who carries on a business of **buying** and **selling** scrap metal, whether the scrap metal is sold in the form in which it is bought or otherwise. S 9

'Scrap metal' includes any old metal, manufactured articles made wholly or partly from metal and any metallic wastes.

S 2 **At each scrap metal store, the dealer must keep a book in which he must enter particulars of:**

1) All scrap metals received at that place

2) All scrap metal either processed at or despatched from that place

The particulars which must be recorded immediately after the processing or despatch are:

Received

- Description and weight of the scrap metal
- Date and time of receipt
- Full name and address of person from whom received
- The price payable (if known)
- Where price is not known, the value as estimated by the dealer
- The registration mark of any vehicle used to deliver the metal

Processed or Despatched

- Description and weight of the scrap metal;
- Date of processing or despatch and, if applicable, the process applied;
- The full name and address of the person to whom it was sold or exchanged and the consideration given for it;
- If processed or despatched other than on sale or exchange, the value of the scrap metal immediately before despatch, as estimated by the dealer

These particulars may be kept in two separate books if preferred. In any case the book must be kept for 2 years from the date of completion

A constable has a right at all reasonable times to enter a scrap metal dealer's business premises and inspect scrap metal, record books and receipts. S 6

It is an offence to obstruct the exercise of the powers of entry and inspection conferred by these provisions. S 6

It is an offence for a person selling scrap metal to a scrap metal dealer to give him a false name and address. S 5

It is an offence for a scrap metal dealer to acquire scrap metal from a person apparently under the age of 16 years. S 5

Vagrancy

THE FOLLOWING ARE OFFENCES UNDER THE VAGRANCY ACT 1824, AMENDED BY THE VAGRANCY ACT 1935

LODGING IN OUTHOUSES

Every person who wanders abroad and lodges in any barn or otherwise, or in any deserted or unoccupied building or in the open air, or under a tent, or in any cart or wagon, and not giving a good account of himself

AND

- He has been directed to a reasonably accessible place of free shelter and has failed to apply or has refused shelter there; or
- He persistently wanders abroad and there is a reasonably accessible place of free shelter; or
- He has caused damage to property, infection with vermin, or other offensive consequence, or lodges in such circumstances as to appear to be likely to do so. S 4

POWER OF ARREST

S 25 POLICE AND CRIMINAL EVIDENCE ACT 1984

VAGRANCY

VAGRANCY ACT 1824

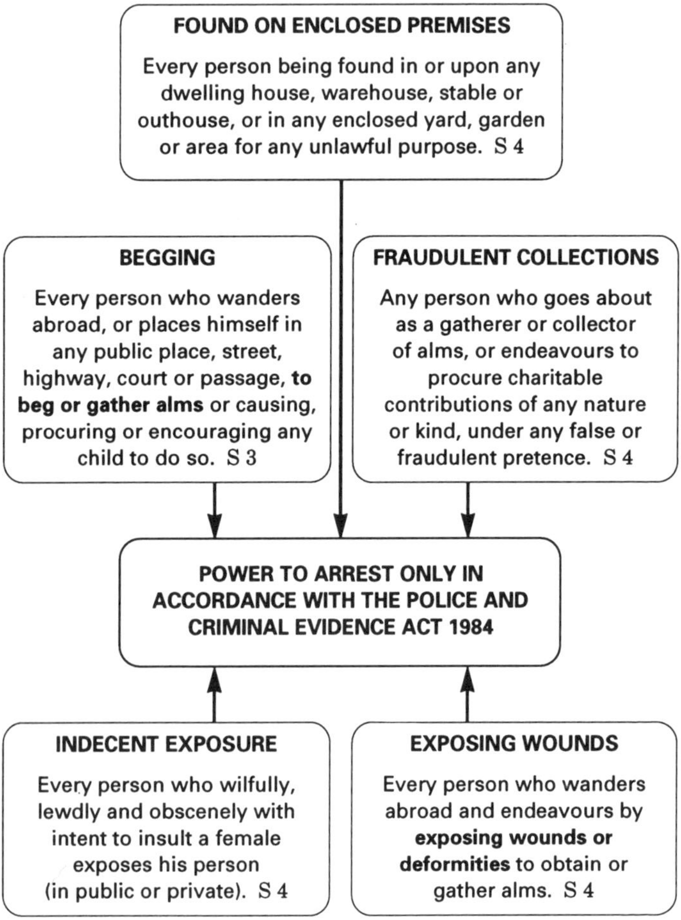
FOUND ON ENCLOSED PREMISES
Every person being found in or upon any dwelling house, warehouse, stable or outhouse, or in any enclosed yard, garden or area for any unlawful purpose. S 4
BEGGING
Every person who wanders abroad, or places himself in any public place, street, highway, court or passage, **to beg or gather alms** or causing, procuring or encouraging any child to do so. S 3
FRAUDULENT COLLECTIONS
Any person who goes about as a gatherer or collector of alms, or endeavours to procure charitable contributions of any nature or kind, under any false or fraudulent pretence. S 4
POWER TO ARREST ONLY IN ACCORDANCE WITH THE POLICE AND CRIMINAL EVIDENCE ACT 1984
INDECENT EXPOSURE
Every person who wilfully, lewdly and obscenely with intent to insult a female exposes his person (in public or private). S 4
EXPOSING WOUNDS
Every person who wanders abroad and endeavours by **exposing wounds or deformities** to obtain or gather alms. S 4

Police

S 90 POLICE ACT 1996

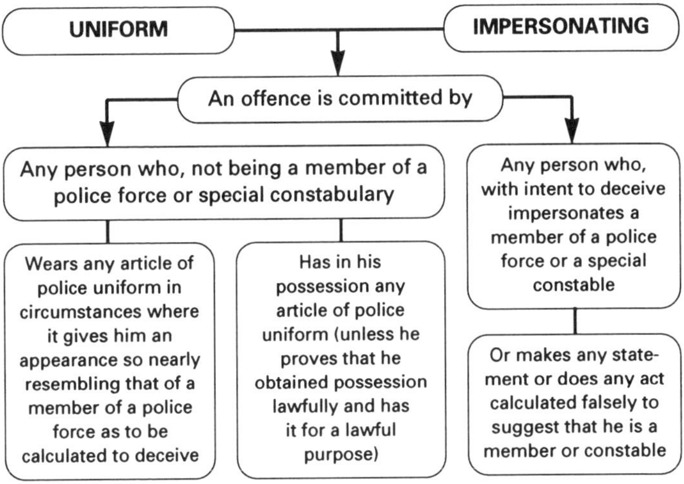

The unauthorised use of any uniform to gain admission to a 'prohibited place' is an offence under s 1 Official Secrets Act 1920

'Article of police uniform' means any article of uniform or any distinctive badge, mark or identification document (or any thing having the appearance of such article etc)

ASSAULT, etc S 89

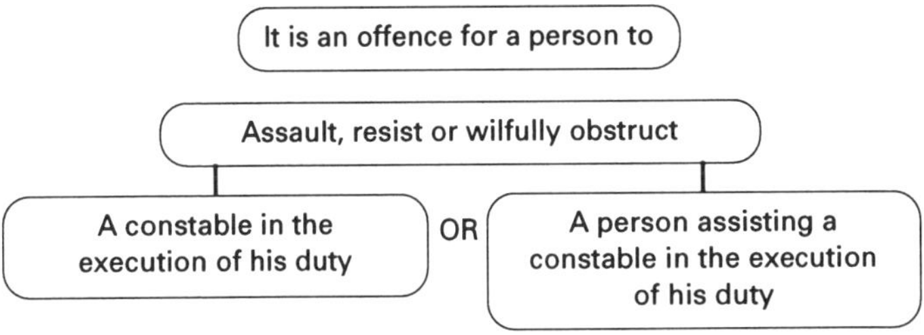

It is a common law offence to refuse to aid and assist a constable in the execution of his duty when called upon to do so, if the person is physically capable of helping and has no lawful excuse for refusing

Chapter 7
Public Order

Litter

S 5 Litter Act 1983,
s 87 Environmental
Protection Act 1990

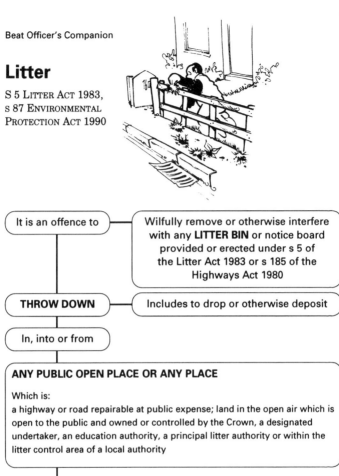

It is an offence to — Wilfully remove or otherwise interfere with any **LITTER BIN** or notice board provided or erected under s 5 of the Litter Act 1983 or s 185 of the Highways Act 1980

THROW DOWN — Includes to drop or otherwise deposit

In, into or from

ANY PUBLIC OPEN PLACE OR ANY PLACE

Which is:
a highway or road repairable at public expense; land in the open air which is open to the public and owned or controlled by the Crown, a designated undertaker, an education authority, a principal litter authority or within the litter control area of a local authority

AND LEAVE

Anything whatsoever in such circumstances as to cause, contribute to, or tend to lead to

DEFACEMENT BY LITTER

Unless authorised by law or consent is obtained from the owner, occupier or person having control of that place

Abandoning Vehicles etc

S 2 REFUSE DISPOSAL (AMENITY) ACT 1978

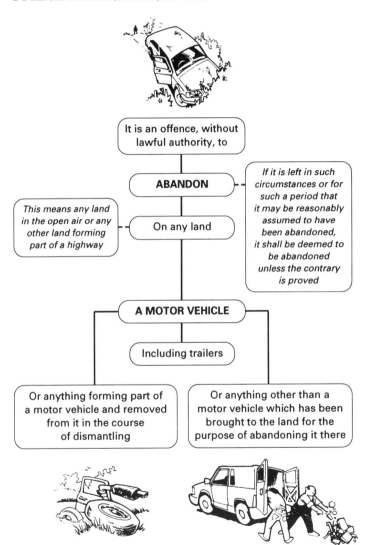

It is an offence, without lawful authority, to

ABANDON

If it is left in such circumstances or for such a period that it may be reasonably assumed to have been abandoned, it shall be deemed to be abandoned unless the contrary is proved

On any land

This means any land in the open air or any other land forming part of a highway

A MOTOR VEHICLE

Including trailers

Or anything forming part of a motor vehicle and removed from it in the course of dismantling

Or anything other than a motor vehicle which has been brought to the land for the purpose of abandoning it there

Noise

S 62 CONTROL OF POLLUTION ACT 1974

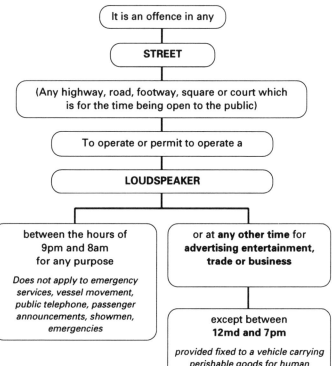

It is an offence in any

STREET

(Any highway, road, footway, square or court which is for the time being open to the public)

To operate or permit to operate a

LOUDSPEAKER

between the hours of 9pm and 8am for any purpose

Does not apply to emergency services, vessel movement, public telephone, passenger announcements, showmen, emergencies

or at **any other time** for **advertising entertainment, trade or business**

except between **12md and 7pm**

provided fixed to a vehicle carrying perishable goods for human consumption and the loudspeaker is used only for the purpose of advertising those goods in a manner which does not cause annoyance. Words may not be used

Trade Disputes

S 241 TRADE UNION AND LABOUR RELATIONS (CONSOLIDATION) ACT 1992

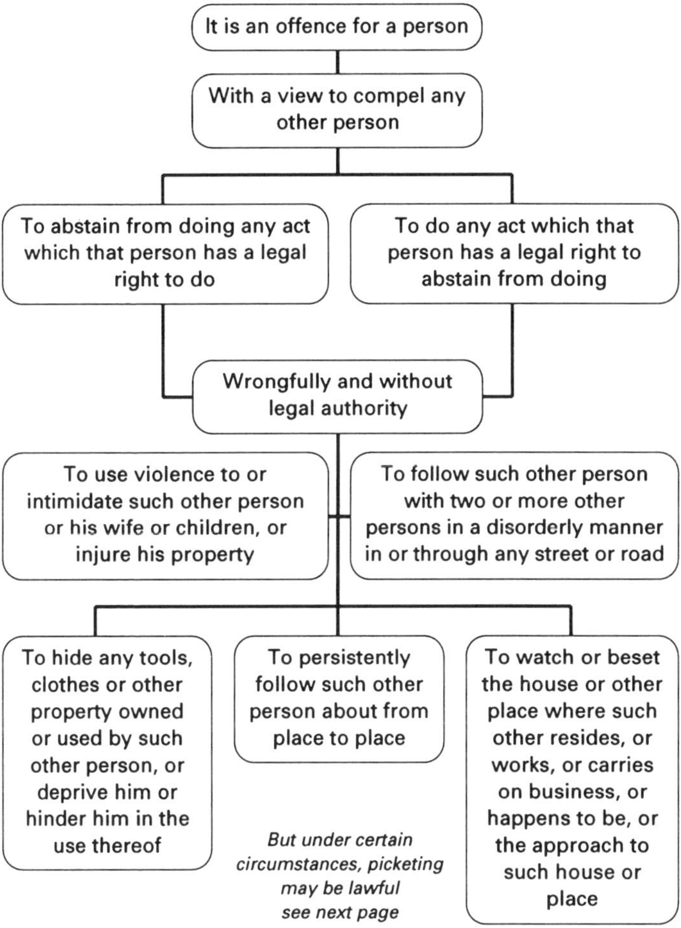
It is an offence for a person
With a view to compel any other person
To abstain from doing any act which that person has a legal right to do
To do any act which that person has a legal right to abstain from doing
Wrongfully and without legal authority
To use violence to or intimidate such other person or his wife or children, or injure his property
To follow such other person with two or more other persons in a disorderly manner in or through any street or road
To hide any tools, clothes or other property owned or used by such other person, or deprive him or hinder him in the use thereof
To persistently follow such other person about from place to place
To watch or beset the house or other place where such other resides, or works, or carries on business, or happens to be, or the approach to such house or place
But under certain circumstances, picketing may be lawful see next page

A constable may arrest without warrant anyone he reasonably suspects is committing one of the above offences

Peaceful Picketing

S 220 Trade Union and Labour Relations (Consolidation) Act 1992

Fear or Provocation of Violence

S 4 Public Order Act 1986

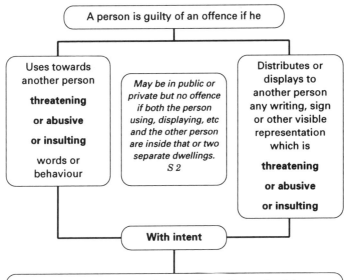

A person is guilty of an offence if he

Uses towards another person **threatening** **or abusive** **or insulting** words or behaviour

May be in public or private but no offence if both the person using, displaying, etc and the other person are inside that or two separate dwellings. S 2

Distributes or displays to another person any writing, sign or other visible representation which is **threatening** **or abusive** **or insulting**

With intent

- To cause that person to believe that immediate unlawful violence will be used against him or another by any person, or
- To provoke the immediate use of unlawful violence by that person or another, or
- Whereby that person is likely to believe that such violence will be used or it is likely that such violence will be provoked

Violence includes conduct towards property. Need not cause, or be intended to cause, injury or damage. S 8

A constable may arrest without warrant anyone he reasonably suspects is committing this offence. S 4(3)

Harassment, Alarm or Distress

S 5 PUBLIC ORDER ACT 1986

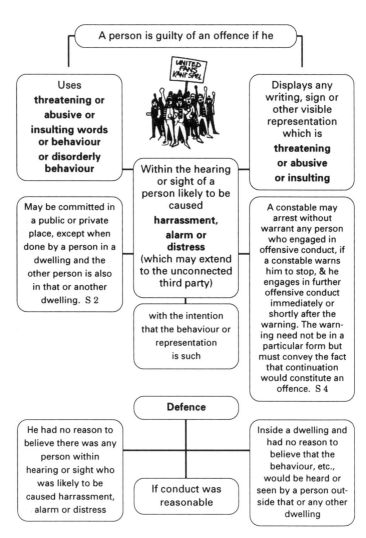

A person is guilty of an offence if he

Uses **threatening or abusive or insulting words or behaviour or disorderly behaviour**

Displays any writing, sign or other visible representation which is **threatening or abusive or insulting**

Within the hearing or sight of a person likely to be caused **harrassment, alarm or distress** (which may extend to the unconnected third party)

with the intention that the behaviour or representation is such

May be committed in a public or private place, except when done by a person in a dwelling and the other person is also in that or another dwelling. S 2

A constable may arrest without warrant any person who engaged in offensive conduct, if a constable warns him to stop, & he engages in further offensive conduct immediately or shortly after the warning. The warning need not be in a particular form but must convey the fact that continuation would constitute an offence. S 4

Defence

He had no reason to believe there was any person within hearing or sight who was likely to be caused harrassment, alarm or distress

If conduct was reasonable

Inside a dwelling and had no reason to believe that the behaviour, etc., would be heard or seen by a person outside that or any other dwelling

INTENTIONAL HARASSMENT, ALARM OR DISTRESS

S 4A PUBLIC ORDER ACT 1986 (INSERTED BY S 154 CRIMINAL JUSTICE AND PUBLIC ORDER ACT 1994)

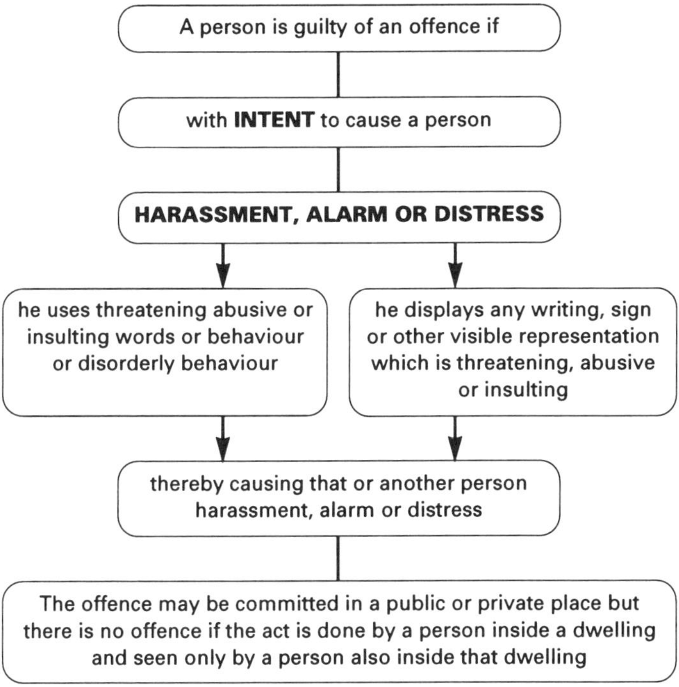

Defences – (i) he was inside the dwelling and had no reason to believe that the act would be seen or heard by someone outside the dwelling
(ii) the conduct was reasonable.

A constable may arrest without warrant anyone whom he reasonably suspects is committing the offence.

Protection from Harassment and Fear of Violence

PROTECTION FROM HARASSMENT ACT 1997

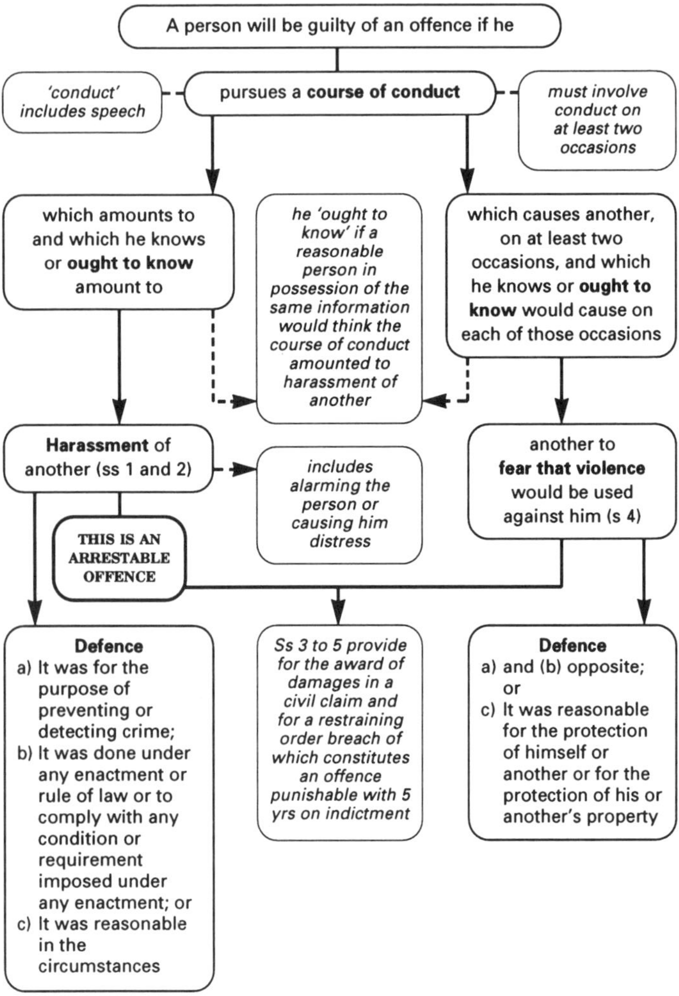
A person will be guilty of an offence if he
'conduct' includes speech
pursues a **course of conduct**
must involve conduct on at least two occasions
which amounts to and which he knows or **ought to know** amount to
he 'ought to know' if a reasonable person in possession of the same information would think the course of conduct amounted to harassment of another
which causes another, on at least two occasions, and which he knows or **ought to know** would cause on each of those occasions
Harassment of another (ss 1 and 2)
includes alarming the person or causing him distress
another to **fear that violence** would be used against him (s 4)
THIS IS AN ARRESTABLE OFFENCE
Defence
a) It was for the purpose of preventing or detecting crime;
b) It was done under any enactment or rule of law or to comply with any condition or requirement imposed under any enactment; or
c) It was reasonable in the circumstances
Ss 3 to 5 provide for the award of damages in a civil claim and for a restraining order breach of which constitutes an offence punishable with 5 yrs on indictment
Defence
a) and (b) opposite; or
c) It was reasonable for the protection of himself or another or for the protection of his or another's property

Football Offences

FOOTBALL (OFFENCES) ACT 1991

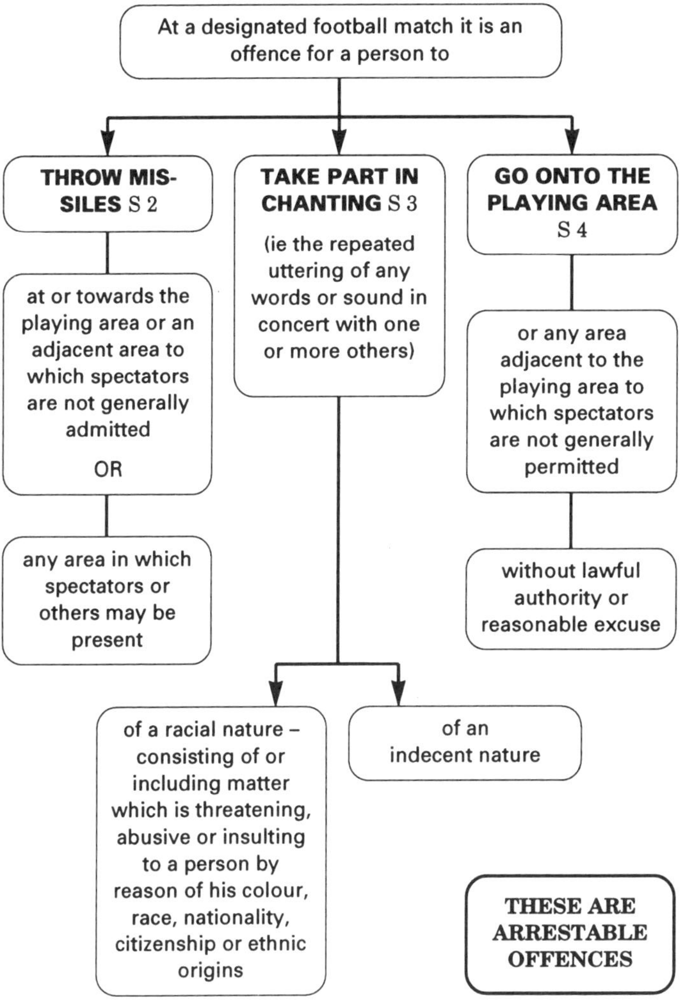
At a designated football match it is an offence for a person to
THROW MISSILES S 2
at or towards the playing area or an adjacent area to which spectators are not generally admitted
OR
any area in which spectators or others may be present
TAKE PART IN CHANTING S 3
(ie the repeated uttering of any words or sound in concert with one or more others)
of a racial nature – consisting of or including matter which is threatening, abusive or insulting to a person by reason of his colour, race, nationality, citizenship or ethnic origins
of an indecent nature
GO ONTO THE PLAYING AREA S 4
or any area adjacent to the playing area to which spectators are not generally permitted
without lawful authority or reasonable excuse
THESE ARE ARRESTABLE OFFENCES

TICKET TOUTS

S 166 Criminal Justice and Public Order Act 1994

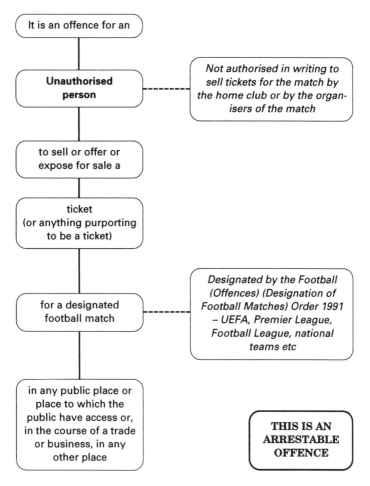

It is an offence for an

Unauthorised person — *Not authorised in writing to sell tickets for the match by the home club or by the organisers of the match*

to sell or offer or expose for sale a

ticket (or anything purporting to be a ticket)

for a designated football match — *Designated by the Football (Offences) (Designation of Football Matches) Order 1991 – UEFA, Premier League, Football League, national teams etc*

in any public place or place to which the public have access or, in the course of a trade or business, in any other place

THIS IS AN ARRESTABLE OFFENCE

Offensive Weapons

S 139 Criminal Justice Act 1988

It is an offence to have an article which has a **blade** or which is **sharply pointed**

Folding pocket-knives are exempt provided the cutting edge of the blade is not longer than 3".

In a public place
(ie any place to which at the material time the public have or are permitted access, whether on payment or otherwise)

*It shall be a **defence** to show that he had good reason or lawful authority for having it, or that he had it with him for use at work, for religious reasons, or as part of a national costume.*

School Premises
An additional offence was created by the Offensive Weapons Act 1996 to include possession of the above articles (or offensive weapons as described above) whilst on **school premises** (s139a Criminal Justice Act 1988).

A constable may **enter** (using reasonable force if necessary) and **search** school premises or any person found theron for weapons if he suspects this offence is being, or has been, committed and to **seize** such articles.

S 1 Prevention of Crime Act 1953

It is an offence to have an **offensive weapon**

Offensive weapons will normally be one of two types:

- *Any article **made or adapted** for causing injury*
- *Or other articles **intended to be used** for such purposes*

whilst in a **public place** without lawful authority or reasonable excuse

Unless acting in the capacity of Crown servant, police, armed services, etc. (Public place means any highway and any other place to which at the material time the public have or are permitted access, whether on payment or otherwise).

Restriction of Offensive Weapons Acts 1959 & 1961

It is an offence for any person to manufacture, import, sell, hire, offer for sale or hire, or hire expose or have in possession for the purpose of sale or hire, or to lend or give to any other person a **flick knife or gravity knife**.

OFFENSIVE WEAPONS – SALE OR SUPPLY

S 141 Criminal Justice Act 1988 and Criminal Justice Act 1988 (Offensive Weapons) Order 1988

It is an offence to
manufacture, sell or hire or offer for sale or hire, expose or have in possession for the purpose of sale or hire or lend or give to any other person

ANY OF THE FOLLOWING WEAPONS

not being antiques (manufactured more than 100 years before the date of the offence)

Balisong, or butterfly knife
being a blade enclosed by its handle, which is designed to split down the middle, without the operation of a spring or other mechanical means, to reveal the blade;

Knuckleduster
that is, a band of metal or other hard material worn on one or more fingers, and designed to cause injury, and any weapon incorporating a knuckleduster;

Telescopic truncheon
being a truncheon which extends automatically by hand pressure applied to a button, spring or other device in or attached to its handle;

Push dagger
being a knife the handle of which fits within a clenched fist and the blade of which protrudes from between two fingers;

Shuriken, shaken, or death star
being a hard non-flexible plate having three or more sharp radiating points and designed to be thrown;

Handclaw
being a band of metal or other hard material from which a number of sharp spikes protrude, and worn around the hand;

continued...

Footclaw
being a bar of metal or other hard material from which a number of sharp spikes protrude, and worn strapped to the foot;

Manrikgusari, or kusari
being a length of rope, cord, wire or chain fastened at each end to a hard weight or hand grip.

Swordstick
that is, a hollow walking-stick or cane containing a blade which may be used as a sword;

Hollow kubatan
being a cylindrical container containing a number of sharp spikes;

Blowpipe, or blowgun
being a hollow tube out of which hard pellets or darts are shot by the use of breath;

Kusari gama
being a length of rope, cord, wire or chain fastened at one end to a sickle;

Kyoketsu shoge
being a length of rope, cord, wire or chain fastened at one end to a hooked knife;

Belt buckle knife
being a buckle which incorporates or conceals a knife.

Sale to Persons Under 16

S 141A Criminal Justice Act 1988

Any person who sells to a person under the age of **16 years** any knife, knife blade, razor blade, axe, or any other article which has a blade or is sharply pointed, and made or adapted for causing injury to any person shall be guilty of an offence.

Marketing of Knives

KNIVES ACT 1997, CRIMINAL JUSTICE AND PUBLIC ORDER ACT 1994, S60

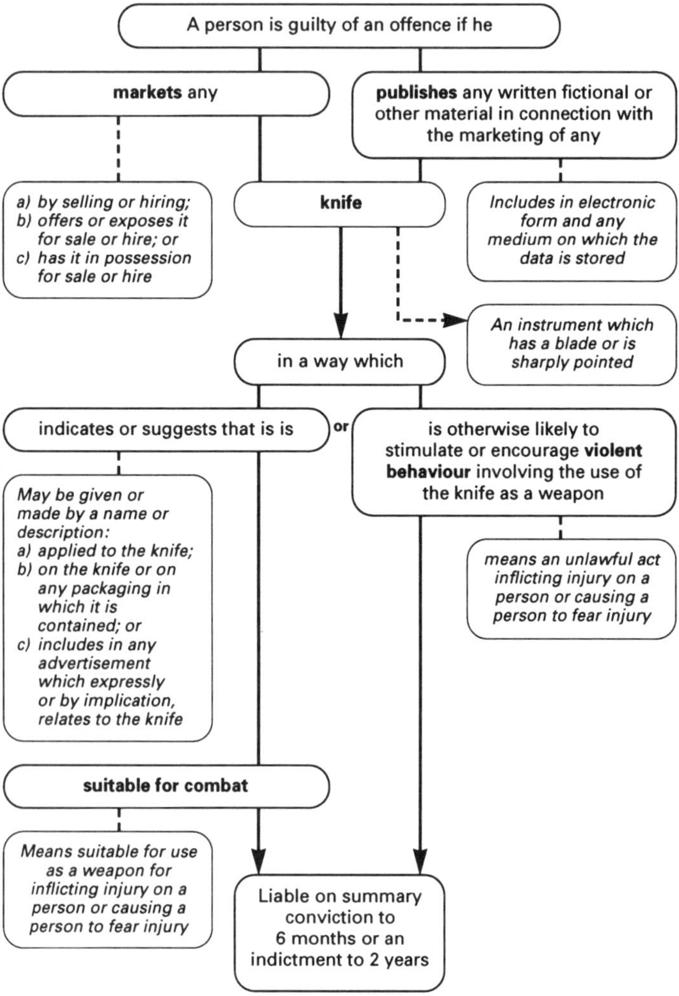
A person is guilty of an offence if he
markets any
publishes any written fictional or other material in connection with the marketing of any
a) by selling or hiring;
b) offers or exposes it for sale or hire; or
c) has it in possession for sale or hire
knife
Includes in electronic form and any medium on which the data is stored
An instrument which has a blade or is sharply pointed
in a way which
indicates or suggests that is is
or
is otherwise likely to stimulate or encourage **violent behaviour** involving the use of the knife as a weapon
May be given or made by a name or description:
a) applied to the knife;
b) on the knife or on any packaging in which it is contained; or
c) includes in any advertisement which expressly or by implication, relates to the knife
means an unlawful act inflicting injury on a person or causing a person to fear injury
suitable for combat
Means suitable for use as a weapon for inflicting injury on a person or causing a person to fear injury
Liable on summary conviction to 6 months or an indictment to 2 years

DEFENCES

Trades:

a) It was marketed:
   - i) for use by the armed forces of any country;
   - ii) as an antique or curio; or
   - iii) as falling within such other category (if any) as may be prescribed;

b) It was reasonable for the knife to be marketed in that way; and

c) There were no grounds to suspect that it would be used for an unlawful purpose.

Others:

He did not know or suspect that the way in which the knife was marketed:

a) amounted to an indication or suggestion that the knife was suitable for combat; or

b) was likely to stimulate or encourage violent behaviour involving the use of the knife as a weapon.

General:

He took all reasonable precautions and exercised all due diligence to avoid committing the offence.

POLICE POWERS

A justices' warrant is required to search premises for knives and to seize them.

An Inspector or above many authorise stopping and searching in anticipation of violence *(see following page)*.

Stop and Search for Knives or Offensive Weapons S60 Justice and Public Order Act 1994 as amended by the Knives Act 1997, s 8

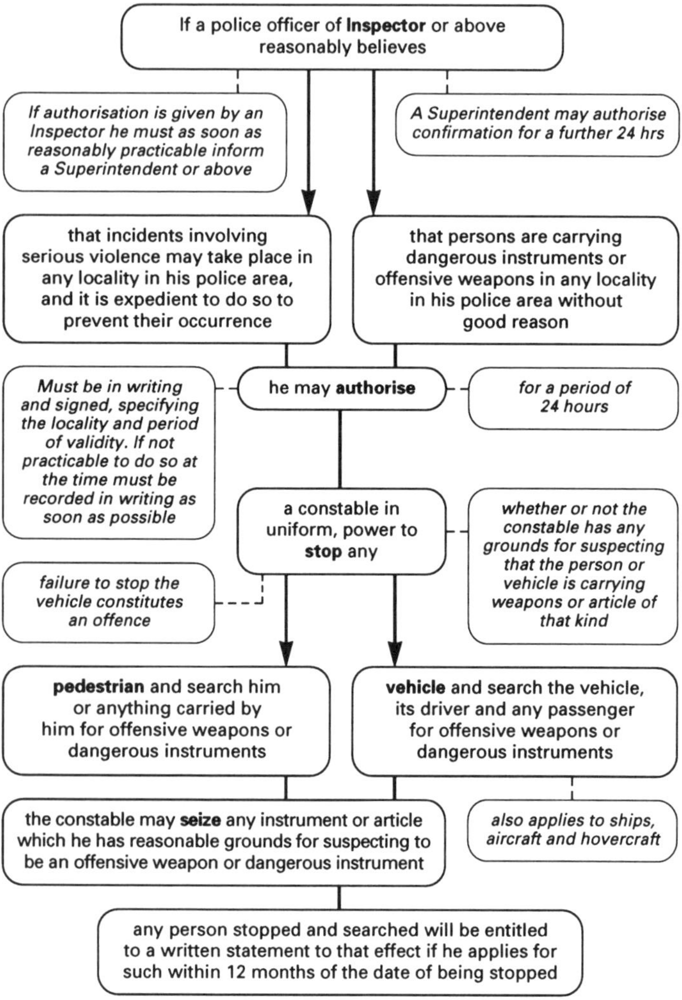
If a police officer of **Inspector** or above reasonably believes
If authorisation is given by an Inspector he must as soon as reasonably practicable inform a Superintendent or above
A Superintendent may authorise confirmation for a further 24 hrs
that incidents involving serious violence may take place in any locality in his police area, and it is expedient to do so to prevent their occurrence
that persons are carrying dangerous instruments or offensive weapons in any locality in his police area without good reason
Must be in writing and signed, specifying the locality and period of validity. If not practicable to do so at the time must be recorded in writing as soon as possible
he may **authorise**
for a period of 24 hours
a constable in uniform, power to **stop** any
whether or not the constable has any grounds for suspecting that the person or vehicle is carrying weapons or article of that kind
failure to stop the vehicle constitutes an offence
pedestrian and search him or anything carried by him for offensive weapons or dangerous instruments
vehicle and search the vehicle, its driver and any passenger for offensive weapons or dangerous instruments
the constable may **seize** any instrument or article which he has reasonable grounds for suspecting to be an offensive weapon or dangerous instrument
also applies to ships, aircraft and hovercraft
any person stopped and searched will be entitled to a written statement to that effect if he applies for such within 12 months of the date of being stopped

Crossbows

CROSSBOWS ACT 1987

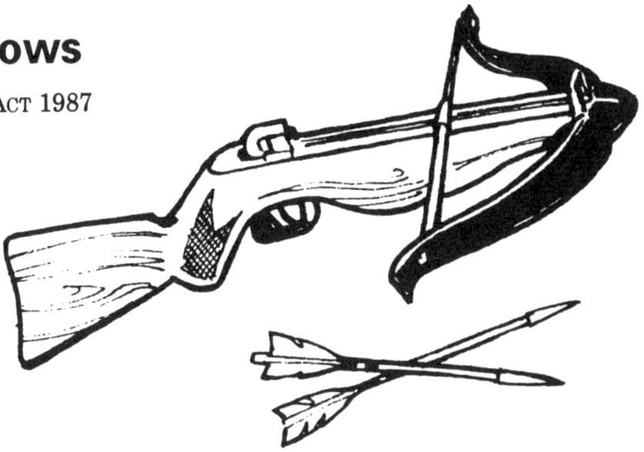

OFFENCES

Sale To sell or hire a crossbow or part of a crossbow to a person under the age of 17 years, unless he believes and has reasonable grounds to believe him to be 17 years.

Purchase For a person under 17 years to buy or hire a crossbow or part of a crossbow

Possession For a person under 17 years to have with him a crossbow (whether assembled to not) capable of discharging a missile unless under the supervision of a person of 21 years or older.

The Act does not apply to crossbows with a draw weight of less than 1.4 Kg.

POLICE POWERS

Search Where a PC suspects with reasonable cause, that a person is committing, or has committed an offence of unlawful possession, he may search that person or vehicle, and may detain the person or vehicle for that purpose.

Seizure PC may seize and retain for the purpose of proceedings any crossbow or part of a crossbow discovered in the course of the search.

Entry For the purpose of exercising the above powers a PC may enter any land **other than a dwelling house**.

Racial Hatred

Ss 17–23 Public Order Act 1986

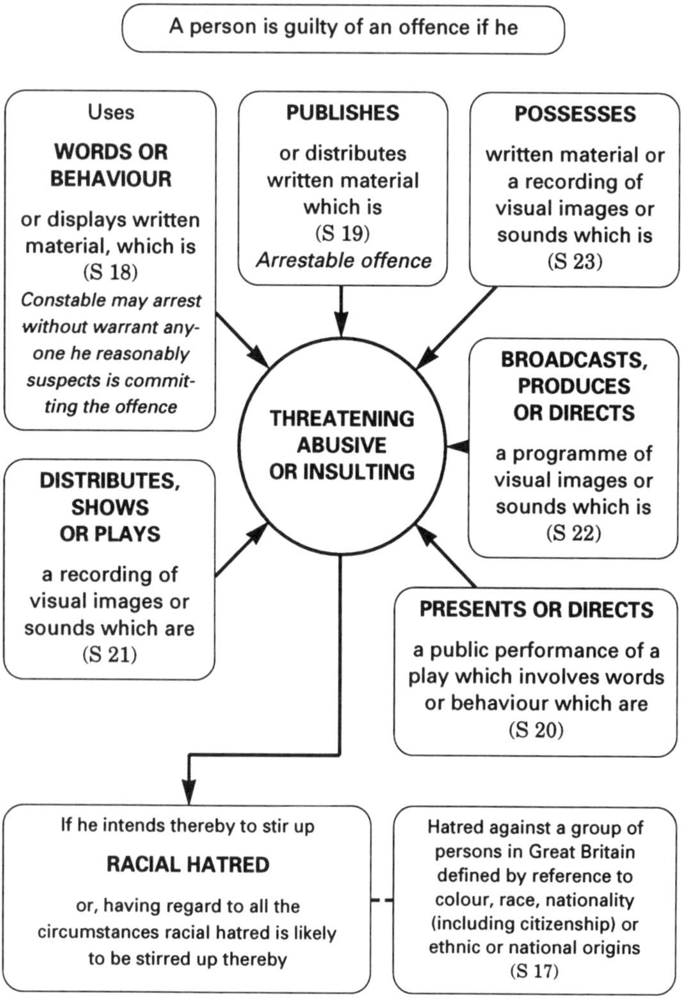
A person is guilty of an offence if he
Uses
WORDS OR BEHAVIOUR
or displays written material, which is
(S 18)
Constable may arrest without warrant anyone he reasonably suspects is committing the offence
PUBLISHES
or distributes written material which is
(S 19)
Arrestable offence
POSSESSES
written material or a recording of visual images or sounds which is
(S 23)
THREATENING
ABUSIVE
OR INSULTING
BROADCASTS, PRODUCES OR DIRECTS
a programme of visual images or sounds which is
(S 22)
DISTRIBUTES, SHOWS OR PLAYS
a recording of visual images or sounds which are
(S 21)
PRESENTS OR DIRECTS
a public performance of a play which involves words or behaviour which are
(S 20)
If he intends thereby to stir up
RACIAL HATRED
or, having regard to all the circumstances racial hatred is likely to be stirred up thereby
Hatred against a group of persons in Great Britain defined by reference to colour, race, nationality (including citizenship) or ethnic or national origins
(S 17)

Trespassers on Land

Ss 61 & 62 Criminal Justice and Public Order Act 1994

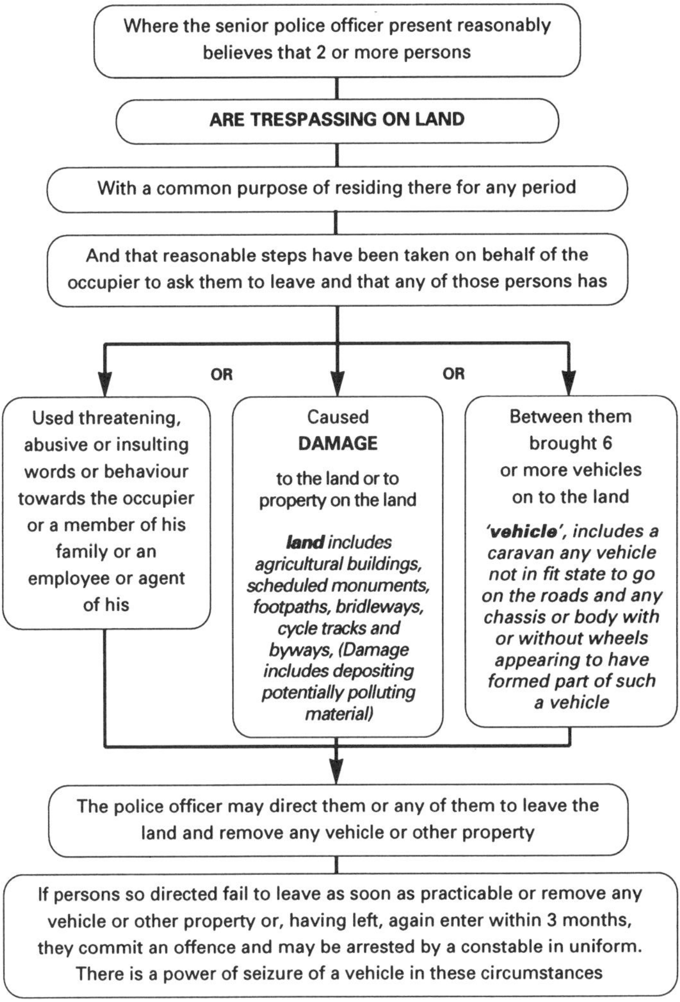
Where the senior police officer present reasonably believes that 2 or more persons
ARE TRESPASSING ON LAND
With a common purpose of residing there for any period
And that reasonable steps have been taken on behalf of the occupier to ask them to leave and that any of those persons has
OR
OR
Used threatening, abusive or insulting words or behaviour towards the occupier or a member of his family or an employee or agent of his
Caused DAMAGE to the land or to property on the land
land includes agricultural buildings, scheduled monuments, footpaths, bridleways, cycle tracks and byways, (Damage includes depositing potentially polluting material)
Between them brought 6 or more vehicles on to the land
'vehicle', includes a caravan any vehicle not in fit state to go on the roads and any chassis or body with or without wheels appearing to have formed part of such a vehicle
The police officer may direct them or any of them to leave the land and remove any vehicle or other property
If persons so directed fail to leave as soon as practicable or remove any vehicle or other property or, having left, again enter within 3 months, they commit an offence and may be arrested by a constable in uniform. There is a power of seizure of a vehicle in these circumstances

Aggravated Trespass

S 68 Criminal Justice and Public Order Act 1994

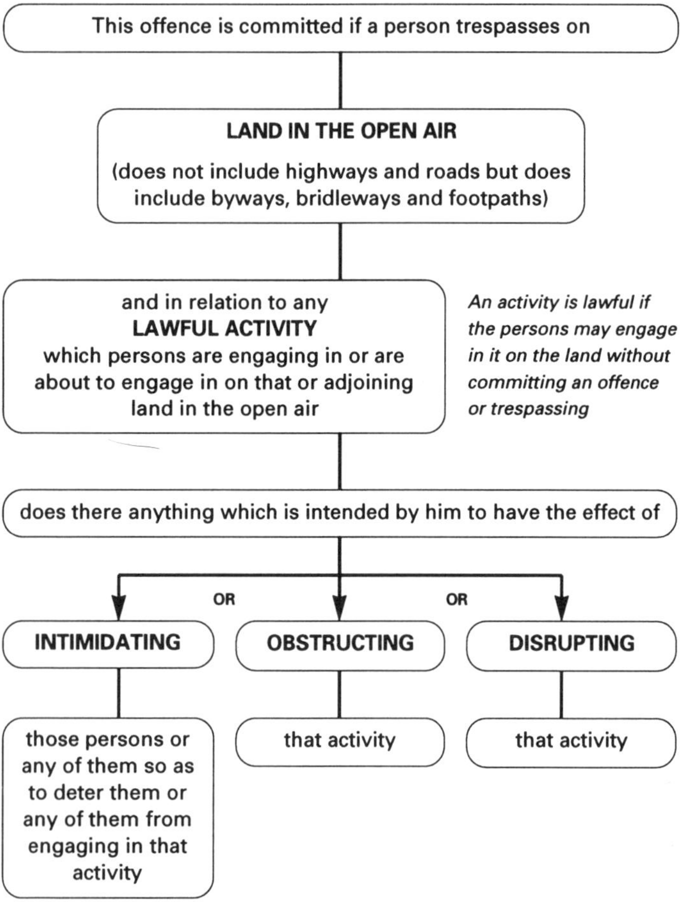
This offence is committed if a person trespasses on
LAND IN THE OPEN AIR
(does not include highways and roads but does include byways, bridleways and footpaths)
and in relation to any LAWFUL ACTIVITY which persons are engaging in or are about to engage in on that or adjoining land in the open air
An activity is lawful if the persons may engage in it on the land without committing an offence or trespassing
does there anything which is intended by him to have the effect of
OR
OR
INTIMIDATING
OBSTRUCTING
DISRUPTING
those persons or any of them so as to deter them or any of them from engaging in that activity
that activity
that activity

A constable in uniform who reasonably suspects that a person is committing this offence may arrest him without a warrant.

AGGRAVATED TRESPASS – REMOVAL OF PERSONS

S 69 Criminal Justice and Public Order Act 1994

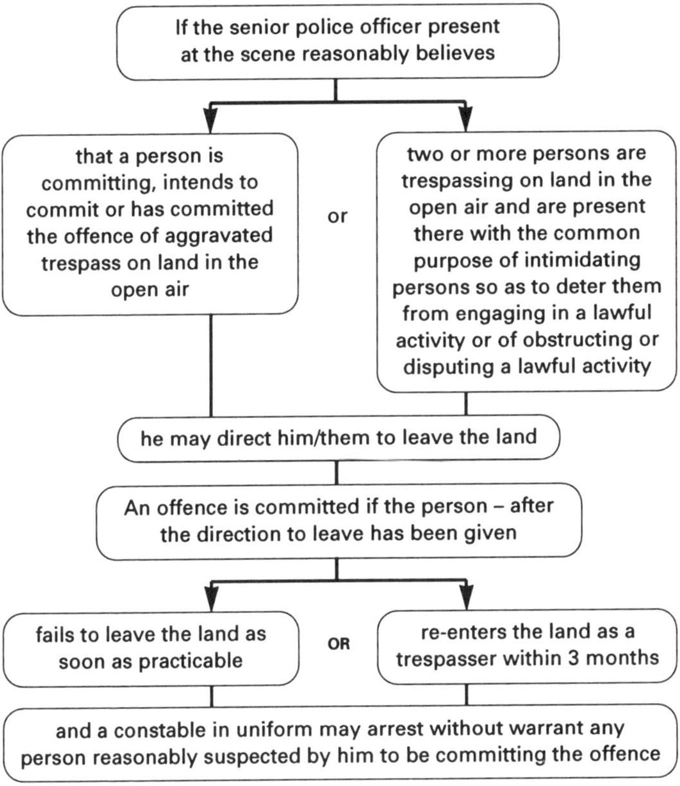
If the senior police officer present at the scene reasonably believes
that a person is committing, intends to commit or has committed the offence of aggravated trespass on land in the open air
or
two or more persons are trespassing on land in the open air and are present there with the common purpose of intimidating persons so as to deter them from engaging in a lawful activity or of obstructing or disputing a lawful activity
he may direct him/them to leave the land
An offence is committed if the person – after the direction to leave has been given
fails to leave the land as soon as practicable
OR
re-enters the land as a trespasser within 3 months
and a constable in uniform may arrest without warrant any person reasonably suspected by him to be committing the offence

The direction to leave may be communicated by a constable at the scene.

Defence

if a person shows he was not trespassing or that he had a reasonable excuse for not leaving or for re-entering.

Trespassory Assemblies

S 14A Public Order Act 1986, inserted by s 70 Criminal Justice and Public Order Act 1994

If the chief officer of police *(or the Commissioner of Police for the City of London or Metropolis)* reasonably believes that an

ASSEMBLY OF 20 OR MORE PERSONS

is intended to be held in any district at a place on land (in the open air) to which the public has no (or limited) right of access and

it is likely to be held without the permission of the occupier of the land or to conduct itself in such a way as to exceed the limits of any permission or right of access

and may result:

(i) in a serious disruption to the life of the community, or

(ii) where the land or a building or monument on it, is of historic, architectural, archaeological or scientific importance

he may apply to the council of the district for an order prohibiting for a specified period the holding of such trespassory assemblies in the specified district or part of it. In the City of London and the Metropolitan area the relevant Commissioner may, with the consent of the Home Secretary, make such an order

The order may only be made for a period not exceeding 4 days and for an area not exceeding 5 miles radius from the specified centre

TRESPASSORY ASSEMBLIES – POWERS

Ss 14B & 14C Public Order Act 1986,
inserted by ss 70-71 Criminal Justice and Public Order Act 1994

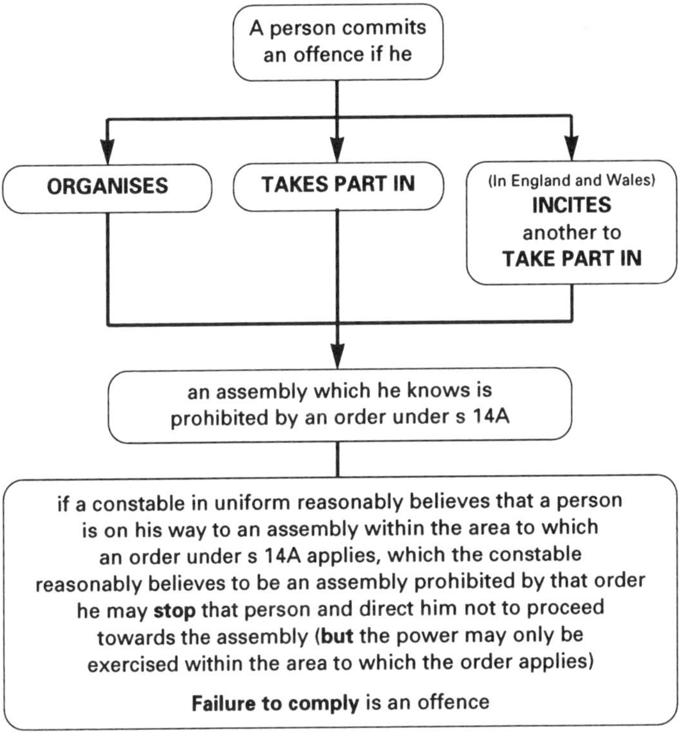
A person commits an offence if he
ORGANISES
TAKES PART IN
(In England and Wales) INCITES another to TAKE PART IN
an assembly which he knows is prohibited by an order under s 14A
if a constable in uniform reasonably believes that a person is on his way to an assembly within the area to which an order under s 14A applies, which the constable reasonably believes to be an assembly prohibited by that order he may stop that person and direct him not to proceed towards the assembly (but the power may only be exercised within the area to which the order applies)
Failure to comply is an offence

A constable in uniform may arrest without warrant any person he reasonably suspects to be committing an offence under ss 14A or 14B.

Raves

S 63 Criminal Justice and Public Order Act 1994

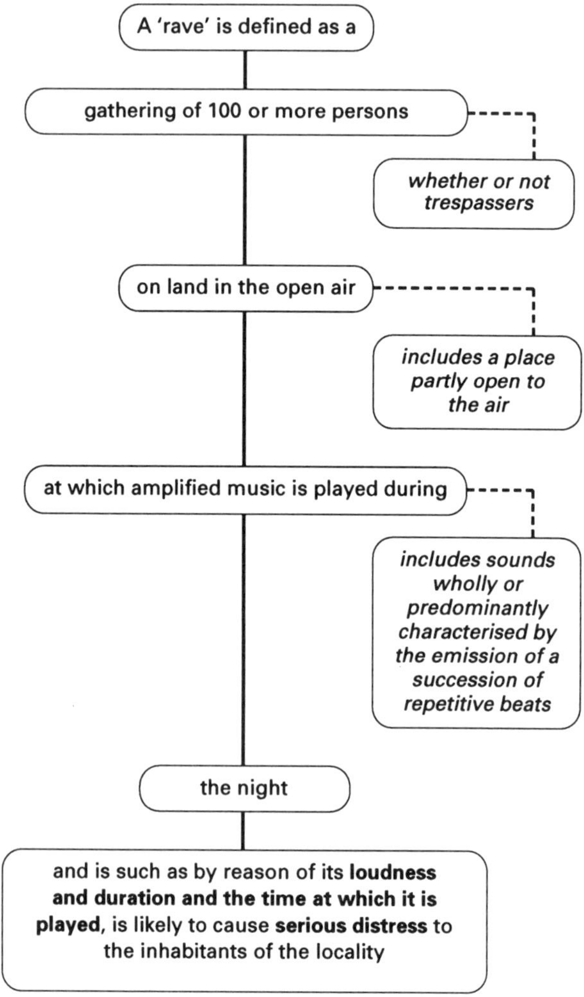
A 'rave' is defined as a
gathering of 100 or more persons
whether or not trespassers
on land in the open air
includes a place partly open to the air
at which amplified music is played during
includes sounds wholly or predominantly characterised by the emission of a succession of repetitive beats
the night
and is such as by reason of its **loudness and duration and the time at which it is played**, is likely to cause **serious distress** to the inhabitants of the locality

RAVES – POWERS

Ss 63 – 65 CRIMINAL JUSTICE AND PUBLIC ORDER ACT 1994

Removal of Persons s 63

A police officer of at least the rank of superintendent who reasonably believes that:

(a) 2 or more persons are making preparations for a rave;

(b) 10 or more persons are waiting for it to begin; or

(c) 10 or more persons are attending a rave in progress;

may **direct** those persons and any other persons who arrive, to leave the land and remove any vehicles or other property that they have with them. The direction may be communicated by any constable at the scene. It will be treated as having been communicated if reasonable steps have been taken to bring it to their attention. Failure to leave or re-entry within 7 days is an offence arrestable by a constable in uniform who reasonably suspects a person to be committing the offence.

Entry and Seizure s 64

A superintendent or above who believes the above direction would be justified in the circumstances, may authorise any constable to enter the land for the purposes of ascertaining whether such circumstances exist and to exercise any of the above powers and to seize and remove a vehicle or sound equipment which the person to whom a direction has been given has failed to remove and which appears to the constable to belong to him or to be in his possession or control. Also applies where a person has re-entered the land with a vehicle and/or sound equipment within 7 days.

Stopping Persons from Attending s 65

If a constable in uniform reasonably believes that a person is on his way to a gathering to which s 63 applies and in respect of which a direction is in force, he may stop that person and direct him not to proceed in the direction of that gathering. This power may be exercised within 5 miles of the boundary of the site of the gathering. Failure to comply is an offence and a constable in uniform who reasonably suspects that a person is committing the offence may arrest him without warrant.

Violent Entry to Premises

S 6 CRIMINAL LAW ACT 1977 AS AMENDED BY S 72 CRIMINAL JUSTICE AND PUBLIC ORDER ACT 1994

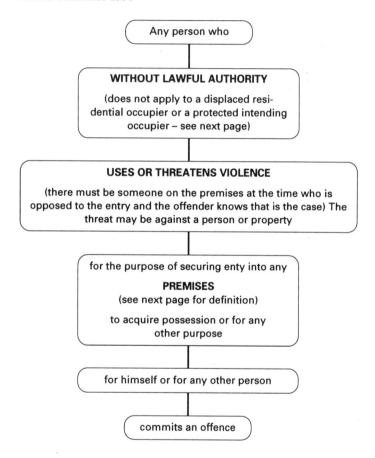

Any person who

WITHOUT LAWFUL AUTHORITY

(does not apply to a displaced residential occupier or a protected intending occupier – see next page)

USES OR THREATENS VIOLENCE

(there must be someone on the premises at the time who is opposed to the entry and the offender knows that is the case) The threat may be against a person or property

for the purpose of securing enty into any

PREMISES

(see next page for definition)

to acquire possession or for any other purpose

for himself or for any other person

commits an offence

A constable in uniform may arrest without warrant anyone who is, or whom he with reasonable cause suspects to be, guilty of this offence.

Squatters

S 7 CRIMINAL LAW ACT 1977, AS SUBSTITUTED BY S 73 CRIMINAL JUSTICE AND PUBLIC ORDER ACT 1994

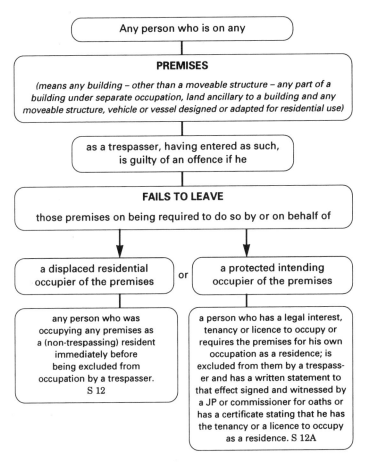

Any person who is on any

PREMISES

(means any building – other than a moveable structure – any part of a building under separate occupation, land ancillary to a building and any moveable structure, vehicle or vessel designed or adapted for residential use)

as a trespasser, having entered as such, is guilty of an offence if he

FAILS TO LEAVE

those premises on being required to do so by or on behalf of

a displaced residential occupier of the premises

or

a protected intending occupier of the premises

any person who was occupying any premises as a (non-trespassing) resident immediately before being excluded from occupation by a trespasser. S 12

a person who has a legal interest, tenancy or licence to occupy or requires the premises for his own occupation as a residence; is excluded from them by a trespasser and has a written statement to that effect signed and witnessed by a JP or commissioner for oaths or has a certificate stating that he has the tenancy or a licence to occupy as a residence. S 12A

Defences – The premises were used mainly for non-residential purposes and offender was not on a residential part. Belief that person requiring him to leave was not a displaced residential occupier or protected intending occupier.

Affray

S 3 Public Order Act 1986

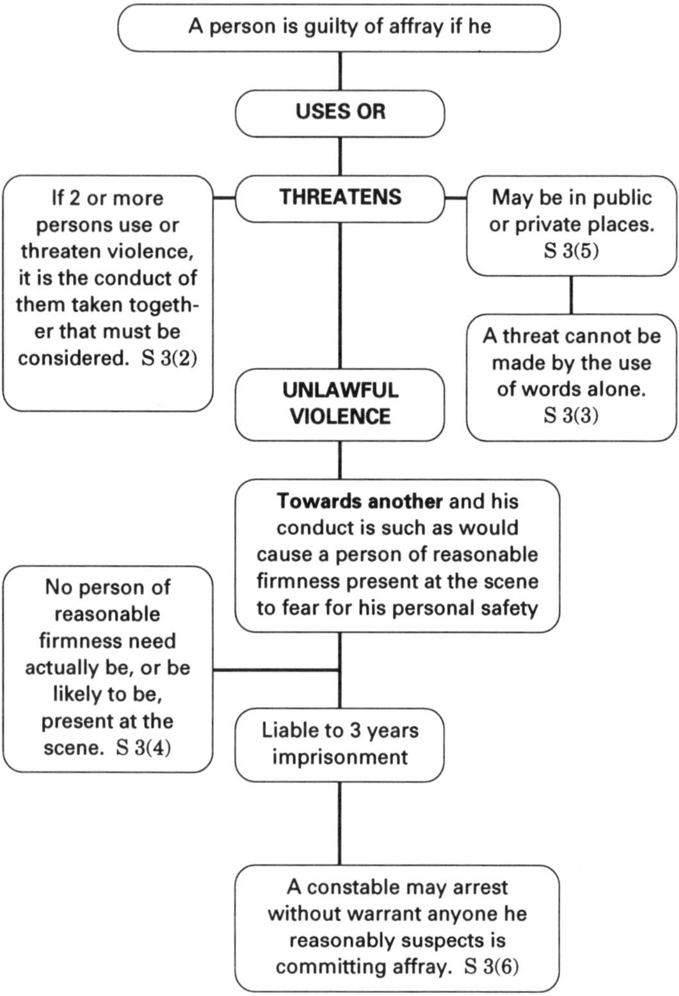
A person is guilty of affray if he
USES OR
THREATENS
UNLAWFUL VIOLENCE
If 2 or more persons use or threaten violence, it is the conduct of them taken together that must be considered. S 3(2)
May be in public or private places. S 3(5)
A threat cannot be made by the use of words alone. S 3(3)
Towards another and his conduct is such as would cause a person of reasonable firmness present at the scene to fear for his personal safety
No person of reasonable firmness need actually be, or be likely to be, present at the scene. S 3(4)
Liable to 3 years imprisonment
A constable may arrest without warrant anyone he reasonably suspects is committing affray. S 3(6)

Riot/Violent Disorder

S 1 & 2 Public Order Act 1986

THESE ARE ARRESTABLE OFFENCES

Where

12 OR MORE PERSONS

If there are 3 or more persons and all the following ingredients except the 'common purpose' are present, then the offence is

VIOLENT DISORDER

contrary to s 2 punishable with 5 years imprisonment

May be in private or public place. S 1(5)

Who are present together

Need not be done simultaneously. S 1(2)

Includes conduct towards property. Need not cause or be intended to cause injury or damage. S 8

USE OR THREATEN UNLAWFUL VIOLENCE

There must be an intention to use violence or be aware that his conduct may be violent

For a common purpose. (may be inferred from conduct) S 1(3)

And the conduct of them (taken together) is such as would cause a person of reasonable firmness present at the scene to

FEAR FOR HIS PERSONAL SAFETY

No person of reasonable firmness need actually be, or be likely to be, present at the scene. S 1(4)

Each of the persons using unlawful violence for the common purpose is guilty of riot. (Liable to 10 years imprisonment)

Public Meetings

S 1 Public Meeting Act 1908

Any person who at a lawful

PUBLIC MEETING

Acts in a disorderly manner for the purpose of preventing the transaction of the business of the meeting shall be guilty of an offence

It is the duty of the police to prevent any action likely to result in a breach of the peace. Refusing to desist is an obstruction of the police in the execution of their duty

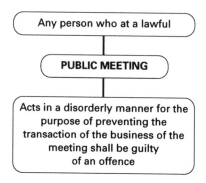

POWER OF ENTRY

The police have a right to enter premises at which the public have been invited to attend if they reasonably apprehend a **breach of the peace**

Any person who incites a person to commit such an offence shall be guilty of a like offence

If a constable reasonably suspects a person to be committing such an offence he may, if requested by the chairman of the meeting, request the offender to give his name and address. If he fails or refuses or gives a false name and address he shall be guilty of an offence

Uniforms

S 1 PUBLIC ORDER ACT 1936

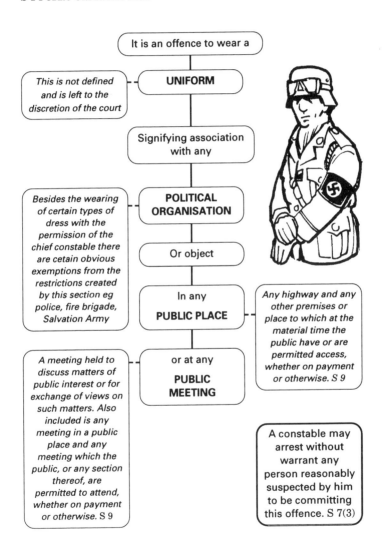

It is an offence to wear a

UNIFORM

This is not defined and is left to the discretion of the court

Signifying association with any

POLITICAL ORGANISATION

Besides the wearing of certain types of dress with the permission of the chief constable there are cetain obvious exemptions from the restrictions created by this section eg police, fire brigade, Salvation Army

Or object

In any **PUBLIC PLACE**

Any highway and any other premises or place to which at the material time the public have or are permitted access, whether on payment or otherwise. S 9

or at any **PUBLIC MEETING**

A meeting held to discuss matters of public interest or for exchange of views on such matters. Also included is any meeting in a public place and any meeting which the public, or any section thereof, are permitted to attend, whether on payment or otherwise. S 9

A constable may arrest without warrant any person reasonably suspected by him to be committing this offence. S 7(3)

Organisations

S 2 Public Order Act 1936

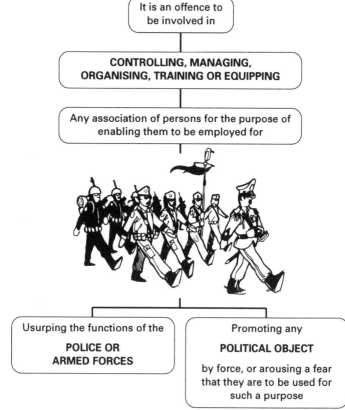

It is an offence to be involved in

CONTROLLING, MANAGING, ORGANISING, TRAINING OR EQUIPPING

Any association of persons for the purpose of enabling them to be employed for

Usurping the functions of the **POLICE OR ARMED FORCES**

Promoting any **POLITICAL OBJECT** by force, or arousing a fear that they are to be used for such a purpose

But this section does not prevent the employment of a reasonable number of stewards to assist in the preservation of order at any public meeting held on private premises, or giving them instruction in their duties, or to giving them badges etc

PROSCRIBED ORGANISATIONS

Ss 1 – 3 Prevention of Terrorism (Temporary Provisions) Act 1989

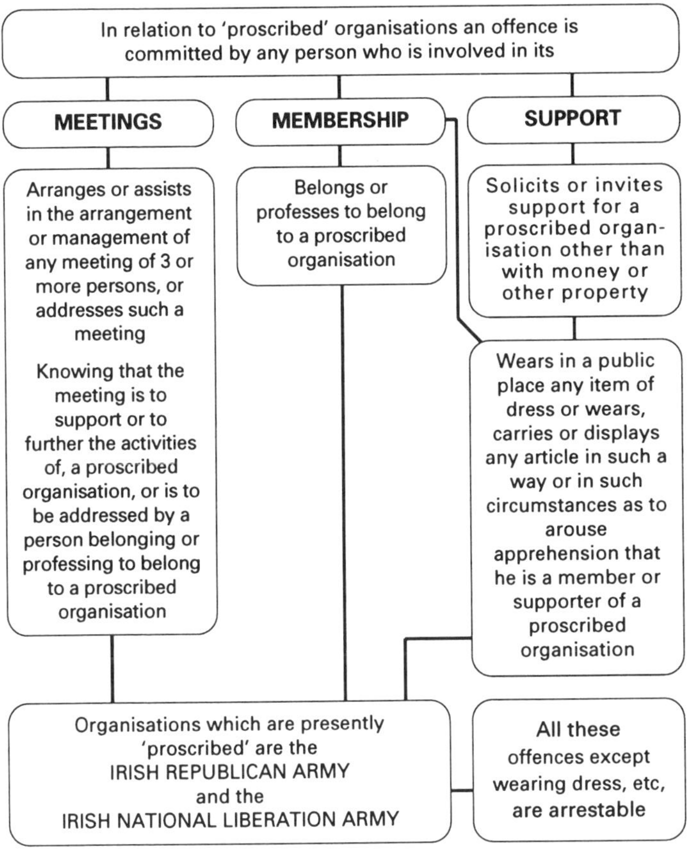
In relation to 'proscribed' organisations an offence is committed by any person who is involved in its
MEETINGS
MEMBERSHIP
SUPPORT
Arranges or assists in the arrangement or management of any meeting of 3 or more persons, or addresses such a meeting
Knowing that the meeting is to support or to further the activities of, a proscribed organisation, or is to be addressed by a person belonging or professing to belong to a proscribed organisation
Belongs or professes to belong to a proscribed organisation
Solicits or invites support for a proscribed organisation other than with money or other property
Wears in a public place any item of dress or wears, carries or displays any article in such a way or in such circumstances as to arouse apprehension that he is a member or supporter of a proscribed organisation
Organisations which are presently 'proscribed' are the IRISH REPUBLICAN ARMY and the IRISH NATIONAL LIBERATION ARMY
All these offences except wearing dress, etc, are arrestable

Public place includes any highway and any premises to which at the material time the public have, or are permitted to have, access whether on payment or otherwise

Chemical Weapons

CHEMICAL WEAPONS ACT 1996

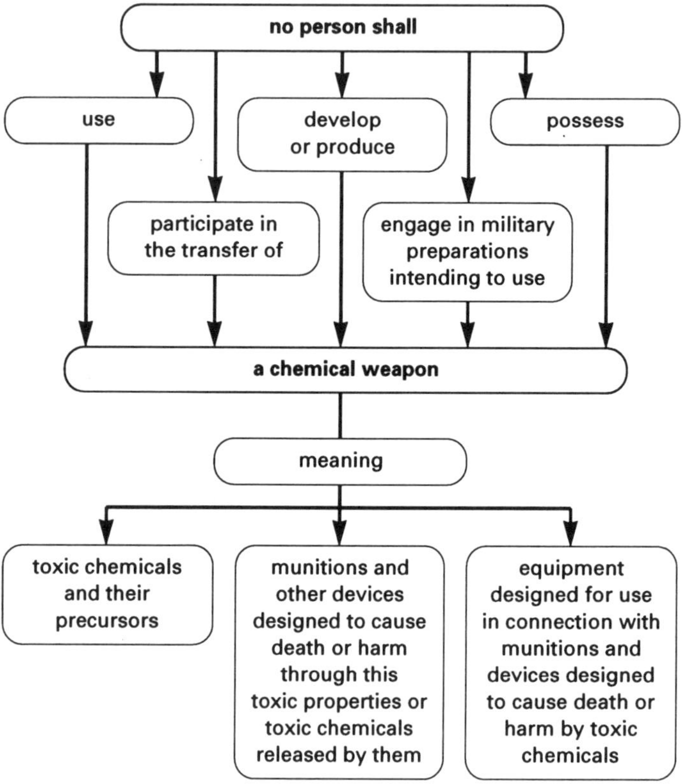

The Act describes various 'permitted purposes' i.e. peaceful purposes; purposes related to protection against toxic chemicals; legitimate military purposes; and purposes of enforcing the law.

Terrorism

SS 8 – 11 PREVENTION OF TERRORISM (TEMPORARY PROVISIONS) ACT 1989

'Terrorism' means the use of violence for political ends, and for the purpose of putting the public or any section of it in fear. S 20

It is an offence for any person to

Solicit or invite any other person to give, lend, or otherwise make available, whether for consideration or not, any money or other property

Receive or accept, whether for consideration or not, any money or other property

Intending

Give, lend or otherwise make available to any other person, whether for consideration or not, or arranges to be made available, any money or other property, knowing or suspecting

That it shall be applied or used for the commission of or in furtherence of, or in connection with, acts of terrorism or for the benefit of a proscribed organisation. Ss 9 & 10

A constable may arrest without warrant any person he reasonably suspects to be guilty of this offence

Fail without reasonable excuse **to disclose information** which he knows or believes might be of material assistance in

- Preventing an act of terrorism; or
- Securing the apprehension, prosecution or conviction of a person for such an act. S 11

Arrestable offence

EXCLUSION ORDER. S 8

Orders may be made by the Secretary of State to exclude from entering GB any persons concerned in terrorism

Where such an order has been made it is an offence to:

Fail to comply with the order

Secure or facilitate entry in contravention

Knowingly harbour an excluded person

A constable may arrest without warrant any person whom he believes to be subject to an exclusion order

TERRORISM – POSSESSION OF ARTICLES AND COLLECTION OF INFORMATION

SS 16A-16B PREVENTION OF TERRORISM (TEMPORARY PROVISIONS) ACT 1989, INSERTED BY S 82 CRIMINAL JUSTICE AND PUBLIC ORDER ACT 1994

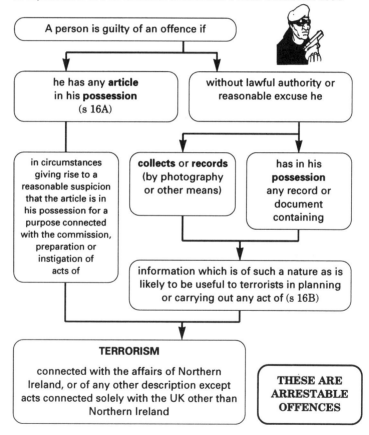

A person is guilty of an offence if

he has any **article** in his **possession** (s 16A)

in circumstances giving rise to a reasonable suspicion that the article is in his possession for a purpose connected with the commission, preparation or instigation of acts of

without lawful authority or reasonable excuse he

collects or **records** (by photography or other means)

has in his **possession** any record or document containing

information which is of such a nature as is likely to be useful to terrorists in planning or carrying out any act of (s 16B)

TERRORISM

connected with the affairs of Northern Ireland, or of any other description except acts connected solely with the UK other than Northern Ireland

THESE ARE ARRESTABLE OFFENCES

Post Office Offences

Ss 42 & 43 Telecommunications Act 1984
S 60 Post Office Act 1953

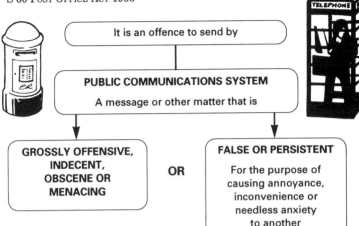

It is an offence to send by

PUBLIC COMMUNICATIONS SYSTEM

A message or other matter that is

GROSSLY OFFENSIVE, INDECENT, OBSCENE OR MENACING

OR

FALSE OR PERSISTENT

For the purpose of causing annoyance, inconvenience or needless anxiety to another

FRAUDULENT USE

It is an offence to make use of any service which is provided by means of a telecommunications system with the intention to avoid payment of any charge. S 42

A person shall not place or attempt to place in or against any post office

LETTER BOX OR TELEPHONE KIOSK

anything likely to damage or soil the box or kiosk, or do anything likely to injure the box or kiosk or its contents or apparatus

Includes any fire, match, light, explosive substance, dangerous substance, filth, noxious or deleterious substance or fluid and shall not **commit** a **nuisance** in or against such a box and shall not do or attempt to do anything likely to injure the box or its contents

Bomb Hoaxes

S 51 CRIMINAL LAW ACT 1977

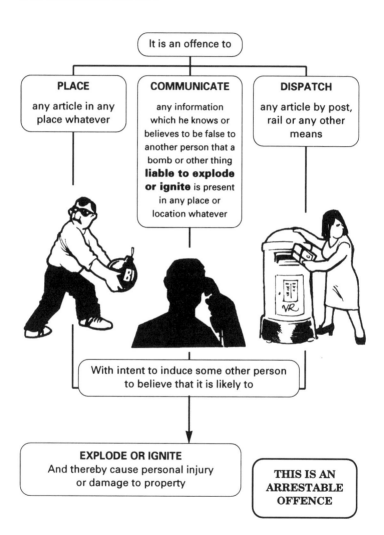

It is an offence to

PLACE

any article in any place whatever

COMMUNICATE

any information which he knows or believes to be false to another person that a bomb or other thing **liable to explode or ignite** is present in any place or location whatever

DISPATCH

any article by post, rail or any other means

With intent to induce some other person to believe that it is likely to

EXPLODE OR IGNITE
And thereby cause personal injury or damage to property

THIS IS AN ARRESTABLE OFFENCE

Contamination of Goods

S 38 Public Order Act 1986

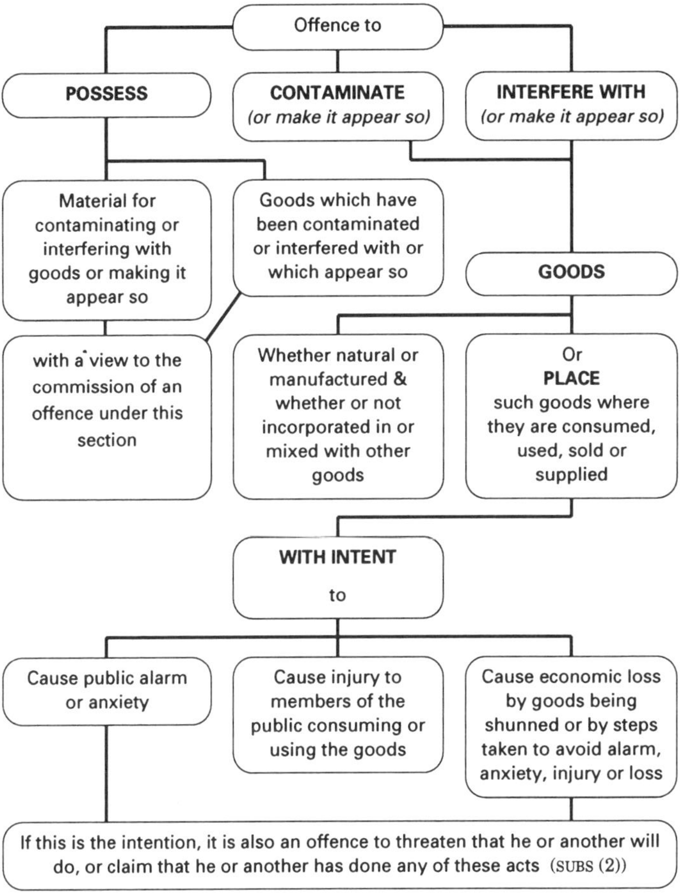
Offence to
POSSESS
CONTAMINATE
(or make it appear so)
INTERFERE WITH
(or make it appear so)
Material for contaminating or interfering with goods or making it appear so
Goods which have been contaminated or interfered with or which appear so
GOODS
with a view to the commission of an offence under this section
Whether natural or manufactured & whether or not incorporated in or mixed with other goods
Or
PLACE
such goods where they are consumed, used, sold or supplied
WITH INTENT
to
Cause public alarm or anxiety
Cause injury to members of the public consuming or using the goods
Cause economic loss by goods being shunned or by steps taken to avoid alarm, anxiety, injury or loss
If this is the intention, it is also an offence to threaten that he or another will do, or claim that he or another has done any of these acts (subs (2))

THIS IS AN ARRESTABLE OFFENCE

Punishment : 10 Years

Taxi Touts

S 167 Criminal Justice and Public Order Act 1994

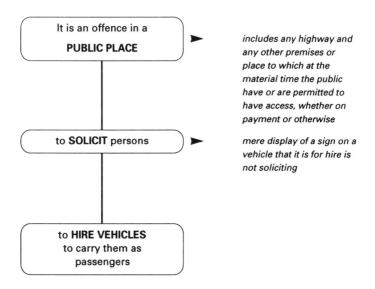

It is an offence in a **PUBLIC PLACE**

► *includes any highway and any other premises or place to which at the material time the public have or are permitted to have access, whether on payment or otherwise*

to **SOLICIT** persons

► *mere display of a sign on a vehicle that it is for hire is not soliciting*

to **HIRE VEHICLES** to carry them as passengers

Does **not** include soliciting persons to hire licensed taxis or public service vehicles on behalf of a holder of a psv operator's licence with his authority.

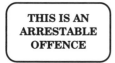

THIS IS AN ARRESTABLE OFFENCE

Intimidation of Witnesses, Jurors and Others

S 51 Criminal Justice and Public Order Act 1994

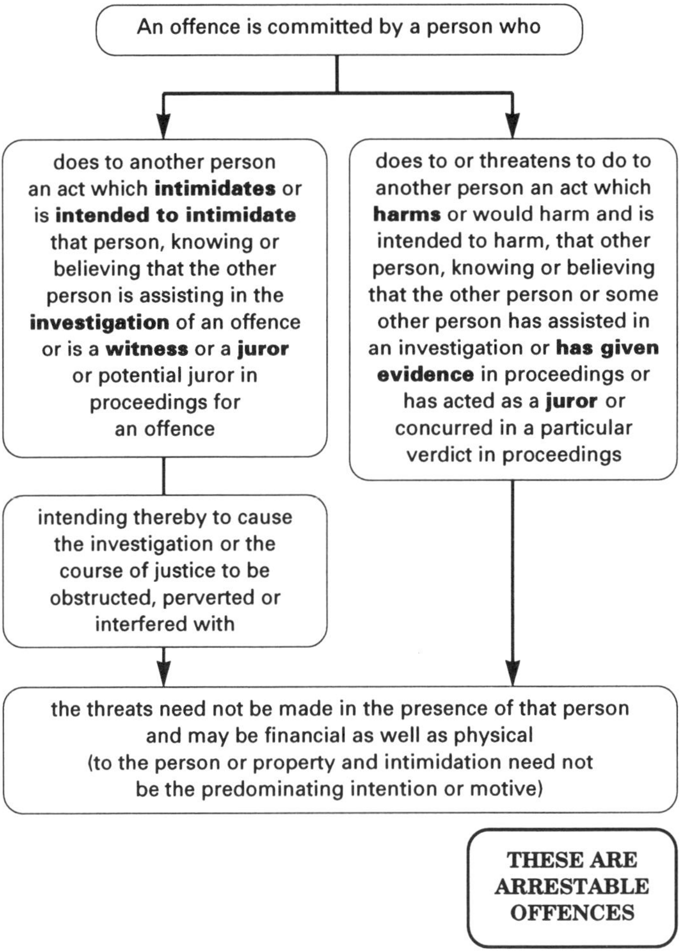
An offence is committed by a person who
does to another person an act which **intimidates** or is **intended to intimidate** that person, knowing or believing that the other person is assisting in the **investigation** of an offence or is a **witness** or a **juror** or potential juror in proceedings for an offence
intending thereby to cause the investigation or the course of justice to be obstructed, perverted or interfered with
does to or threatens to do to another person an act which **harms** or would harm and is intended to harm, that other person, knowing or believing that the other person or some other person has assisted in an investigation or **has given evidence** in proceedings or has acted as a **juror** or concurred in a particular verdict in proceedings
the threats need not be made in the presence of that person and may be financial as well as physical (to the person or property and intimidation need not be the predominating intention or motive)
THESE ARE ARRESTABLE OFFENCES

Chapter 8
Procedure

Questioning of Offenders

POLICE AND CRIMINAL EVIDENCE ACT 1984, CODES OF PRACTICE, CODE C

CAUTIONS

A person should be cautioned if:

SUSPECTED OF AN OFFENCE
Before any questions about it (or further questions if it is his answers to previous questions that provide grounds for suspicion) are put to him for the purpose of obtaining evidence which may be given to a court in a prosecution

ARRESTED FOR AN OFFENCE
Unless:

- Impracticable because of his condition or behaviour, or
- He has already been cautioned (when suspected of the offence)

The revised wording of the caution is:

'You do not have to say anything. But it may harm your defence if you do not mention when questioned something which you later rely on in court. Anything you do say may be give in evidence'

Minor deviations do not constitute a breach of this requirement provided the sense of the caution is preserved. If it appears he does not understand, explain it in your own words. An interpreter must be called in if necessary

If on being questioned under caution or charged with an offence a person fails to mention any fact subsequently relied on in his defence, which he might reasonably have been expected to mention, a court or jury may draw such inferences from the failure as appear proper (s 34 Criminal Justice and Public Order Act 1994)

When there is a break in questioning the person must be made aware that he is still under caution. If in doubt, caution again

When not under arrest it is not necessary to caution again when telling him he may be prosecuted. If not under arrest and at a police station or other premises the person must be told he is not under arrest and not obliged to remain but that if he does, he may obtain free legal advice if he wishes.
A person need not be cautioned if questioned for other purposes, eg to establish identity.

Interviews

INTERVIEWS: GENERAL Codes of Practice, Code C

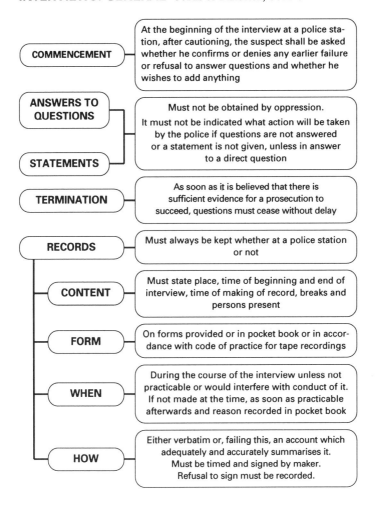

COMMENCEMENT — At the beginning of the interview at a police station, after cautioning, the suspect shall be asked whether he confirms or denies any earlier failure or refusal to answer questions and whether he wishes to add anything

ANSWERS TO QUESTIONS / **STATEMENTS** — Must not be obtained by oppression.
It must not be indicated what action will be taken by the police if questions are not answered or a statement is not given, unless in answer to a direct question

TERMINATION — As soon as it is believed that there is sufficient evidence for a prosecution to succeed, questions must cease without delay

RECORDS — Must always be kept whether at a police station or not

- **CONTENT** — Must state place, time of beginning and end of interview, time of making of record, breaks and persons present
- **FORM** — On forms provided or in pocket book or in accordance with code of practice for tape recordings
- **WHEN** — During the course of the interview unless not practicable or would interfere with conduct of it. If not made at the time, as soon as practicable afterwards and reason recorded in pocket book
- **HOW** — Either verbatim or, failing this, an account which adequately and accurately summarises it. Must be timed and signed by maker. Refusal to sign must be recorded.

INTERVIEWS AT POLICE STATIONS

CODES OF PRACTICE, CODE C

The following requirements must be complied with when carrying out interviews in police stations:

Rest — In any period of 24 hours a detained person must be allowed a continuous period of at least 8 hours for rest, free from questioning, travel or any interruption (visits arising in accordance with the requirements of the Codes of Practice or on medical advice do not constitute an interruption) arising out of the investigation. The period should normally be at night. May only be interrupted or delayed if it would:

Break — Break of at least 45 minutes shall be made at recognised meal times and small breaks of at least 15 minutes for refreshments approx. every 2 hours. A break may be delayed if it would:

- Involve risk or harm to persons or serious loss or damage to property; or
- Delay unnecessarily the person's release from custody; or
- Otherwise prejudice the outcome of the investigation

Alcohol — Detained person may not be supplied with intoxicating liquor except on medical directions. If he is unfit through drink or drugs to the extent that he is unable to appreciate the significance of questions put to him or the answers, he shall not be questioned unless the police surgeon advises that he is fit to be interviewed

Venue — As far as practicable shall take place in interview rooms, adequately heated, lit and ventilated

Conduct — Interviewee shall not be required to stand. Each interviewing officer to identify himself and any other officers present by name and rank

INTERVIEWS: STATEMENTS

CODES OF PRACTICE, CODE C, ANNEX D

If written by a person under caution

he should be invited to write it himself, to sign the declaration and should not be prompted except that a police officer may indicate to him material matters or question any ambiguity

If written by a police officer

the declaration must be signed beforehand. The officer must take down the exact words spoken, without editing or paraphrasing. Necessary questions and answers given must be recorded contemporaneously. When the statement is finished the certificate at the end must be written out and signed by him.

If the person cannot read or refuses to write and sign the certificate

the senior officer present shall read it to him, invite him to sign or make his mark and then certify on the statement what has occurred

INTERVIEWS OF PERSONS AT RISK

If there is any suspicion that the person may be in one of these categories then he must be treated as such

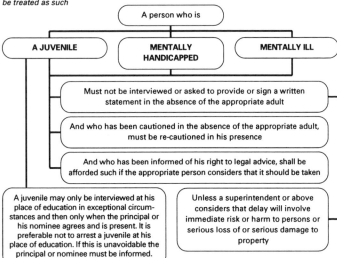

A person who is

A JUVENILE

MENTALLY HANDICAPPED

MENTALLY ILL

Must not be interviewed or asked to provide or sign a written statement in the absence of the appropriate adult

And who has been cautioned in the absence of the appropriate adult, must be re-cautioned in his presence

And who has been informed of his right to legal advice, shall be afforded such if the appropriate person considers that it should be taken

A juvenile may only be interviewed at his place of education in exceptional circumstances and then only when the principal or his nominee agrees and is present. It is preferable not to arrest a juvenile at his place of education. If this is unavoidable the principal or nominee must be informed.

Unless a superintendent or above considers that delay will involve immediate risk or harm to persons or serious loss of or serious damage to property

THE APPROPRIATE ADULT

Means

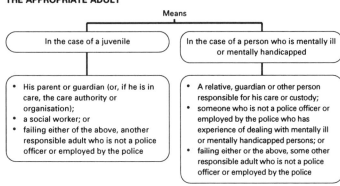

In the case of a juvenile

- His parent or guardian (or, if he is in care, the care authority or organisation);
- a social worker; or
- failing either of the above, another responsible adult who is not a police officer or employed by the police

In the case of a person who is mentally ill or mentally handicapped

- A relative, guardian or other person responsible for his care or custody;
- someone who is not a police officer or employed by the police who has experience of dealing with mentally ill or mentally handicapped persons; or
- failing either or the above, some other responsible adult who is not a police officer or employed by the police

Interpreters

An interpreter is required if

The person has difficulty in understanding English,

the interviewing officer cannot speak the person's language

and

the person wishes an interpreter to be present

The person is deaf or there is doubt about his hearing ability, unless he agrees in writing to be interviewed without one

Unless a superintendent or above considers that delay will involve immediate risk or harm to persons or serious loss of or serious damage to property

The interpreter shall take down the statement in the language in which it is made; the person making it shall be invited to sign it; and an official English translation shall be made in due course

The interpreter must make a note of the interview at the time in the language of the person being interviewed and certify its accuracy. The person must be given the opportunity to read it and sign it as correct or to indicate the respects in which it is inaccurate

Powers of Arrest

S 24 Police & Criminal Evidence Act 1984

WITHOUT WARRANT

Any person may arrest

- Anyone who is in the act of committing an arrestable offence
- Where an arrestable offence has been committed:
  - Anyone who is guilty of the offence
  - Anyone whom he has reasonable grounds for suspecting to be guilty of it
- Anyone whom he has reasonable grounds for suspecting to be committing an arrestable offence

A constable may arrest

- (where he has reasonable grounds for suspecting an arrestable offence has been committed) anyone who he has reasonable grounds for suspecting to be guilty of the offence
- Anyone who is about to commit an arrestable offence or whom he has reasonable grounds for suspecting to be about to commit an arrestable offence

ARRESTABLE OFFENCE

See following page.........

ARRESTABLE OFFENCE

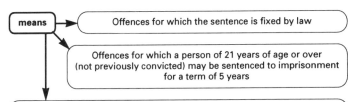

means

- Offences for which the sentence is fixed by law
- Offences for which a person of 21 years of age or over (not previously convicted) may be sentenced to imprisonment for a term of 5 years
- Committing; conspiring to commit; attempting to commit; or inciting, aiding, abetting, counselling or procuring, any of the following offences:
  - Offences for which a person may be arrested under the Customs and Excise Acts, as defined in s 1(1) of the Customs and Excise Management Act 1979.
  - Offences under the Official Secrets Act 1989, except s 8(1), (4) or (5) (unauthorised disclosure, etc, of a Crown servant or government contractor).
  - Offences under the Official Secrets Act 1920 or 1989 that are not arrestable offences by virtue of the term of imprisonment for which a person may be sentenced in respect of them.
  - Offences under section 22 (causing prostitution of women) or 23 (procuration of girl under 21) of the Sexual Offences Act 1956.
  - Offences under section 12(1) (taking motor vehicle or other conveyance without authority etc) or 25(1) (going equipped for stealing, etc) of the Theft Act 1968.
  - Offences under the Football (Offences) Act 1991.
  - Offences under s 2 Obscene Publication Act 1959 (publishing obscene matter) or s 1 Protection of Children Act 1978 (indecent photographs and pseudo-photographs of children).
  - Offences under s 19 Public Order Act 1986 (publishing etc material likely to cause racial hatred).
  - Offences under S166 Criminal Justice and Public Order Act 1994 (unauthorised sale of tickets).
  - Offences under S167 Criminal Justice and PublicOrder Act 1994 (touting for hire car services).
  - Offences under S1 Prevention of Crime Act 1953 (prohibition of the carrying of offensive weapons).
  - Offences under S139 Criminal Justice Act 1988 (having an article with blade or point in public place).
  - Offences under S139A Criminal Justice Act 1988 (having an article with blade or point or an offensive weapon on school premises).
  - Offences under S2 Protection from Harassment Act 1997 (harassment).

SERIOUS ARRESTABLE OFFENCES

S 116, Sched 5 Police and Criminal Evidence Act 1984, amended by s 85 Criminal Justice and Public Order Act 1994

The following are defined as being always serious arrestable offences:

treason, murder, manslaughter, kidnapping, rape, incest or intercourse with a girl under 13, buggery with a person under 16 or a person who has not consented, indecent assault amounting to gross indecency;

production, supply, possession for supply, import or export of controlled drugs, assisting or inducing commission of drugs offence outside UK, assisting another to retain benefit of drugs trafficking;

firearms – possession with intent to injure, carrying with criminal intent, using to resist arrest;

hostage-taking; aircraft or ship hijacking;

torture;

causing death by dangerous driving or by careless driving under the influence;

indecent photographs or pseudo-photographs of children, publication of obscene material;

various offences relating to terrorism.

Other arrestable offences are serious only if their commission leads to serious harm to State security or public order; the death of any person; serious injury to any person; substantial financial gain to any person; or serious financial loss to any person; or serious interference with the administration of justice or the investigation of an offence;

If a serious arrestable offence has been committed this is one of the grounds for applying for a search warrant

POWERS OF ARREST

SS 24 & 25 POLICE AND CRIMINAL EVIDENCE ACT 1984

WITHOUT WARRANT

(not an arrestable offence)

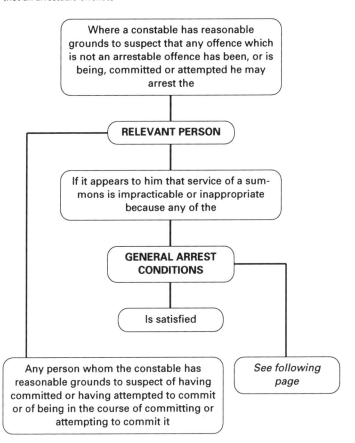

Where a constable has reasonable grounds to suspect that any offence which is not an arrestable offence has been, or is being, committed or attempted he may arrest the

RELEVANT PERSON

If it appears to him that service of a summons is impracticable or inappropriate because any of the

GENERAL ARREST CONDITIONS

Is satisfied

Any person whom the constable has reasonable grounds to suspect of having committed or having attempted to commit or of being in the course of committing or attempting to commit it

See following page

POWERS OF ARREST – CROSS-BORDER

S 137 CRIMINAL JUSTICE AND PUBLIC ORDER ACT 1994

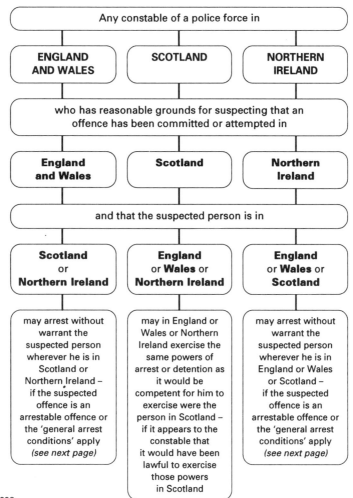

Any constable of a police force in

ENGLAND AND WALES	SCOTLAND	NORTHERN IRELAND
who has reasonable grounds for suspecting that an offence has been committed or attempted in		
England and Wales	**Scotland**	**Northern Ireland**
and that the suspected person is in		
Scotland or **Northern Ireland**	**England** or **Wales** or **Northern Ireland**	**England** or **Wales** or **Scotland**
may arrest without warrant the suspected person wherever he is in Scotland or Northern Ireland – if the suspected offence is an arrestable offence or the 'general arrest conditions' apply *(see next page)*	may in England or Wales or Northern Ireland exercise the same powers of arrest or detention as it would be competent for him to exercise were the person in Scotland – if it appears to the constable that it would have been lawful to exercise those powers in Scotland	may arrest without warrant the suspected person wherever he is in England or Wales or Scotland – if the suspected offence is an arrestable offence or the 'general arrest conditions' apply *(see next page)*

GENERAL ARREST CONDITIONS

S 25 Police and Criminal Evidence Act 1984

IDENTITY

That the name of the relevant person is unknown to, and cannot be readily ascertained by, the constable; or

That the constable has reasonable grounds for doubting whether a name furnished by the relevant person is his real name

ADDRESS FOR SERVICE

That:

- The relevant person has failed to furnish a satisfactory address for service; or
- The constable has reasonable grounds for doubting whether an address furnished by the relevant person is a satisfactory address for service

'Satisfactory for service' means that the relevant person will be at that address sufficiently long to serve a summons; or that some other specified person will accept service for him

PREVENTATIVE MEASURES

That the constable has reasonable grounds for believing that arrest is necessary to prevent the relevant person

- Causing physical injury to himself or any other person
- Suffering physical injury
- Causing loss of or damage to property
- Committing an offence against public decency where members of the public could not be expected to avoid him
- Causing an unlawful obstruction of the highway

PROTECTION

That the constable has reasonable grounds for believing that arrest is necessary to protect a child or other vulnerable person from the relevant person

MODE OF ARREST

SS 28 AND 30 POLICE AND CRIMINAL EVIDENCE ACT 1984

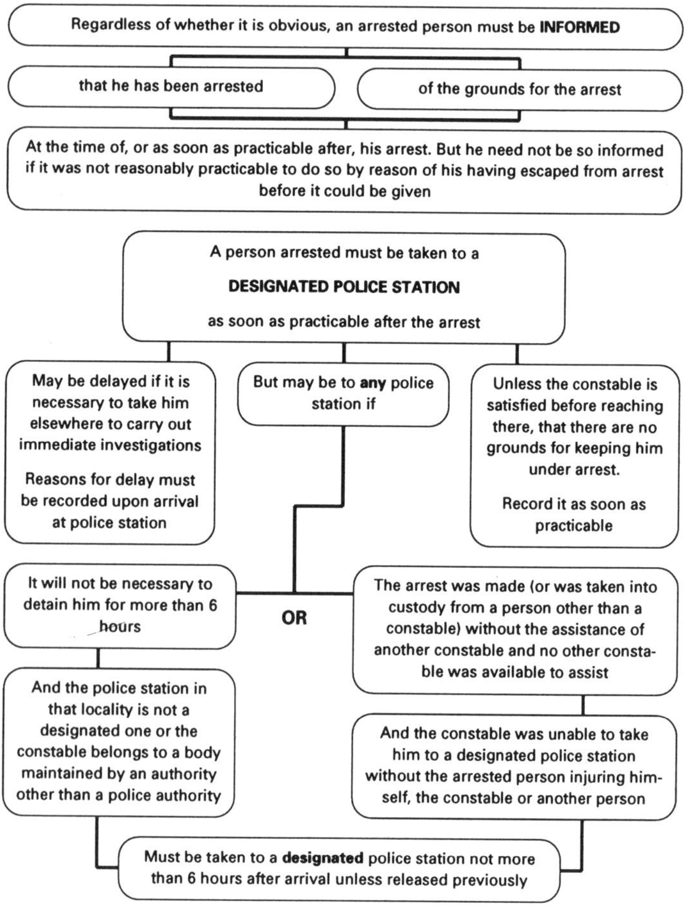
Regardless of whether it is obvious, an arrested person must be **INFORMED**
that he has been arrested
of the grounds for the arrest
At the time of, or as soon as practicable after, his arrest. But he need not be so informed if it was not reasonably practicable to do so by reason of his having escaped from arrest before it could be given
A person arrested must be taken to a **DESIGNATED POLICE STATION** as soon as practicable after the arrest
May be delayed if it is necessary to take him elsewhere to carry out immediate investigations
Reasons for delay must be recorded upon arrival at police station
But may be to **any** police station if
Unless the constable is satisfied before reaching there, that there are no grounds for keeping him under arrest.
Record it as soon as practicable
It will not be necessary to detain him for more than 6 hours
OR
The arrest was made (or was taken into custody from a person other than a constable) without the assistance of another constable and no other constable was available to assist
And the police station in that locality is not a designated one or the constable belongs to a body maintained by an authority other than a police authority
And the constable was unable to take him to a designated police station without the arrested person injuring himself, the constable or another person
Must be taken to a **designated** police station not more than 6 hours after arrival unless released previously

Searches

CONDUCT OF A SEARCH

S 2 POLICE AND CRIMINAL EVIDENCE ACT 1984

If a constable contemplates a

SEARCH
under any power without first making an arrest

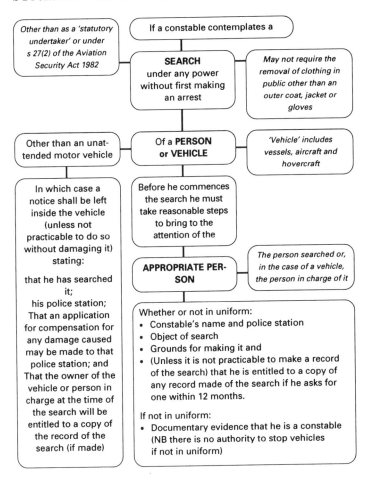

Other than as a 'statutory undertaker' or under s 27(2) of the Aviation Security Act 1982

May not require the removal of clothing in public other than an outer coat, jacket or gloves

Of a **PERSON or VEHICLE**

Other than an unattended motor vehicle

'Vehicle' includes vessels, aircraft and hovercraft

In which case a notice shall be left inside the vehicle (unless not practicable to do so without damaging it) stating:

that he has searched it;
his police station;
That an application for compensation for any damage caused may be made to that police station; and
That the owner of the vehicle or person in charge at the time of the search will be entitled to a copy of the record of the search (if made)

Before he commences the search he must take reasonable steps to bring to the attention of the

APPROPRIATE PERSON

The person searched or, in the case of a vehicle, the person in charge of it

Whether or not in uniform:
- Constable's name and police station
- Object of search
- Grounds for making it and
- (Unless it is not practicable to make a record of the search) that he is entitled to a copy of any record made of the search if he asks for one within 12 months.

If not in uniform:
- Documentary evidence that he is a constable (NB there is no authority to stop vehicles if not in uniform)

CONDUCT OF A SEARCH

Police and Criminal Evidence Act 1984

Codes of Practice, Code A

Embarrassment:
Every reasonable effort must be made to reduce the embarrassment of the person being searched.

Co-operation and force:
Co-operation must be sought and reasonable force may only be used if the person is unwilling to co-operate or resists. Although force may only be used as a last resort, reasonable force may be used if necessary to conduct a search or to detain a person or vehicle for the purposes of a search.

Extent of search:
The thoroughness and extent of the search depends on what is suspected of being carried and by whom. The length of time for which a person or vehicle may be detained must in all circumstances be reasonable and not extend beyond the time taken for the search.

Place:
The search must be carried out at or near the place where the person/vehicle was first detained.

Clothing:
Searches in public may require no more than the removal of outer coat, jacket or gloves. Where it is reasonable to conduct a more thorough search this must be done out of public view. The removal of more than an outer coat, jacket, gloves, headgear or footwear may only be made by an officer of the same sex.

Suspected terrorists:
If a pedestrian is stopped under s 13A Prevention of Terrorism (Temporary Provisions) Act 1989, the search must be confined to bags or other things carried by him. This would not however, prevent a search being carried out under other powers.

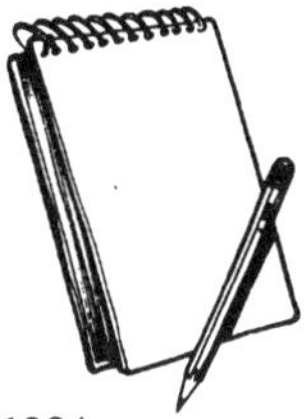

RECORDS OF SEARCHES

S 3 Police and Criminal Evidence Act 1984

Where a constable has carried out a

SEARCH under any power

Other than as a 'statutory undertaker' or under s 27(2) of the Aviation Security Act 1982

He shall make a **RECORD** of it in writing unless it is **NOT PRACTICABLE** to do so

- Stating the name of the person searched (but he may not be detained to find out his name)
- Including (if name not known by constable) a description of the person
- Including a description of any vehicle searched
- Stating
  - object of the search
  - grounds for making it
  - date and time made
  - place made
  - whether anything found, and if so, what
  - any injury to a person or damage to property which appears to the constable to have resulted from the search
  - identity of constable

If it could be made, but not practicable to make it on the spot, he shall make it as soon as practicable afterwards

The person who was searched, and the owner or person in charge of a vehicle at the time it was searched, are entitled to a **COPY** of any record made if he asks for one within 12 months

'Vehicle' includes vessels, aircraft and hovercraft

SELECTOR

The subject of searching, etc. Is rather involved and the reader may be assisted by selecting the appropriate circumstances below and referring to the relevant section in the following pages. In addition, specific powers relating to Firearms, Drugs, Crossbows, Game and Offensive Weapons may be found in the relevant pages of this book.

HAS AN ARREST BEEN MADE?	REASON FOR SEARCH?	TYPE OF SEARCH PERSON	PREMISES	VEHICLE
YES	Material valuable to the investigation and relevant evidence		F	
	Evidence on premises occupied or controlled by arrested person		C	C
	Offender, potential offender or witness to serious arrestable offence, or person unlawfully at large			G
YES, OTHER THAN AT A POLICE STATION	Anything which might cause injury	E		
	Evidence of offence for which arrested		E	
NO	Arresting a person, saving life or preventing damage		B	B
	Stolen or prohibited articles	A		A
	Securing evidence or seizing anything obtained in commission of an offence		D	D
	Material valuable to the investigation and relevant evidence		F	
	Offender, potential offender or witness to serious arrestable offence, or person unlawfully at large			G
	Prevention of terrorism	H		H
	Prevention of serious violence/offensive weapons	H		H

For conduct and recording of a search see section 'A'

(A)

STOP AND SEARCH

S 1 POLICE AND CRIMINAL EVIDENCE ACT 1984

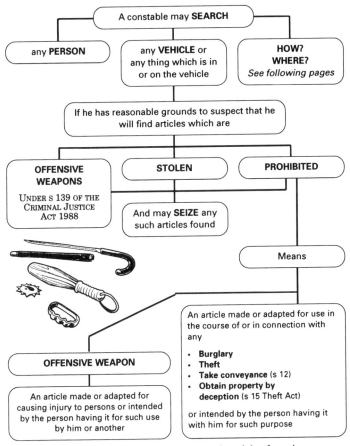

A constable may **SEARCH**

- any **PERSON**
- any **VEHICLE** or any thing which is in or on the vehicle
- **HOW? WHERE?** *See following pages*

If he has reasonable grounds to suspect that he will find articles which are

- **OFFENSIVE WEAPONS** UNDER S 139 OF THE CRIMINAL JUSTICE ACT 1988
- **STOLEN**
- **PROHIBITED**

And may **SEIZE** any such articles found

PROHIBITED Means

OFFENSIVE WEAPON

An article made or adapted for causing injury to persons or intended by the person having it for such use by him or another

An article made or adapted for use in the course of or in connection with any

- **Burglary**
- **Theft**
- **Take conveyance** (s 12)
- **Obtain property by deception** (s 15 Theft Act)

or intended by the person having it with him for such purpose

There is a power to seize any such articles found

Ⓐ

STOP AND SEARCH

S 1 Police and Criminal Evidence Act 1984

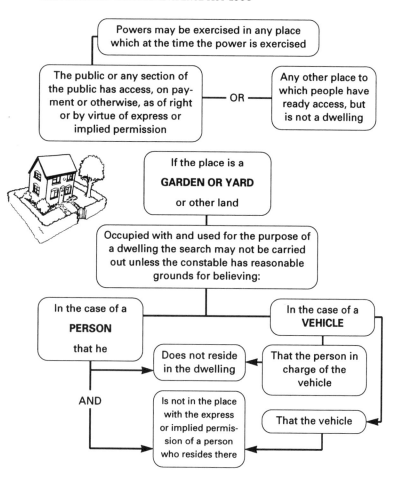

Powers may be exercised in any place which at the time the power is exercised

The public or any section of the public has access, on payment or otherwise, as of right or by virtue of express or implied permission

OR

Any other place to which people have ready access, but is not a dwelling

If the place is a **GARDEN OR YARD** or other land

Occupied with and used for the purpose of a dwelling the search may not be carried out unless the constable has reasonable grounds for believing:

In the case of a **PERSON** that he

In the case of a **VEHICLE**

Does not reside in the dwelling

That the person in charge of the vehicle

AND

Is not in the place with the express or implied permission of a person who resides there

That the vehicle

STOP AND SEARCH

Ⓐ

POLICE AND CRIMINAL EVIDENCE ACT 1984

CODE OF PRACTICE, CODE A

Powers requiring reasonable suspicion:
reasonable suspicion cannot be founded on personal factors alone. Whether a reasonable suspicion exists will depend upon the nature of the article suspected of being carried in the context of other factors such as the time and place and the behaviour of the persons concerned. Reasonable suspicion may be based on reliable information or intelligence which indicates a habitual carrying of unlawful knives, weapons or drugs.

Detention:
if reasonable grounds for suspicion exist an officer may detain the person in order to search him. He may not be stopped or detained in order to find grounds for a search. There is no power to stop or detain a person against his will in order to find grounds for a search.

Questioning:
before being searched, a person may be questioned. If he gives an explanation whereby grounds for reasonable suspicion cease then he may not be searched. Retrospective grounds for searching cannot be provided during questioning where no grounds existed previously.

Serious violence:
s 60 Criminal Justice and Public Order Act 1984 will provide a stop and search power where it is reasonably believed that an incident involving serious violence may take place and the exercise of the power has been duly authorised.

Terrorism:
S 13A Prevention of Terrorism (Temporary Provisions) Act 1989 (added by s 81 Criminal Justice and Public Order Act 1994) established a power to stop and search person, vehicles, ships and aircraft where an assistant chief constable (or equivalent) considers it expedient to do so to prevent acts of terrorism. A constable may make any search he thinks fit.

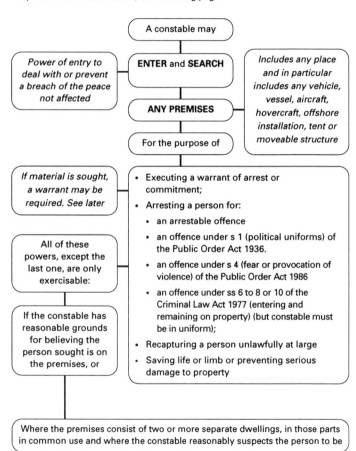

(B)

ENTRY AND SEARCH

S 17 POLICE AND CRIMINAL EVIDENCE ACT 1984

If a person has been arrested, see following page

A constable may

ENTER and **SEARCH**

Power of entry to deal with or prevent a breach of the peace not affected

ANY PREMISES

Includes any place and in particular includes any vehicle, vessel, aircraft, hovercraft, offshore installation, tent or moveable structure

For the purpose of

- Executing a warrant of arrest or commitment;
- Arresting a person for:
  - an arrestable offence
  - an offence under s 1 (political uniforms) of the Public Order Act 1936.
  - an offence under s 4 (fear or provocation of violence) of the Public Order Act 1986
  - an offence under ss 6 to 8 or 10 of the Criminal Law Act 1977 (entering and remaining on property) (but constable must be in uniform);
- Recapturing a person unlawfully at large
- Saving life or limb or preventing serious damage to property

If material is sought, a warrant may be required. See later

All of these powers, except the last one, are only exercisable:

If the constable has reasonable grounds for believing the person sought is on the premises, or

Where the premises consist of two or more separate dwellings, in those parts in common use and where the constable reasonably suspects the person to be

Ⓒ

ENTRY AND SEARCH FOR EVIDENCE

S 18 POLICE AND CRIMINAL EVIDENCE ACT 1984

See also s 32 relating to search of arrested person and premises upon arrest

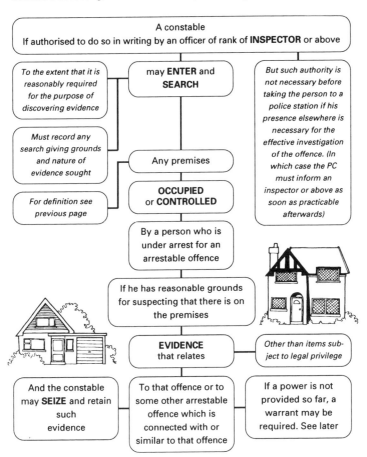

A constable
If authorised to do so in writing by an officer of rank of **INSPECTOR** or above

To the extent that it is reasonably required for the purpose of discovering evidence

may **ENTER** and **SEARCH**

But such authority is not necessary before taking the person to a police station if his presence elsewhere is necessary for the effective investigation of the offence. (In which case the PC must inform an inspector or above as soon as practicable afterwards)

Must record any search giving grounds and nature of evidence sought

Any premises

For definition see previous page

OCCUPIED or **CONTROLLED**

By a person who is under arrest for an arrestable offence

If he has reasonable grounds for suspecting that there is on the premises

EVIDENCE that relates

Other than items subject to legal privilege

And the constable may **SEIZE** and retain such evidence

To that offence or to some other arrestable offence which is connected with or similar to that offence

If a power is not provided so far, a warrant may be required. See later

SEIZURE

Ⓓ

S 19 Police and Criminal Act 1984

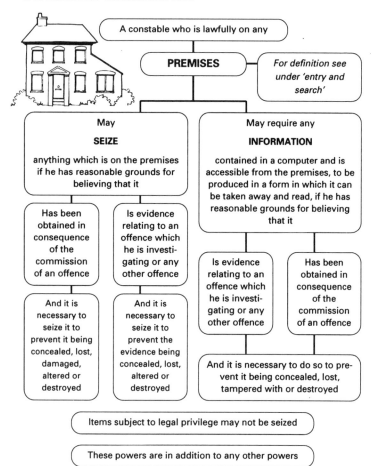

A constable who is lawfully on any

PREMISES

For definition see under 'entry and search'

May **SEIZE** anything which is on the premises if he has reasonable grounds for believing that it

- Has been obtained in consequence of the commission of an offence
  - And it is necessary to seize it to prevent it being concealed, lost, damaged, altered or destroyed
- Is evidence relating to an offence which he is investigating or any other offence
  - And it is necessary to seize it to prevent the evidence being concealed, lost, altered or destroyed

May require any **INFORMATION** contained in a computer and is accessible from the premises, to be produced in a form in which it can be taken away and read, if he has reasonable grounds for believing that it

- Is evidence relating to an offence which he is investigating or any other offence
- Has been obtained in consequence of the commission of an offence

And it is necessary to do so to prevent it being concealed, lost, tampered with or destroyed

Items subject to legal privilege may not be seized

These powers are in addition to any other powers

SEARCH UPON ARREST

S 32 POLICE AND CRIMINAL EVIDENCE ACT 1984 AS AMENDED BY S 59 CRIMINAL JUSTICE AND PUBLIC ORDER ACT 1994 (E)

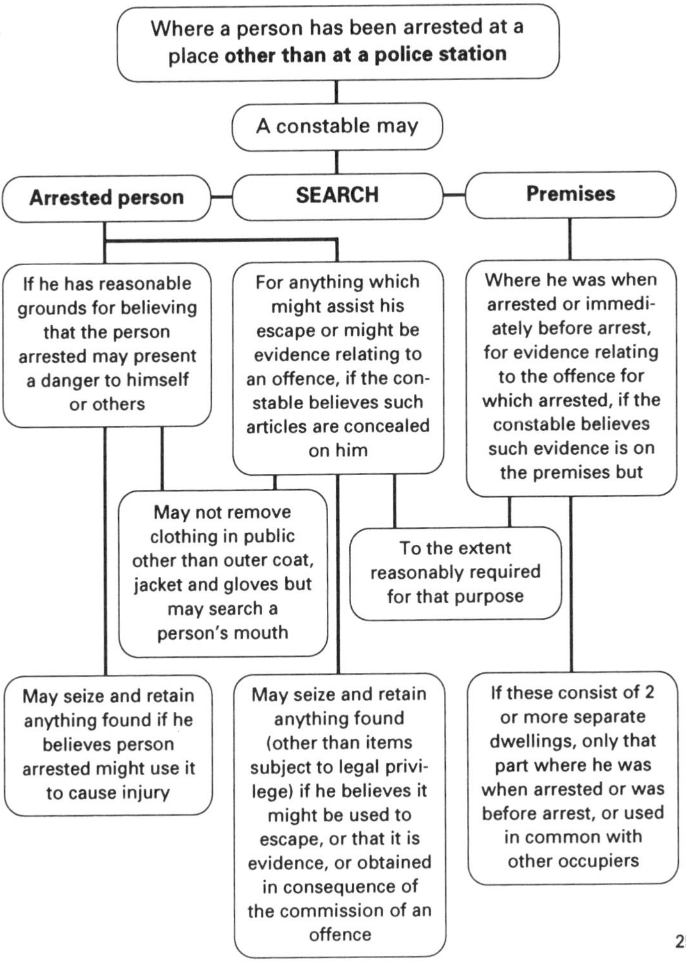
Where a person has been arrested at a place other than at a police station
A constable may
Arrested person
SEARCH
Premises
If he has reasonable grounds for believing that the person arrested may present a danger to himself or others
For anything which might assist his escape or might be evidence relating to an offence, if the constable believes such articles are concealed on him
Where he was when arrested or immediately before arrest, for evidence relating to the offence for which arrested, if the constable believes such evidence is on the premises but
May not remove clothing in public other than outer coat, jacket and gloves but may search a person's mouth
To the extent reasonably required for that purpose
May seize and retain anything found if he believes person arrested might use it to cause injury
May seize and retain anything found (other than items subject to legal privilege) if he believes it might be used to escape, or that it is evidence, or obtained in consequence of the commission of an offence
If these consist of 2 or more separate dwellings, only that part where he was when arrested or was before arrest, or used in common with other occupiers

SEARCH WARRANTS

S 8 Police and Criminal Evidence Act 1984

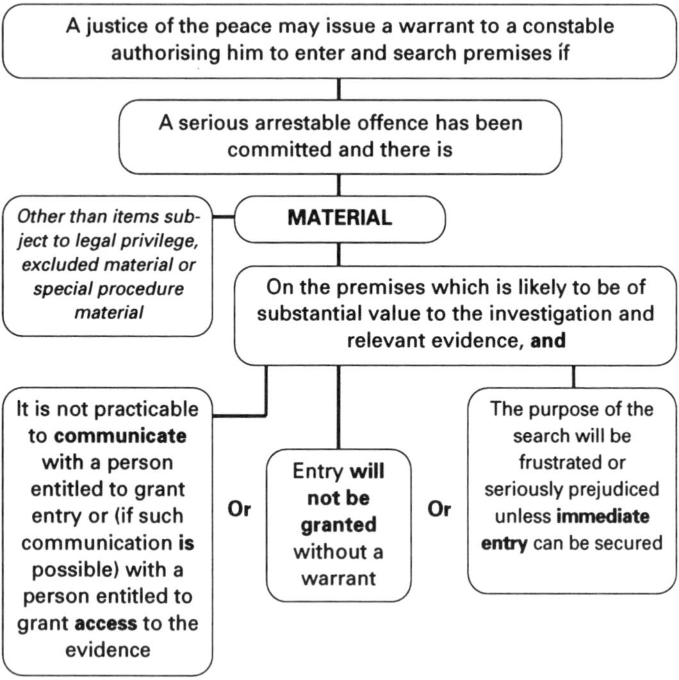
A justice of the peace may issue a warrant to a constable authorising him to enter and search premises if
A serious arrestable offence has been committed and there is
MATERIAL
Other than items subject to legal privilege, excluded material or special procedure material
On the premises which is likely to be of substantial value to the investigation and relevant evidence, and
It is not practicable to communicate with a person entitled to grant entry or (if such communication is possible) with a person entitled to grant access to the evidence
Or
Entry will not be granted without a warrant
Or
The purpose of the search will be frustrated or seriously prejudiced unless immediate entry can be secured

EXECUTION S 16

Must be within **1 month** of issue.
Must be at a **reasonable hour** unless the purpose may be frustrated by doing so.
Where occupier or person in charge of the premises is present, constable must **identify himself, produce the warrant** and supply him with a copy. If no such person present, copy must be left in a prominent place on the premises.

ROAD CHECKS

(G)

S 4 Police and Criminal Evidence Act 1984

Under certain circumstances, a PC needs authority to carry out a road check

WHAT IS A ROAD CHECK?

The exercise in a locality of the power conferred by s 163 of the Road Traffic Act 1988, to stop either all vehicles or vehicles selected by any criterion

WHAT TYPE OF CHECK NEEDS TO BE AUTHORISED?

Where it is necessary to ascertain whether a vehicle is carrying:

- A person who has committed a serious arrestable offence (other than a traffic or excise offence) and may be in the locality
- A person who is a witness to a serious arrestable offence
- A person who intends to commit a serious arrestable offence and may be in the locality
- A person who is unlawfully at large any may be in the locality

WHO CAN AUTHORISE IT?

Normally a superintendent must authorise it in writing. But may be authorised by an officer below that rank as a matter of urgency, in which case, as soon as practicable, he must make a written record of the time he gives it and cause a superintendent to be informed

The locality at which the check is to be carried out must be specified

HOW LONG MAY IT LAST?

The superintendent or above (not below) must specify a period, not exceeding seven days, during which it may take place (may be renewed in writing). He may direct whether it shall be continuous or conducted at specified times

STOP AND SEARCH

Ⓗ

Serious Violence/Offensive Weapons

Where an Inspector or above reasonably believes that incidents involving serious violence may take place in his area and it is expedient to prevent their occurrence, or that persons are carrying dangerous instruments or offensive weapons without good reason, he may authorise (in writing) stopping and searching of persons and vehicles in that locality for a period not exceeding 24 hours for offensive weapons or dangerous instruments. If the authorisation is given by an Inspector he must as soon as practicable inform an officer of or above the rank of Superintendent. A constable may stop any person or vehicle and make any search he thinks fit whether or not he has any grounds for suspecting that weapons or articles of that kind are present.
(For a fuller explanation see under 'Knives – stop and search').

S 60 Criminal Justice and Public Order Act 1994, As amended by the Knives Act 1997 – when in force

PREVENTION OF TERRORISM

Where it appears to an officer of the rank of commander/assistant chief constable that it is expedient in order to prevent acts of terrorism (connected with Northern Ireland or of any description but not connected solely with the affairs of the UK) he may authorise the stopping and searching of person or vehicles (including ships and aircraft) for up to 28 days in a specified locality. In the exercise of these powers a constable may stop any vehicle or person and make any search he thinks fit whether or not he has any grounds for suspecting that articles of terrorism are being carried.

S 81 Criminal Justice and Public Order Act 1994

Chapter 9

Detention and Treatment of Persons

Custody Officers

S 36 Police and Criminal Evidence Act 1984

Are appointed by the chief officer of police or other police officer directed by the chief officer

WHO MAY BE A CUSTODY OFFICER?

Must be at least the rank of sergeant. However, functions may be performed by any rank if a custody officer is not readily available

WHO MAY NOT BE?

None of the functions of a custody officer may be performed by an officer who is involved in the investigation of the offence for which the person is in detention, except:

A custody officer
- Performing a function assigned to him by the Act or a Code of Practice;
- Carrying out duties imposed by s 39 of the Act;
- Doing anything connected with the identification of a suspect; or
- Doing anything under ss 7 & 8 of the RTA 1988

Where a person is taken to a non designated police station, and an officer not involved in the investigation of the offence is not available, any officer may perform the functions of the custody officer. If that officer is the officer taking the arrested person to the police station, he must inform an inspector or above who is attached to a designated police station, as soon as practicable, that he is to do so

Custody Records

POLICE AND CRIMINAL EVIDENCE ACT 1984
CODE OF PRACTICE, CODE C

REQUIREMENT

A separate custody record must be opened as soon as practicable for each person who is brought to a police station under arrest or is arrested at the police station having attended there voluntarily. All information which has to be recorded under this code must be recorded as soon as practicable, in the custody record unless otherwise specified

Where a person is transferred to another police station the record or a copy of it must accompany him. The record shall show the time and reason for the transfer and the time of release from detention

AUTHORITY

In the case of any action requiring the authority of an officer of a specified rank, his name and rank must be noted in the custody record

ACCURACY

The custody officer is responsible for the accuracy and completness of the custody record

All entries in custody and written interview records must be timed and signed by the maker

Any refusal by a person to sign either a custody or an interview record when asked to do so in accordance with the provisions of this code must itself be recorded

SUPPLY OF COPY

When a person leaves police detention he or his legal representative shall be supplied on request with a copy of the custody record as soon as practicable. This entitlement lasts for twelve months after his release

Responsibility for Detained Persons

S 39 Police and Criminal Evidence Act 1984

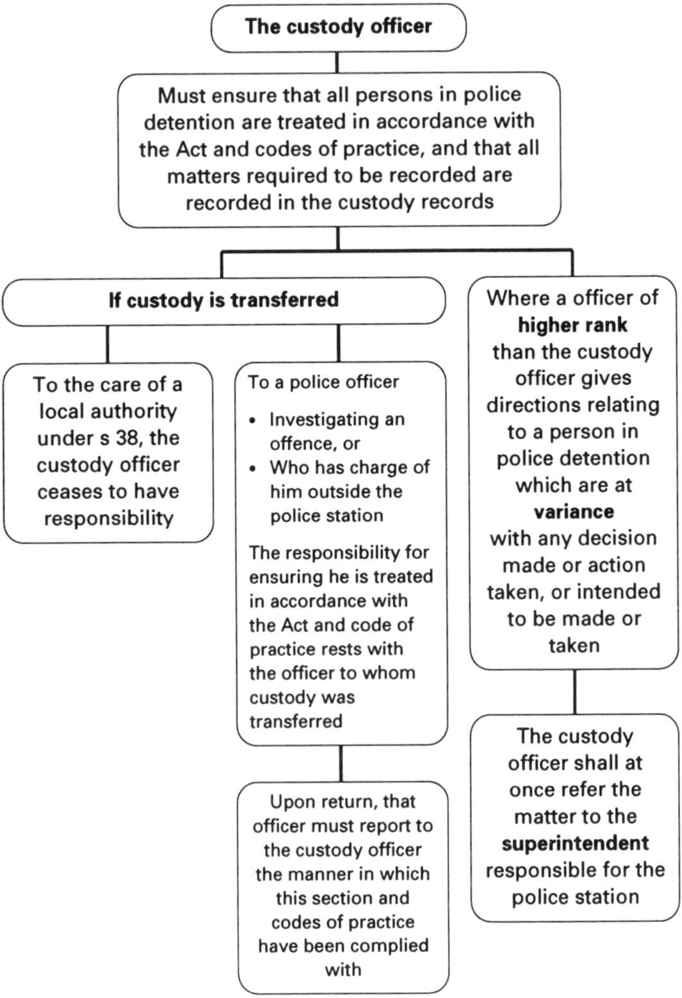
The custody officer
Must ensure that all persons in police detention are treated in accordance with the Act and codes of practice, and that all matters required to be recorded are recorded in the custody records
If custody is transferred
To the care of a local authority under s 38, the custody officer ceases to have responsibility
To a police officer
• Investigating an offence, or
• Who has charge of him outside the police station
The responsibility for ensuring he is treated in accordance with the Act and code of practice rests with the officer to whom custody was transferred
Upon return, that officer must report to the custody officer the manner in which this section and codes of practice have been complied with
Where a officer of higher rank than the custody officer gives directions relating to a person in police detention which are at variance with any decision made or action taken, or intended to be made or taken
The custody officer shall at once refer the matter to the superintendent responsible for the police station

Initial Action

POLICE AND CRIMINAL EVIDENCE ACT 1984, CODES OF PRACTICE, CODE C

Normal

When a person is brought to a police station under arrest or is arrested at the police station having gone there voluntarily, the custody officer must inform him of the following rights and of the fact that they are continuing rights.

- The right to have someone informed of his arrest
- The right to consult a solicitor and that independent legal advice is available free of charge
- The right to consult the Codes of Practice

The custody officer must also give the person a written notice setting out the above three rights, the right to a copy of the custody record and the caution, how to obtain legal advice, and an additional notice briefly setting out his entitlements. The custody officer shall ask the person to sign the custody record to acknowledge receipt of this notice

If the custody officer authorises a person's detention he must inform him of the grounds as soon as practicable and in any case before that person is then questioned about any offence. The person shall be asked to sign on the custody record to signify whether or not he wants legal advice at this point (and tick one of the alternative boxes). The custody officer must act without delay to secure the provision of such advice when requested. Should the person decline legal advice he should be asked the reason for waiving his right.

The grounds for a person's detention shall be recorded, in his presence if practicable

Special groups

If the person does not understand English or appears to be deaf and the custody officer cannot communicate with him then the custody officer must as soon as practicable call an interpreter, and ask him to provide the information required above.

If the person is a juvenile, is mentally handicapped or is suffering from mental illness then the custody officer must as soon as practicable inform the appropriate adult of the grounds for his detention and his whereabouts, and ask the adult to come to the police station to see the person. If the appropriate adult is already at the police station when information is given to the person as required above, then the information must be given to the detained person in his presence. If the appropriate adult is not at the police station when the information is given, then the information must be given to the detained person again in the presence of the appropriate adult once that person arrives.

If the person is blind or seriously visually handicapped or is unable to read, the custody officer must ensure that his solicitor, relative, the appropriate adult or some other person likely to take an interest in him is available to help in checking any documentation. Where this code requires written consent or signification, then the person who is assisting may be asked to sign instead if the detained person so wishes.

In the case of a juvenile who is known to be subject to a supervision order, reasonable steps must also be taken to notify the person supervising him. Action taken shall be recorded

Responsible person

If the person is a juvenile, the custody officer must ascertain the identity of a person responsible for his welfare. That person may be his parent or guardian (or, if he is in care, the care authority or voluntary organisation) or any other person who has for the time being, assumed responsibility for his welfare.

Persons attending voluntarily

Any person attending a police station voluntarily for the purpose of assisting with an investigation may leave at will unless placed under arrest. If it is decided that he would not be allowed to do so then he must be informed at once that he is under arrest and be brought before the custody officer. If he is not placed under arrest but is cautioned, the officer who gives the caution must at the same time inform him that he is not under arrest, that he is not obliged to remain at the police station but that if he remains at the police station he may obtain legal advice if he wishes

Legal Advice

POLICE AND CRIMINAL EVIDENCE ACT 1984, CODE OF PRACTICE C

GENERAL

Any person may at any time consult and communicate privately in person, in writing or on the telephone, with a solicitor unless a delay has been authorised. (See later). No attempt should be made to dissuade the suspect from obtaining legal advice. It should be pointed out to him that the advice is free and he may speak to a solicitor on the telephone. If he continues to waive his right he should be asked his reason for doing so. Where a solicitor arrives at a police station and asks to see a particular person, that person must (unless a delay has been authorised) be informed of the solicitor's arrival and asked whether he would like to see him. The solicitor's attendance and the detained person's decision must be entered on the custody record.

INTERVIEWS

A person who asks for legal advice may not be interviewed or continue to be interviewed until he has received it unless:

(a) A delay has been authorised; or
(b) An officer of the rank of superintendent or above has reasonable grounds for believing that:
  (i) Delay will involve an immediate risk of harm to persons or serious loss of, or damage to, property (once sufficient information to avert the risk has been obtained, questioning must cease until legal advice is given, unless other reasons for not receiving it exist); or
  (ii) Where a solicitor has agreed to attend, but awaiting his arrival would cause unreasonable delay to the processes of investigation; or
(c) The solicitor selected:
  (i) Cannot be contacted;
  (ii) Has previously indicated that he does not wish to be contacted; or
  (iii) Having been contacted, has declined to attend; and the person has been advised of the duty solicitor scheme (if in operation) but has declined to ask for the duty solicitor, or he is unavailable; or

Where (c) applies and the person indicated that he does not want legal advice, the interview may be started or continued without further delay provided that an officer of the rank of inspector or above has agreed that the interview may proceed.

(d) If the person who wanted legal advice changes his mind then the interview may start or continue provided he consents in writing or on tape and an officer of at least the rank of inspector has agreed after inquiring into the reasons for the suspect's change of mind.

Where a person has been permitted to consult a solicitor and the solicitor is available at the time the interview begins or is in progress, he must be allowed to have his solicitor present while he is interviewed.

Legal Advice *continued...*

SOLICITOR

In this code 'solicitor' means a solicitor qualified to practise in accordance with the Solicitors Act 1974, a trainee, a clerk or a legal executive. If the solicitor sends a non-accredited or probationary representative then he shall be admitted to the police station for this purpose unless an officer of the rank of inspector of above considers that such a visit will hinder the investigation of crime and directs otherwise. Once admitted to the police station, the provisions relating to solicitors apply. For matters to be taken into account in reaching this decision, refer to Code of Practice C para 6.13.

If the inspector refuses access to a non-accredited or probationary representative or a decision is taken that such a person should not be permitted to remain at an interview, he must forthwith notify a solicitor on whose behalf the person was to have acted or was acting, and give him an opportunity to make alternative arrangements.

REQUIREMENT TO LEAVE

The solicitor may only be required to leave the interview if his conduct is such that the investigating officer is unable properly to put questions to the suspect. If this happens the investigating officer will stop the interview and consult an officer not below the rank of superintendent, if readily available, otherwise an officer not below the rank of inspector, who is not connected with the investigation. That officer will decide, after speaking to the solicitor, whether or not the interview should continue in the presence of that solicitor. If he decides that it should not, the suspect will be given the opportunity to consult another solicitor before the interview continues and that solicitor will be given an opportunity to be present at the interview. The removal of a solicitor from an interview is a serious step and if it occurs, the officer who took the decision will consider whether the incident should be reported to the Law Society. If the decision to remove the solicitor has been taken by an officer below the rank of superintendent, the facts must be reported to an officer of at least superintendent rank who will consider whether a report to the Law Society would be appropriate. In the case of a duty solicitor a report should also be made to the Legal Aid Board

RECORDS

Any request for legal advice and the action taken on it shall be recorded.

If a person has asked for legal advice and an interview is commenced in the absence of a solicitor or his representative (or the solicitor or his representative has been required to leave an interview) this must be recorded in the interview record.

Delay: Notifying of Arrest and Access to Legal Advice PACE 1984, Code C, Annex B

AUTHORITY

The rights to have someone notified of the arrest, or to have access to legal advice may be delayed if the person is in police detention in connection with a serious arrestable offence, has not yet been charged with an offence and an officer of the rank of superintendent or above has reasonable grounds for believing that the exercise of either right:

(i) will interfere with or harm evidence connected with a serious arrestable offence or interference with or physical harm to other persons;
(ii) will alert other persons suspected of having committed such an offence but not yet arrested for it; or
(iii) will hinder the recovery of property obtained in consequence of the commission of such an offence;
(iv) where the serious arrestable offence is either one of drugs trafficking or to which a confiscation order under Pt VI CJA 1988 applies.

LIMITATION

Access to a solicitor may not be delayed on the grounds that he might advise the person not to answer any questions or that the solicitor was initially asked to attend the police station by someone else, provided that the person himself then wishes to see the solicitor.

PERIOD

These rights may be delayed only for as long as is necessary and in no case beyond 36 hours after the relevant time. If the above grounds cease to apply within this time, the person must as soon as practicable be asked if he wishes to exercise either right, the custody record must be noted accordingly and action taken. A detained person shall be allowed to consult a solicitor before any court hearing.

TERRORISM

If the above conditions to authorise delay exist, rights may be delayed for up to 48 hours if an officer of the rank of superintendent or above has reasonable grounds for believing that the exercise of either right will interfere with gathering information about terrorist acts or make it more difficult to prevent acts of terrorism or apprehend suspects.

If the above grounds cease to apply within this time, the person must as soon as practicable be asked if he wishes to exercise either right and appropriate action must be taken.

RECORDS

The grounds for delay shall be recorded and the person informed of them as soon as practicable. Any reply given must be recorded and the person asked whether he wants to endorse the record as to whether he wishes to receive legal advice.

Treatment of Detained Persons

PACE 1984

GENERAL

If a complaint is made about a detained person's treatment since his arrest, or it comes to the notice of any officer that he may have been treated improperly, a report must be made as soon as practicable to an officer of the rank of inspector or above who is not connected with the investigation. If a possible assault or the possibility of the unnecessary or unreasonable use of force is involved then the police surgeon must also be called as soon as practicable.

ILLNESS

The custody officer must immediately call the police surgeon (or, in urgent cases, send the person to hospital or call the nearest available medical practitioner) if a person brought to a police station or already detained there appears to be ill (mental or physical), injured, insensible (other than through drunkenness alone) or appears to need medical attention; whether or not the person requests medical attention.

INFECTIOUS DISEASE

If it appears that a person brought to the police station under arrest may be suffering from a significant infectious disease the custody officer should isolate the person and his property until he has obtained medical directions as to where the person should be taken, whether fumigation should take place and what precautions should be taken by officers.

MEDICAL EXAMINATION

If a detained person requests a medical examination the police surgeon must be called as soon as practicable. He may also be examined by his own doctor at his own expense.

MEDICATION

If a person is required to take or apply any medication in compliance with medical directions, the custody officer is responsible for its safe keeping and for ensuring that he is given the opportunity to take or apply it at the appropriate times. No police officer may administer controlled drugs subject to the Misuse of Drugs Act 1971 for this purpose.

RECORDS

A record must be made of any arrangements made for an examination by a police surgeon, any complaint reported and medical directions to the police.

The custody record shall detail the medicines the person has with him on arrival at the police station and any which he claims to need but does not have.

Conditions of Detention

(CODE OF PRACTICE) POLICE AND CRIMINAL EVIDENCE ACT 1984

CELLS
So far as is practicable, not more than one person shall be detained in each cell. Cells must be adequately heated, cleaned and ventilated. No additional restraints should be used within a locked cell unless absolutely necessary, and then only approved handcuffs.

BEDDING
Bedding should be of a reasonable standard and in a clean and sanitary condition.

TOILETS
Access to toilet and washing facilities must be provided.

CLOTHING
If a person's clothes have to be removed for investigation, hygiene or health reasons or for cleaning, replacement clothing of a reasonable standard of comfort and cleanliness shall be provided. A person may not be interviewed unless adequate clothing has been offered to him.

MEALS
At least two light meals and one main meal shall be offered in any period of 24 hours. Drinks should be provided at mealtimes and upon reasonable request between meals. Whenever necessary, advice shall be sought from the police surgeon on medical or dietary matters. Special dietary needs or religious beliefs should be met where practicable. Meals may be supplied by family or friends at the prisoner's, or their, expense.

EXERCISE
Brief daily, outdoor exercise where practicable.

JUVENILES
Should not be put in a cell unless no other secure accommodation available and impracticable to supervise. May not share a cell with an adult.

FORCE
Reasonable force may be used if necessary:

- to secure compliance with reasonable instructions, or
- to prevent escape, injury, damage to property or the destruction of evidence.

CHECKS
Persons detained should be visited every hour, and those who are drunk at least every 30 minutes and spoken to every time.

RECORDS
Replacement clothing and meals offered must be recorded. If a juvenile is placed in a cell, the reason must be recorded.

Intimate Searches

S 65 POLICE AND CRIMINAL EVIDENCE ACT 1984, CODE C, ANNEX A

AUTHORITY

Body orifices other than the mouth may be searched only if an officer of the rank of superintendent or above has reasonable grounds for believing:

a) that an article which could cause physical injury to a detained person or others has been concealed; or

b) a class A drug has been concealed and

c) an intimate search is the only practicable means of removing it

An intimate search may only be carried out by a registered medical practitioner or registered nurse, unless an officer of at least the rank of superintendent considers that this is not practicable and the risk of physical injury exists, in which case the officer carrying out the search must be of the same sex as the person searched.

PERSONS AT RISK

An intimate search at a police station of a juvenile or a mentally disordered or mentally handicapped person may take place only in the presence of the appropriate adult of the same sex (unless the person specifically requests the presence of a particular adult of the opposite sex who is readily available). But in relation to a juvenile the search may take place without the appropriate adult's presence if the juvenile so indicates and the appropriate adult agrees.

STRIP SEARCH

A strip search involves the removal of more than outer clothing and may take place only if the custody officer considers it to be necessary to find an article which the detained person would not be allowed to keep. The officer carrying out the search must be of the same sex as the person he is searching and where possible there should only be two people present in addition to the suspect.

RECORDS

After an intimate search the custody officer shall record which parts of the person's body were searched, who carried out the search, who was present, the reasons for the search and its result. In the case of a strip search he shall record the reasons for the search and its result.

If an intimate search is carried out by a police officer, the reason why it is impracticable for a suitably qualified person to conduct it must be recorded.

Intimate Samples

Ss 62, 65 Police and Criminal Justice Act 1984, as amended by s 54 Criminal Justice and Public Order Act 1994

An
INTIMATE SAMPLE

is a sample of blood, semen, any other tissue fluid, urine, saliva or pubic hair or a swab taken from a person's body orifices (other than the mouth) or a dental impression

And may be taken from a **person in police detention**

if authorised by an officer of at least the rank of superintendent who has reasonable grounds for suspecting the person's involvement in a recordable offence and for believing that the sample will tend to prove or disprove his involvement

and if the appropriate consent is given in writing

And may be taken from a person **not** in police detention

if in the course of the investigation two or more non-intimate samples suitable for the same means of analysis have been taken, and have proved insufficient and a superintendent or above authorises it and the appropriate consent is given

A sample, other than of urine, may only be taken by a registered medical practitioner and a dental impression may only be taken by a registered dentist

Non-Intimate Samples

S 63 Police and Criminal Evidence Act 1984, as amended by s 55 & Sched 10 Criminal Justice and Public Order Act 1994

A NON-INTIMATE SAMPLE

is a sample of hair (other than pubic hair), taken from or from under a nail, a swab taken from any part of the body including the mouth (but no other body orifice), saliva, a footprint or similar impression of any part of the body except the hand.

It may not be taken without written consent unless he is in police detention or being held in custody by authority of a court; and a Superintendent or above authorises it. It may be taken from a person without the appropriate consent (whether or not he is in police detention) if he has been charged with a recordable offence or informed that he will be reported for such an offence and:

(a) he has not had a non-intimate sample taken;

(b) it proved unsuitable or insufficient;

(c) or he has been convicted of a recordable offence;

(d) has been detained following acquittal on grounds of insanity or being unfit to plead.

FINGERPRINTS AND SAMPLES

Ss 63A, 64 Police and Criminal Evidence Act 1984, amended by the Criminal Justice and Public Order Act 1994

Fingerprints or samples or the information derived from samples taken from a person arrested for a recordable offence may be checked against other fingerprints or samples or the information derived from them contained in records held by or on behalf of the police or in connection with the investigation of an offence

Fingerprints may be taken without consent from a person aged over ten if the conditions set out above exist, and reasonable force may be used.

Destruction - s 64 PACE requires the destruction of fingerprints or samples as soon as is practicable after the conclusion of proceedings except that samples need not be destroyed if they were taken for the purpose of the same investigation of an offence for which a person from whom one was taken has been convicted.

Urgent Interviews

POLICE AND CRIMINAL EVIDENCE ACT 1984

If, and only if, an officer of the rank of superintendent or above considers that delay will involve an immediate risk of harm to persons or serious loss of or serious damage to property:

(i) A person **heavily under the influence of drink** or drugs may be interviewed in that state.

(ii) An **arrested juvenile** or a person who is **mentally disordered** or **mentally handicapped** may be interviewed in the absence of the appropriate adult.

(iii) A person who has difficulty in **understanding English** or who has a **hearing disability** may be interviewd in the absence of an interpreter.

Questioning in these circumstances may not continue once sufficient information to avert the immediate risk has been obtained.

A record shall be made of the grounds for any decision to interview a person as above.

Incommunicado

CODE C

A person arrested and held in custody may request that one person known to him or who is likely to take an interest in his welfare be informed of his whereabouts as soon as is practicable.

Limits on Detention

S 34 Police and Criminal Evidence Act 1984, as amended by s 29 Criminal Justice and Public Order Act 1994

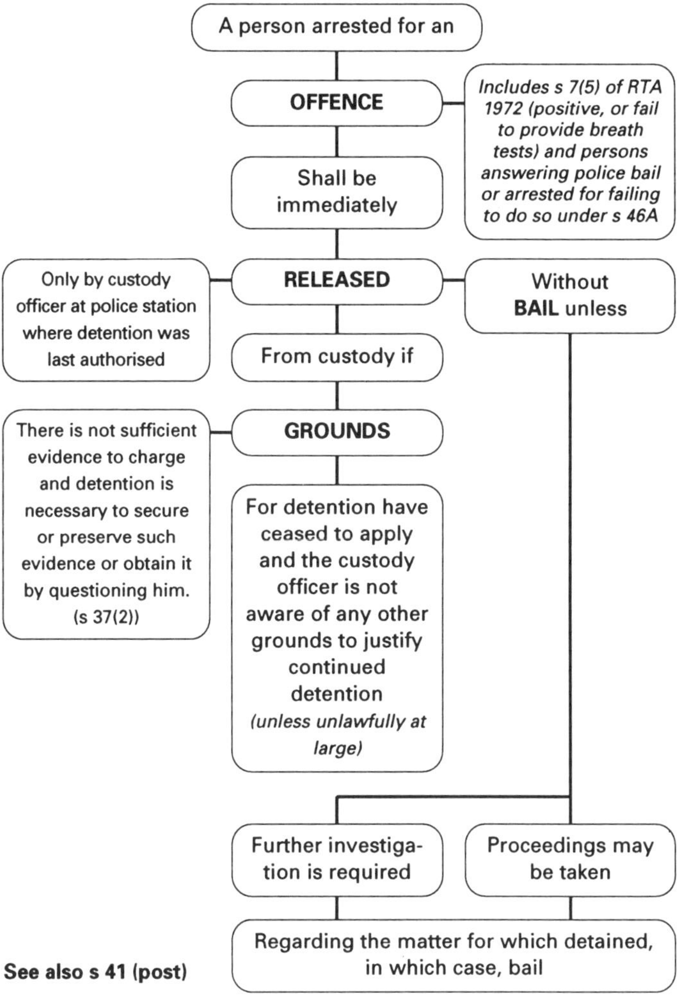
A person arrested for an
OFFENCE
Includes s 7(5) of RTA 1972 (positive, or fail to provide breath tests) and persons answering police bail or arrested for failing to do so under s 46A
Shall be immediately
RELEASED
Only by custody officer at police station where detention was last authorised
Without BAIL unless
From custody if
GROUNDS
There is not sufficient evidence to charge and detention is necessary to secure or preserve such evidence or obtain it by questioning him. (s 37(2))
For detention have ceased to apply and the custody officer is not aware of any other grounds to justify continued detention (unless unlawfully at large)
Further investigation is required
Proceedings may be taken
Regarding the matter for which detained, in which case, bail

See also s 41 (post)

Reviews of Detention

S 40 Police and Criminal Evidence Act 1984

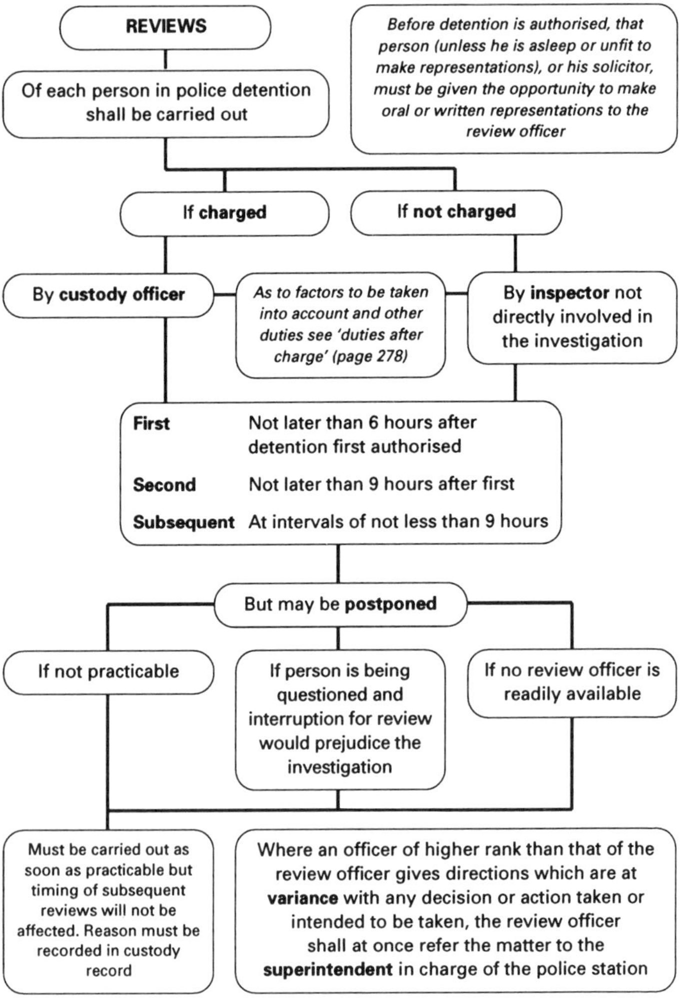
REVIEWS
Of each person in police detention shall be carried out
Before detention is authorised, that person (unless he is asleep or unfit to make representations), or his solicitor, must be given the opportunity to make oral or written representations to the review officer
If charged
If not charged
By custody officer
As to factors to be taken into account and other duties see 'duties after charge' (page 278)
By inspector not directly involved in the investigation
First
Not later than 6 hours after detention first authorised
Second
Not later than 9 hours after first
Subsequent
At intervals of not less than 9 hours
But may be postponed
If not practicable
If person is being questioned and interruption for review would prejudice the investigation
If no review officer is readily available
Must be carried out as soon as practicable but timing of subsequent reviews will not be affected. Reason must be recorded in custody record
Where an officer of higher rank than that of the review officer gives directions which are at variance with any decision or action taken or intended to be taken, the review officer shall at once refer the matter to the superintendent in charge of the police station

Relevant Time

S 41 Police and Criminal Evidence Act 1984

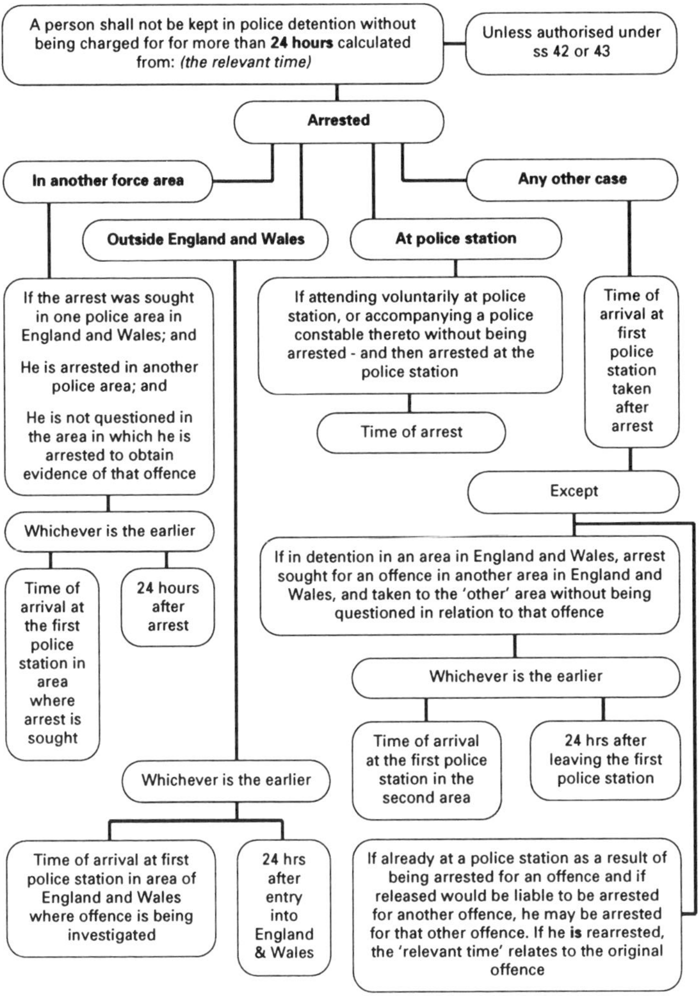
A person shall not be kept in police detention without being charged for for more than **24 hours** calculated from: *(the relevant time)*
Unless authorised under ss 42 or 43
Arrested
In another force area
Outside England and Wales
At police station
Any other case
If the arrest was sought in one police area in England and Wales; and
He is arrested in another police area; and
He is not questioned in the area in which he is arrested to obtain evidence of that offence
Whichever is the earlier
Time of arrival at the first police station in area where arrest is sought
24 hours after arrest
If attending voluntarily at police station, or accompanying a police constable thereto without being arrested - and then arrested at the police station
Time of arrest
Time of arrival at first police station taken after arrest
Except
If in detention in an area in England and Wales, arrest sought for an offence in another area in England and Wales, and taken to the 'other' area without being questioned in relation to that offence
Whichever is the earlier
Time of arrival at the first police station in the second area
24 hrs after leaving the first police station
Whichever is the earlier
Time of arrival at first police station in area of England and Wales where offence is being investigated
24 hrs after entry into England & Wales
If already at a police station as a result of being arrested for an offence and if released would be liable to be arrested for another offence, he may be arrested for that other offence. If he **is** rearrested, the 'relevant time' relates to the original offence

Continued Detention

S 42 POLICE AND CRIMINAL EVIDENCE ACT 1984

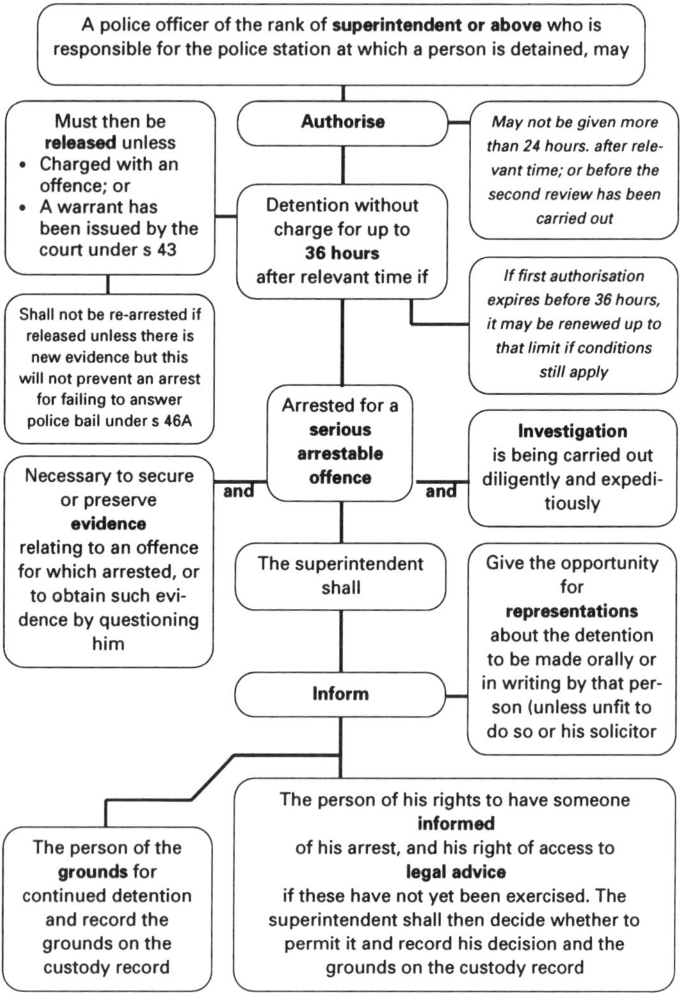
A police officer of the rank of **superintendent or above** who is responsible for the police station at which a person is detained, may
Authorise
May not be given more than 24 hours. after relevant time; or before the second review has been carried out
Must then be **released** unless
• Charged with an offence; or
• A warrant has been issued by the court under s 43
Detention without charge for up to **36 hours** after relevant time if
If first authorisation expires before 36 hours, it may be renewed up to that limit if conditions still apply
Shall not be re-arrested if released unless there is new evidence but this will not prevent an arrest for failing to answer police bail under s 46A
Arrested for a **serious arrestable offence**
and
and
Necessary to secure or preserve **evidence** relating to an offence for which arrested, or to obtain such evidence by questioning him
Investigation is being carried out diligently and expeditiously
The superintendent shall
Give the opportunity for **representations** about the detention to be made orally or in writing by that person (unless unfit to do so or his solicitor
Inform
The person of the **grounds** for continued detention and record the grounds on the custody record
The person of his rights to have someone **informed** of his arrest, and his right of access to **legal advice** if these have not yet been exercised. The superintendent shall then decide whether to permit it and record his decision and the grounds on the custody record

Warrant of Further Detention

S 43 Police and Criminal Evidence Act 1984

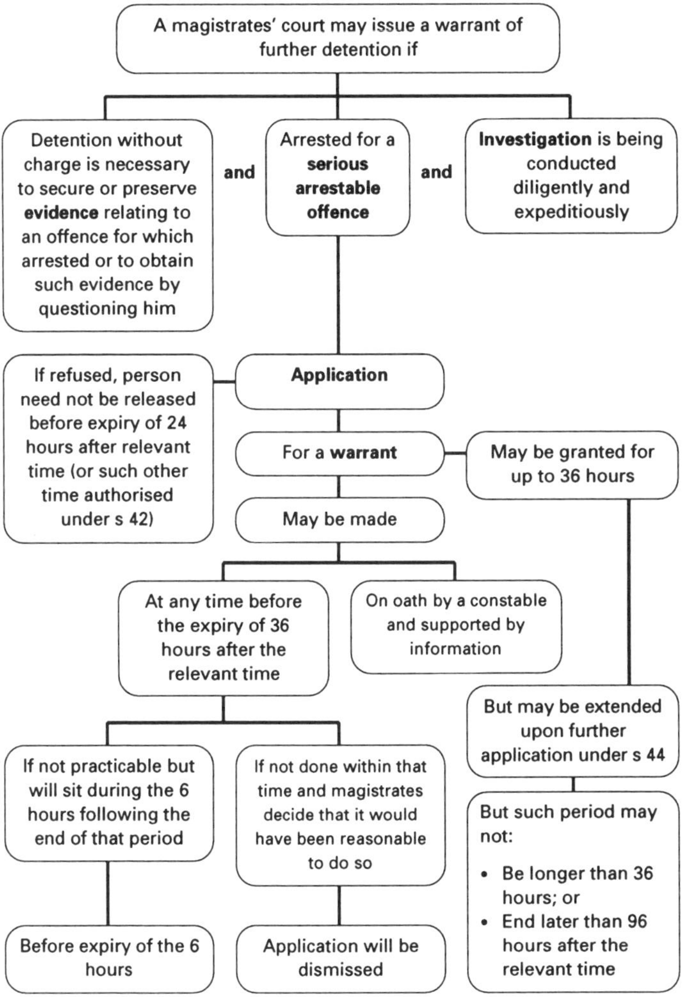
A magistrates' court may issue a warrant of further detention if
Detention without charge is necessary to secure or preserve **evidence** relating to an offence for which arrested or to obtain such evidence by questioning him
and
Arrested for a **serious arrestable offence**
and
Investigation is being conducted diligently and expeditiously
If refused, person need not be released before expiry of 24 hours after relevant time (or such other time authorised under s 42)
Application
For a **warrant**
May be granted for up to 36 hours
May be made
At any time before the expiry of 36 hours after the relevant time
On oath by a constable and supported by information
But may be extended upon further application under s 44
If not practicable but will sit during the 6 hours following the end of that period
If not done within that time and magistrates decide that it would have been reasonable to do so
But such period may not:
• Be longer than 36 hours; or
• End later than 96 hours after the relevant time
Before expiry of the 6 hours
Application will be dismissed

Duties Before Charge

S 37 Police and Criminal Evidence Act 1984

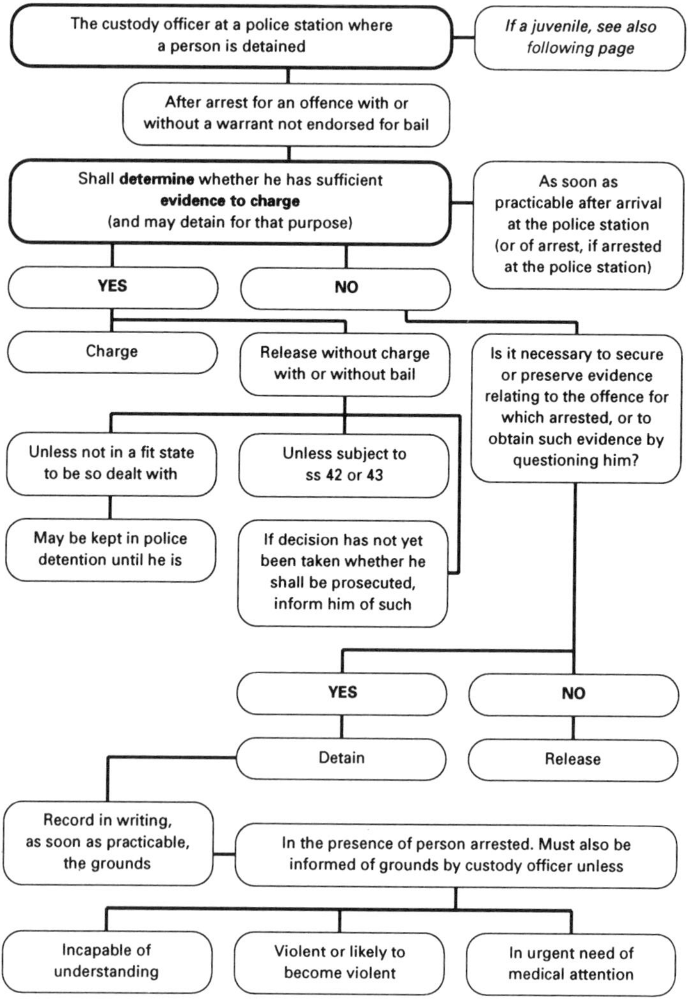
The custody officer at a police station where a person is detained
If a juvenile, see also following page
After arrest for an offence with or without a warrant not endorsed for bail
Shall **determine** whether he has sufficient **evidence to charge** (and may detain for that purpose)
As soon as practicable after arrival at the police station (or of arrest, if arrested at the police station)
YES
NO
Charge
Release without charge with or without bail
Is it necessary to secure or preserve evidence relating to the offence for which arrested, or to obtain such evidence by questioning him?
Unless not in a fit state to be so dealt with
Unless subject to ss 42 or 43
May be kept in police detention until he is
If decision has not yet been taken whether he shall be prosecuted, inform him of such
YES
NO
Detain
Release
Record in writing, as soon as practicable, the grounds
In the presence of person arrested. Must also be informed of grounds by custody officer unless
Incapable of understanding
Violent or likely to become violent
In urgent need of medical attention

Duties Before Charge (juveniles)

S 37 POLICE AND CRIMINAL EVIDENCE ACT 1984

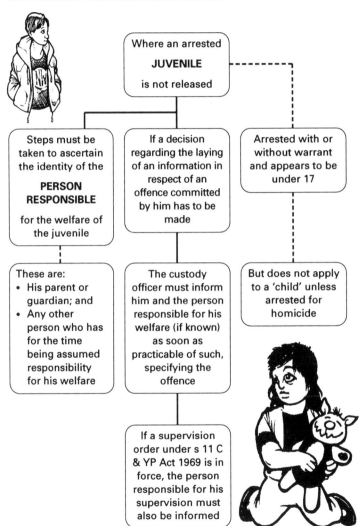

Where an arrested **JUVENILE** is not released

Steps must be taken to ascertain the identity of the **PERSON RESPONSIBLE** for the welfare of the juvenile

These are:
- His parent or guardian; and
- Any other person who has for the time being assumed responsibility for his welfare

If a decision regarding the laying of an information in respect of an offence committed by him has to be made

The custody officer must inform him and the person responsible for his welfare (if known) as soon as practicable of such, specifying the offence

If a supervision order under s 11 C & YP Act 1969 is in force, the person responsible for his supervision must also be informed

Arrested with or without warrant and appears to be under 17

But does not apply to a 'child' unless arrested for homicide

Charging

POLICE AND CRIMINAL EVIDENCE ACT 1984

GENERAL

When an officer considers that there is sufficient evidence to prosecute a detained person, and that there is sufficient evidence for a prosecution to succeed, and that the person has said all that he wishes to say about the offence, he should without delay bring him before the custody officer who shall then be responsible for considering whether or not he should be charged. Where a detained person is suspected of more than one offence it is permissible to delay bringing him before the custody officer until the above conditions are satisfied in respect of all the offences. Any resulting action should be taken in the presence of the appropriate adult if the person is a juvenile or mentally disordered or mentally handicapped.

Caution

When a detained person is charged with or informed that he may be prosecuted for an offence he shall be cautioned in the following terms:

> *'You do not have to say anything unless you wish to do so, but what you say may be given in evidence.' (but see new caution below)*

Notice

At the time a person is charged he shall be given a written notice showing particulars of the offence with which he is charged and including the name of the officer in the case, his police station and the reference number for the case. So far as possible the particulars of the charge shall be stated in simple terms, but they shall also show the precise offence in law with which he is charged. The notice shall begin with the following words:

> *'You are charged with the offence(s) shown below. You do not have to say anything unless you wish to do so, but what you say may be given in evidence.'* **(But see new caution next page.)**

If the person is a juvenile or is mentally ill or mentally handicapped the notice shall be given to the appropriate adult.

STATEMENTS OF OTHER PERSONS

If after a person has been charged with or informed he may be prosecuted for an offence a police officer wishes to bring to his notice any written statement made by another person or the content of an interview with another person, he shall be handed a true copy of any such written statement or have brought to his attention the content of the interview record.

Charging *continued...*

CAUTION

'You do not have to say anything. But it may harm your defence if you do not mention now something which you later rely on in court. Anything you do say may be given in evidence.'

QUESTIONS AFTER CHARGING

Question relating to an offence may not be put to a person after he has been charged with that offence, or informed that he may be prosecuted for it, except for the purpose of preventing or minimising harm or loss to some other person or to the public or for clearing up an ambiguity in a previous answer or statement, or where it is in the interests of justice. He should be cautioned before any such questions are asked of him.

JUVENILES

If a juvenile is charged with an offence and his continuing detention is authorised he should be taken into the care of a local authority to be detained pending the court appearance unless the custody officer certifies that it is impracticable to do so, or in the case of a juvenile aged at least 12, that no secure accommodation is available and there is a risk of serious harm to the public from that juvenile, in accordance with s 38(6) Police and Criminal Evidence Act 1984, as amended by s 59 Criminal Justice Act 1991 and s 24 Criminal Justice and Public Order Act 1994.

RECORDS

A record shall be made of anything a detained person says when charged. Any questions put after charge and answers given relating to the offence shall be contemporaneously recorded in full on the forms provided and the record signed by that person or, if he refuses, by the interviewing officer and any third parties present. If the questions are tape recorded the arrangements set out in the relevant Code of Practice (E) apply.

If a juvenile cannot be transferred into local authority care the custody officer must record the reasons and make out a certificate to be produced before the court together with juvenile.

Duties After Charge

S 38 Police and Criminal Evidence Act 1984, as amended by s 28 Criminal Justice and Public Order Act 1994

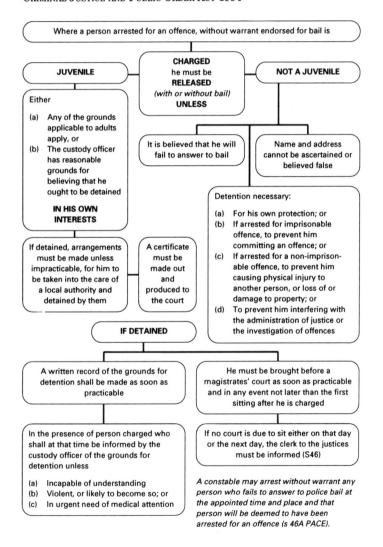

Where a person arrested for an offence, without warrant endorsed for bail is

CHARGED he must be **RELEASED** *(with or without bail)* **UNLESS**

JUVENILE

Either

(a) Any of the grounds applicable to adults apply, or
(b) The custody officer has reasonable grounds for believing that he ought to be detained

IN HIS OWN INTERESTS

If detained, arrangements must be made unless impracticable, for him to be taken into the care of a local authority and detained by them

A certificate must be made out and produced to the court

NOT A JUVENILE

It is believed that he will fail to answer to bail

Name and address cannot be ascertained or believed false

Detention necessary:

(a) For his own protection; or
(b) If arrested for imprisonable offence, to prevent him committing an offence; or
(c) If arrested for a non-imprisonable offence, to prevent him causing physical injury to another person, or loss of or damage to property; or
(d) To prevent him interfering with the administration of justice or the investigation of offences

IF DETAINED

A written record of the grounds for detention shall be made as soon as practicable

In the presence of person charged who shall at that time be informed by the custody officer of the grounds for detention unless

(a) Incapable of understanding
(b) Violent, or likely to become so; or
(c) In urgent need of medical attention

He must be brought before a magistrates' court as soon as practicable and in any event not later than the first sitting after he is charged

If no court is due to sit either on that day or the next day, the clerk to the justices must be informed (S46)

A constable may arrest without warrant any person who fails to answer to police bail at the appointed time and place and that person will be deemed to have been arrested for an offence (s 46A PACE).

Index